Managing your school library and information service
A practical handbook

Managing your school library and information service
A practical handbook

Anthony Tilke

ʃ

facet publishing

Published by
Facet Publishing
7 Ridgmount Street
London WC1E 7AE

Facet Publishing (formerly Library Association Publishing) is wholly owned
by CILIP: the Chartered Institute of Library and Information Professionals.

First published 2002

British Library Cataloguing in Publication Data

A catalogue record for this book is available from the British Library.

ISBN 1-85604-437-8

Typeset in 11/15pt Aldine 401 BT and Syntax by Facet Publishing.
Printed and made in Great Britain by MPG Books Ltd, Bodmin, Cornwall.

CONTENTS

FOREWORD

Good school libraries are full of energy and inspiration. Over the last 20 years I have been lucky to visit many, all over the world, and I have always come away amazed and enthusiastic. There is an unmistakable 'buzz' about a good library; a combination of exuberance and order, of purpose and openness. It celebrates the infinite variety of the world and the joy of being able to home in on a particular aspect of that variety.

We are asking an enormous amount of the young people being educated today. They are being launched into a rich and complex global culture, which generates an incredible amount of information. There are more things to know – and more ways of knowing – than ever before. Students are encouraged to take control of their own learning, and they need a wide range of resources to help them develop their learning skills.

Supporting this kind of learning places enormous demands on school libraries. Often working on very limited budgets, librarians are asked to provide a rich environment in which students will be stretched and stimulated without being swamped. They must respond to ever-changing situations while offering a safe harbour from which to explore the vast and bewildering sea of information.

Those are challenging demands and this book discusses them in detail and in depth. It is entirely appropriate that it has been written by Anthony Tilke, whose own school library is a delightful and exciting place, at the very heart of the school it serves.

Gillian Cross

ACKNOWLEDGEMENTS

I am indebted to a number of individuals and organizations who have helped with the development of this book. A feature of this book is the 'voice of the librarian', and although comments, advice and tips may have appeared first in other publications, a number of people were kind enough to give direct and original comments. In addition, other librarians provided information, help and contacts. I am grateful to them all. They include:

Lynn Barrett, Librarian, Dixons City Technology College, Bradford (and a national committee member of CILIP School Libraries Group (SLG)), together with the Finance Director of Dixons City Technology School, Bradford

Helen Boothroyd, Head of the Schools Library Service, Suffolk

Darelyn Dawson, school librarian in Sydney and Convenor, IB (International Baccalaureate) Librarians Group of Australasia

Sue Jones, Head of Hertfordshire Schools Library Service

Kathy Lemaire, Chief Executive, School Library Association

Marianne McCartney, Librarian, Hampton School, London

Helen Pallett, school librarian, English Midlands, and school library trainer

Helen Pugh, Librarian at King's College School, Wimbledon, London and formerly Chair of CILIP SLG (London and Home Counties Branch)

Elspeth S. Scott, school librarian in Dundee, Scotland, and a national committee member of the School Library Association

Anne-Marie Tarter, Librarian, Ripon Grammar School, Yorkshire and Secretary of CILIP SLG

Sue Ward, school librarian, Nottingham, national committee member of the CILIP School Libraries Group, and ex-Group Councillor, The Library Association

Lynn Winkworth, School Librarian, Headington School, Oxford, and a national committee member of the School Library Association.

I am also grateful to the following individuals and organizations for use of specific material.

Hertfordshire Schools Library Service, for permission to use a job description which the service produced for school librarians in the county, and which appeared in Hertfordshire Schools Library Service (1995).

IFLA Section for School Libraries and School Resource Centres: Glenys Willars (Principal Educational Librarian, Leicestershire County Council, Chair of CILIP SLG), Chair of the School Library Section, International Federation of Library Associations, for permission to reproduce text from the UNESCO School Library Manifesto, which was developed by the Section.

CILIP: the Chartered Institute of Library and Information Professionals, especially:

- *Library & Information Update*: Elspeth Hyams (Editor), for permission to use a diagram headed 'Information literacy' in an article by Hilary Johnson (*Library Association Record*, **103** (12) (December 2001), 753), and with thanks to Rachel Middleton
- Marketing Department: for permission to use a specimen press release for the Carnegie and Kate Greenaway Awards in the Appendices
- Workplace and Solo Adviser, Lyndsay Rees-Jones, concerning a survey of employment issues for solo librarians. The questionnaire is provided in the Appendices.

David V. Loertscher, for permission to reproduce a table on collaborative planning (which originally appeared in California School Library Association (1997) *From library skills to information literacy: a handbook for the 21st century*, 2nd edn, San José, California, Hi Willow Research and Publishing, 35). And a diagram showing a new way of working for a school library, both of which appeared in Loertscher (1999).

Price Waterhouse Coopers, for permission to reproduce a survey undertaken at Dixons City Technology School (to whom thanks are also due) as part of their study in 2001 of a survey of innovations in city technology colleges, for the Department for Education and Employment. This survey is reproduced in the Appendices.

Professional, Research and Teaching Group, based at Yokohama International School, Japan, for notes of their discussion concerning the essential elements of a school, which were used as a basis for material included in Chapter 1.

Finally, and not least, to Rebecca Casey, my editor, and Helen Carley and other colleagues at Facet Publishing, with thanks for all their help and advice during the process of writing this book.

GLOSSARY

The following acronyms and abbreviations are found in this book:

AASL	American Association of School Librarians
CILIP	Chartered Institute of Library and Information Professionals
GNVQ	General National Vocational Qualification
GCSE	General Certificate of Secondary Education
IT-ICT	Information (and communication) technology
LEA	Local education authority
LMS	Library Media Specialist (USA)
OPAC	Open public access catalogue (computer terminal)
SLRC	School Library Resource Centre/Center
SLS	Schools Library Service (UK)

INTRODUCTION

One writer excels at a plan or a title page, another works away the body of the book, and a third is a dab at an index.

Oliver Goldsmith, *The Bee*, 1 [1759]

As the single author of all the elements of this handbook, it falls to me to define its terms of reference, and to discuss its relevance to its intended audience. The first part of this introduction looks at the scope of the book and the second part discusses some features and issues concerning school librarianship.

The scope of the book

The title of this book contains words and terms that are no strangers to most prospective readers. But we may be blasé about these terms, forgetting that a title for a book usually takes some thought and naturally each word in this title has been carefully chosen. The title reflects the technical and professional nature of the text, the aim of which is to blend the important educational role of the school librarian with the practical and managerial aspects of the profession. Both are necessary to function effectively as a school librarian. Essentially written for the secondary school librarian, nevertheless the points made in the book would be of relevance to anyone working in a school library. So, if we look at the words of the title individually we find the following:

School

Obviously this sets the context. The word school comes first, and logically so. The library serves the school and should be an integral part of the school. In reality, however, this role varies from school to school. What do we define a school as? A place for learning, for socialization, for self-discovery . . . all these and more? This topic would fill a book quite easily, so readers of this book may accept that a secondary or high school, for the purposes of this book, will concentrate on learning, research and study. However, the book will aim to identify some of the other factors of that complex organization: the school.

Library

While a school library may be named a study, media, resource, cyber or information centre, at the end of the day, the word library is still well understood by many people. However, its image may not be all that one would wish. Nevertheless, whatever connotation the term may have for users and others, it is recognized and understood by many. This book celebrates such a recognition and the word is used deliberately and proudly.

Information

Since information is the stuff of books and other resources, libraries should, after all, be information-rich. In order for information to become knowledge interaction with a user is necessary, hence information literacy or more familiarly information skills. Whether this term is also seen as a subset of study or research skills can be debated, but the term is often cited and has been an interest of professionals concerned with school libraries for a number of years.

Service

It may be argued that a library offers a service to the school community. In doing this, is the school library offering something different from other parts of the school? Does the library service ethos support school values? To put it another way, a school library may look different from other parts of school, but is still part of a school, with all the tensions that accepted rules, discipline and behaviour patterns may bring. In such a scenario, the library may be more a room to accommodate pupils for a range of functions, rather than a place where services can be effectively provided to a range of client groups.

Practical

This book aims to be practical. It will not offer a blueprint for the 'perfect school library', but should aid reflection, tease out issues, offer some ways forward, enabling the manager of a school library and information service to be in control. It is hoped that this is – in the end – more practical than merely saying 'Do this in all situations'. After all, how many times have you heard (and spoken) the sentence 'This year's Grade 8 is very different from last year's'. Perhaps the 'perfect' school library does not and cannot exist. It may be more pertinent to aim for a relevant and effective school library.

Handbook

This word brings expectations of comprehensiveness, and hopefully this book will live up to such expectations. It cannot be complete though. Given the changes that have affected school libraries and other aspects of professional life in librarianship in the last few years, no handbook could make such a claim. It does, naturally, aim to cover the major issues and aspects of school librarianship.

In common with other handbooks, this book may be referred to for specific information. However, the book has a structure and the intention is that it will also be read in a logical order. The aspects of a library manager's role are built up in many ways in the book incrementally, so that a concept is introduced in one chapter and built on in others. This reflects the nature of the school librarian's job – while there are specific job activities, most relate to other aspects of the role. The book therefore aims to reflect such a reality.

School librarianship: features and issues

The following features and issues are pertinent to the main concerns of the author in writing this book. Its aim is not to provide detail of a transient nature, such as specific curricula, but to focus on more lasting aspects of the methodology behind school librarianship.

British school librarianship

We live in a global age, and though a trend for standardization may be the ideal, in reality there are differences, often associated with nationality or region. We can think of many examples of non-standardization, such as mobile phones, video recording systems, currencies. Even within the UK, educational systems vary: consider Scotland. School library systems, training and education, expectations and roles also vary. This handbook cannot seek to provide a global perspective, but focuses on offering a British approach in terms of skills, opportunities and initiatives. It will not be better or worse than other countries' systems, simply different, yet hopefully relevant and effective.

The literature on school librarianship includes a wide range of documents that cite research, standards and good practice. Documents have been cited here to provide supporting evidence and a source for further information. It is invidious to single out one source, but a very practical one is a survey of secondary school libraries in the UK (Sheffield Hallam University, 2000). An initial survey (significantly drawn from a one-in-three sample) of secondary school libraries was funded by The Library Association in 1997 and a second survey, published in 2000, crucially allows trends to be identified. The report of the latter survey includes very useful and hitherto unavailable national data on the provision and development of secondary school libraries in Britain.

At the same time, professional practice and ideas can be transferred from other parts of the world. Where relevant, good practice and equitable standards concerning school libraries from other countries have been included in the book. Of particular importance are school library guidelines from Australia (Australian School Library Association, 2001) and the USA (American Association of School Librarians, 1998b). Each document is excellent, but they both represent different situations, and have different things to say. They are used extensively in this book, together with British school library guidelines (Tilke, 1998a).

Curricula

Although offering a British point of view, this handbook will not focus on the 'National Curriculum', not least because it is not followed in all of Britain. For instance, Scotland has a different curriculum (5–14 Curriculum). Public examination names in England and Wales include a host of acronyms and abbreviations: GCSE, AS, A2 and GNVQ. Scottish schools offer courses at Standard and Higher levels. Indeed in maintained (state) and private (independent) schools in the UK, International Baccalaureate and other curricula are now offered. With the pace of change in curricula, it would be foolish for a school library handbook to identify purely or even mainly with one curriculum model. What is important is possibly to identify examples of good practice from a variety of systems, but certainly to tease out strategies that can be employed whatever the curriculum of the school.

History of school libraries and librarianship

The history of schools is long, complex and honourable. The history of education is even more so. Is this also true of school librarianship? Mention of libraries in schools will no doubt be found in historical literature, but does it tell us what school libraries did and provide information about services offered? Relatively infrequently, will be the conclusion. Examples of particular movements and initiatives to improve the state of school libraries, reforming individuals and attempts to provide a service to pupils and teachers could be cited. For the purposes of this book, it may be accepted that school libraries have *generally* moved from the parlous situation often found in the last century. Nowadays, we are not looking for zealous missionaries so much as managers who are adept at developing curriculum-relevant services and working in the complex organization that is a school. This handbook therefore is concerned with the librarian rather than the library per se – it is the librarian's interaction that turns a library into a library and information *service*.

Professional v. academic

An aspect of the development of British librarianship has been the trend – shared with other professions – for entrants to the profession to be trained not only via a purely professional qualification, but to require beforehand specific education at a tertiary level in library science. There is also an expectation of continuing professional development, and this is a significant issue for librarians in schools, who typically have needs associated with input and updating of technological and other skills, together with an understanding of teaching and learning processes.

In addition, the book draws, where appropriate, on sources from the wider educational world, as it is important to relate school library issues to the library's setting.

Pressures and opportunities for school libraries and librarians

A handbook, to be successful, must not ignore the fact that there have been and are many pressures on school libraries and librarians to succeed and even to survive. These could be because of financial constraints, low or high expectations, curriculum/examination pressures, political policy, etc. The other side of the coin, however, is the fact that there are many opportunities for libraries in schools to develop relevant, useful and value-added services.

Information and communication technology (ICT)

Given the present and future role of technology in the development of school libraries, the reader may be surprised that there is no comprehensive chapter in this book on this important aspect of today's libraries. However, it is precisely because technology is so prevalent and important that references to ICT are to be found throughout the book. It would be folly to focus on particular aspects of technology as the pace of technological change is so great that the words would be out of date by the time the book is published. In addition, the book focuses on management implications of technology, rather than technology itself.

The librarian's voice

A feature of this handbook will be the attempt – through comments and examples – to provide views, comments, advice and warnings from librarians themselves. This enables readers to consider different points of views and situations.

Students' needs

The student's voice will be heard in the book, albeit indirectly. After all students form one of the key groups for whom school libraries exist. They could hardly be left out of the equation!

Debunking the 'holy grail' or holding on to Shangri-La?

The concept of a whole-school policy for a library has exercised the minds of librarians for a number of years. It seems self-evident and logical, but may have proved elusive in many cases. This handbook supports the idea of the whole-school policy, yet argues that school libraries may de facto be successful without such a development. After all, what has been gained if a document propounding a whole-school policy for the library has been duly ratified but the library service is not held in the 'hearts and minds' of the school community? An added aspect is the amount of time and effort that librarians may put into developing such policies, at the expense of their motivation and morale.

Common aspects of school library development will be referred to throughout the book. These ingredients are commonly understood to feature:

- head teacher, governing body and senior management support
- curricular relevance
- policy and planned development
- finance
- accommodation, resources and equipment
- access
- monitoring and evaluation.

A standard and simple enough recipe, yet in practice it requires a considerable amount of effort to get the mixture right, and it *is* a mixture – consider a case where money was no obstacle, yet support and recognized policy for the library are not present. Or where teacher and curricular involvement is high, yet there are insufficient funds to reasonably satisfy demand. There are many variations and no single optimum mix, but the recipe needs both input and output. This is because while a secondary school library requires 'input' in the form of funding, in particular to purchase resources, this enables it to produce 'output' in the form of effective learning.

Essential skills for a secondary school librarian are those of management, for it is by judging, evaluating and managing that a librarian will enable a school library to consistently develop as a relevant and essential facility within a school.

1

THE SCHOOL AS AN ORGANIZATION

Organizations are many things at once!
They are complex and multifaceted.
They are paradoxical.
That's why the challenges facing managers and practitioners are often so difficult.

Morgan, 1998, 3

To function successfully in an organization, it is essential for an individual to understand just how the organization works. Without knowledge of this sort, an individual will find it difficult to cope, manage and ultimately succeed. Understanding or knowledge such as this is even more pertinent to solo workers. By solo worker is meant a member of a particular kind of profession who, by training, education and experience, may be in the minority in the organization in which they are employed. Such a situation is true for librarians in secondary schools. This first chapter sets the scene for the existence and purpose of a library and information service in a secondary or high school. More than that, the chapter shows why the library needs to focus on the purpose of the parent body – the school – and introduces aspects of the library manager's functions that will be explored throughout this book.

At first glance, it is simple enough to provide answers to questions: what does a school consist of? What does a school do? A school consists of teachers, pupils and buildings. A school educates children and young people.

In reality, though, organizations are complex entities. First of all, it is important to understand what an organization is. A key concept in business studies, we find that an organization is 'a social grouping designed to achieve certain goals'. Furthermore, formal organizations 'exist independently of the individuals who belong to them at any given time, and the roles and activities of organization members are formally prescribed at least to some extent' (Pass, 1995, 460).

More particularly, it is important to analyse what is involved in the make-up of a school organization. Murphy (1992, 167) records that a school may be 'a collection of individual entrepreneurs (teachers) surrounded by a common parking lot' or 'a group of classrooms held together by a common heating . . . system'. Essentially, they could be considered as loosely linked organizations. However, he does indicate that research exists to suggest that 'better schools are more tightly linked – structurally, symbolically and culturally' and 'operate more as an organic whole'. A librarian needs to work with most if not all parts of a school and at times any of the descriptions given above may apply to his or her organization.

Structures

Nevertheless, it is often easier to see an organization in structural, functional and network terms. In this context, we can see that a school includes the following.

Management and administration

Head teacher; finance; communication; vision; accountability.
These are generally understood to be immoveable. They are needed to allow an organization to function and develop. Schmoker (1996, 20) found that schools could 'lack clear, common direction and communication that promotes people working toward mutually intelligible goals' though Reynolds and Packer (1992, 177) considered that head teachers who have been appointed since the 1990s recognize the importance of motivating and relating to constituent groups within the organization. Whether for pub-

lic or private organizations, funding is a key resource and management is accountable to the governing body of the organization for this as for other aspects of school provision.

Partners

Staff; students; parents; alumni; governors or trustees; volunteers; local community; professional community; local support, advisory services; inspection; government (local/regional and central).

All have a role in helping a school evolve and function to a greater or lesser degree. Some roles have and will change radically but, typically, all are involved in shaping school provision.

Resources, facilities, buildings, environment

The physical environment can be seen with the human eye and tends to be clearly perceived and understood, so it is relatively easy to evaluate what we see before us.

Regulations, laws and discipline

The environment of a school also involves more intangible aspects, such as regulations, rules and discipline. All organizations need a modus operandi. Schools have complex structures and these need to work effectively to put in place an environment that allows an academic and social organization to function well.

Curriculum

Arguably, this is the heart of a school. In practice, and in detail, it is rarely 'set in stone' and evolves and develops to suit changing needs. The curriculum is also a structure, is codified or written, and is developed by co-ordinators, curriculum managers and in detail by departmental colleagues.

Enrolment

This may range from automatic to selective intake. Optimum enrolment provides a good mix of funding and use of available resources. Achieving such a balance may be difficult, so that tensions occur, for example a short-fall could result in a restriction in available funding, while there may be accommodation and other shortages in an over-subscribed school.

Communication, public relations, marketing

In an organization where, typically, workers function on their own (i.e. in a classroom), the result may be, as Schmoker (1996, 9) identifies, 'teacher isolation'. In order to make the organization cohesive, effective communication is essential. Public relations and marketing are different from communication, as they involve putting across ideas and concepts; they may be undertaken as much within an organization as within the wider community.

Methodology, assessment

Assessment is essential for promoting effective learning and in practice is an on-going job function for formal educators who continually assess student progress. Assessment may also, as in all organizations, be job based, often through a structural hierarchy. In addition, external evaluation of the organization is very valuable. This may be at the organization's request, i.e. using advisers and consultants, or required of it, i.e. using inspectors.

Professional development

Providing continuing professional development for members of an organization recognizes the fact that the skills, knowledge and expertise of staff are the most valuable assets of an organization.

Ethos

Less easy to identify, but just as real is the ethos of a school. It is easier to 'know it' than to say what it includes. Nevertheless it may have a number of features. To identify the ethos of a school presumes the ability to obtain an understanding of its *sense* of: responsibility, vision, history of an organization, status of an organization and its component parts, teacher/staff culture, morale, curriculum and its relationships, leadership, mission and philosophy, support networks and public relations, together with a sense of community.

Community

An organization needs members, user groups or a community. A school's community consists of staff, students, parents/guardians and families, and those responsible for governance and support. They can all work together and this will be most apparent, for instance, at large events, such as school inspections and special ceremonies, and also at poignant times, such as the unexpected death of a member of the school community.

Spirituality or values

In addition, a sense of a school's spirituality is represented in its values. These tend to vary from school to school and may be partly conditional, for instance, depending on the local or prevailing culture (Drake, 1998, 162). As Drake considers that a value system does not arise without a 'considered proactive policy', values may be identified by considering answers to the following questions:

- What does a school value and acknowledge in its students?
- What is valued in its staff?
- Are support staff valued?

- Is there a clear sense of the value of education within the organization?
- What does it consider to be the goal of education – is it to develop a working mind or to inculcate skills in order for an individual to make a successful living?
- Is communication valued?
- What is the importance given to developing students' self-esteem?
- Is an ability to learn and to analyse valued?
- Is an ability to adapt monitored?
- What behaviours are relevant?
- Is a sense of social awareness promoted?

It is therefore possible to identify a range of values that a school implicitly or directly supports and promotes.

We may consider it fundamental for a solo worker, employed in a school, to understand what sort of school s/he works and functions within, but in practice does this apply to all such workers? Surely a librarian possesses a degree of technical and specialized knowledge and can function equally well whatever the surrounding. Does a library in a school need to relate slavishly to its surroundings? After all, a library is a library is a library: library functions and procedures surely continue whatever the setting for the library.

Let us take the simplest and most standard or accepted functions of a library – to provide a selection of resources and a system for the loan of these items. In one sense, this is a professional function and technical procedure, common to many types of library, but look at it from the point of view of the borrower. Clearly, this could be a civic duty or an onus on any member of an organization. But relate it to a school's curriculum and we find that it involves, on the part of the student, exercising choice and accepting responsibility for the care and due return of items on loan. Thus, on a daily basis, the library is supporting the ethos and sense of values of a school by providing a facility where life skills of choice and responsibility may be exercised.

If we look again at the list of structures of a school, we can see that the librarian, as manager of a central school facility, supports, uses and relates to many if not all structural aspects of the organization that were identified above, viz.:

Management and administration

Head teacher; finance; communication; vision; accountability.
A librarian, as a member of the staff in charge of a central facility, is ultimately responsible to a head teacher for the management of the library service in the school.

A library should sensibly use a proportion of available funding. The head teacher and finance managers should reasonably expect a librarian to account and plan for the use of funding. Equally, a librarian should expect access to and involvement with the financial decision-making process in order to present reasons why a library should receive appropriate funding.

From very practical day-to-day matters to policy concerns, a librarian needs to be aware of plans and developments in the school, so that the library may helpfully reflect what is happening in the institution. Good communication will enable the librarian to be aware of the vision of the school, and communication structures will enable the solo worker to contribute to the vision-development process. The librarian should be accountable for the good management of the library and information service in the school, for health and safety implications and perhaps for pastoral aspects of school life.

Partners

Staff; students; parents; alumni; governors or trustees; volunteers; local community; professional community; local support, advisory services; inspection; government.
As secondary school library guidelines (Tilke, 1998a, 1) identify, a librarian should have relationships with all these user groups, although perhaps not all to the same extent. Staff and students will be daily users of the facility. Parents may be library users, or support the facility in some way (e.g. as volunteers or by raising funding through a parent and teacher support group). Alumni or former pupils may well support the library through gifts and donations. Governors should receive a report on the library and a nominated

member of the governing body may have a special relationship with the library. The librarian may provide information and be aware of resources in the local community; likewise, the librarian should have links with the professional community, e.g. the local public library service. The librarian may use localized support and advisory services, e.g. support library services and specialist education advisers. The school library and its librarian may well (and, in the view of many librarians and others, should) be included in inspection arrangements for schools. Finally, there should be central and local government policies for school libraries, though they may need teasing out on occasion.

Resources, facilities, buildings, environment

A library is or should be a main asset for the school, in terms of learning resources and a facility for study. It will occupy appropriate building space in a school. It also should provide an appropriate and different environment for the school, perhaps giving a sense of an academic, studious atmosphere. It may be an area that shows considerable investment in furnishing and décor, and in time and thought in identifying use of the library. By this, the school could show the value it feels in and for its library.

Regulations, laws and discipline

A library is a part of the school, and regulations and disciplinary standards that apply throughout the school will also be relevant in the library. Take, for instance, supervision of pupils[1] where the rules of conduct need to be observed within the library as much as elsewhere in the school. Equally, there are particular regulations or conventions that are adopted when using a library, e.g. accepting that it may be a quiet area, to aid study, thought and reflection. Knowledge and understanding of such aspects is helpful for all user groups if a library is to function effectively within the institution.

Curriculum

If the library does not support and extend the school curriculum, through appropriate resources, research exercises and the promotion of individual study, it does little or nothing. In addition, there may be a 'library curriculum' in terms of information skills development. Therefore a librarian needs to be aware of the curriculum and in addition to receiving knowledge and information of this sort, should be able to input library curriculum implications to curriculum managers and others.

Enrolment

In a school with high enrolment levels, there may be pressure on accommodation for teaching purposes. As a 'non-teaching' area, the library may be a casualty in such a scenario and the space may be taken over for timetabled teaching purposes. However, in a school seeking to expand pupil enrolment, a good and attractive library may act as a selling-point in any marketing exercise, however simple or basic.

Communication, public relations, marketing

As identified above, the librarian may develop the school library as a marketable aspect of the school. A librarian may play a more pro-active role in terms of public relations, for instance, in organizing special events (e.g. a visit by an author) and drafting press releases in order to promote them. As well as benefiting from good communication, a librarian needs to be adept at using various methods and judging when, what and how to communicate to colleagues.

Methodology, assessment

Although their job is demonstrably different to that of the majority of workers in a school, a librarian should be included in any job evaluation processes that may take place in the organization. Equally, the library should be fully included in external evaluations of a school's performance. The librarian should have a role in the overall assessment of students' progress by indicating how effective an individual student is in terms of the acquisition and development of study and information skills. The librarian can also contribute towards the evaluation of any curriculum-related study skills programme, and personally assess the performance and quality of the library and information service itself.

Professional development

While there may be specific librarianship training and development needs, a school librarian will benefit from specific curricular and technological training that may be provided to all or selected staff members who are involved with the education of students. A librarian may also provide training to help teachers progress strategies to develop use of the library in support of specific curricula. In addition, the librarian may develop a resource bank of material of a professional nature to assist individual colleagues following formal courses of study.

Conclusion

It may be seen, therefore, that a library, managed by its librarian, should and must relate *specifically* to the school environment. It is not sufficient merely to administer a library without any regard for the context, situation, aims and purpose of the parent body. The features discussed above provide the setting for aspects of the role of the school librarian that will be explored and developed further in this book.

Notes

1   Library Association advice note 'Supervision of pupils in the library outside formal lesson times', reproduced as an appendix in Tilke, Anthony (1998b) *On-the-job sourcebook for school librarians*, London, Library Association Publishing.

2
THE SCHOOL LIBRARIAN

Not that libraries aren't also the greatest cultural institutions of all time: they
are – just as librarians are unsung heroes and saints.   Dirda, 2001

The librarian is the head of the school's library and information service. As
a service provider, s/he can be the major factor in enabling the library to move
from being a static collection of resources that is contained within a room to
a dynamic, active and focused central facility that is of relevance to and valued by the school.

A school librarian needs to possess knowledge and technical expertise,
management skills and a number of competencies. These skills and competencies, in particular, enable the librarian to be:

- an effective communicator within the institution
- pro-active with colleagues in the organization
- politically skilful in order to develop and maintain relationships with individuals and take account of the differing power bases that exist within each
  institution.

The librarian of the central facility makes the school library relevant, meaningful and useful. S/he does not do this by being skilful and experienced only
in traditional skills and attributes of librarianship – cataloguing, classification and indexing – important though they are, but in a wide range of skills
and qualities that are not specific to librarianship but generic. These skills

– qualities, even – include listening, watching, talking in a focused manner, understanding the 'big picture', flexibility, appreciating that priorities shift, tolerance and constructive selfishness (i.e. understanding how and when to press for change and improvement) (Tilke, 1999).

Competencies, skills and aptitudes

A competency may be regarded as the ability or capacity to carry out a skill to an agreed or high standard. If this is related to *any* skill then it could make for a long list for librarians (as for any professional group). However, it is more practical to limit an analysis of competencies to *core* skills. For librarians, these competencies can be defined in various ways. One example is a list provided by the New England Educational Media Association in the USA (Markuson, 1999, 136):

> The school [librarian] understands, promotes, and can provide evidence to support the fact that:

- Information literacy is an integral part of the curriculum.
- Collaborative planning and teaching between the librarian and classroom teachers is the norm rather than the exception.
- Resource based learning experiences and environments are the foundation of the educational and instructional process.
- Literatures, in all formats, are valid, valuable bases for learning in all subject areas, and a robust collection of resources has been developed to achieve this.
- Technology is used as a tool or resource to facilitate student learning.
- The library staff continues to seize opportunities for professional growth and development.
- The resources are organized, managed, and easily accessible to students, faculty, and the school community.
- An advocacy programme that communicates the role of the library to the educational and parent community is strong and productive.
- Ethical use of ideas and information is fostered at every turn.

The above list, while succinct, may nevertheless appear daunting. However, it will be seen that such competencies span the spectrum of the school librarian's job, from resource provision to communication, teaching to technology.

In order to fully appreciate the different roles played by a school librarian, it is useful to look at a job description. A job description outlines the main functions and responsibilities of a post. There are many job descriptions for school librarians – some comprehensive, others brief, some accurate, others vague. One job description, developed by a schools library service in England whose local education authority or board had developed a programme of appointing qualified librarians to secondary schools, was recommended as a standard job description for librarians in the authority's schools. It identified three main job activities – learning, management and consultation (Hertfordshire Schools Library Service, 1995).

Let us take these activities in turn. Firstly, the school librarian is responsible for providing learning opportunities. By providing a range of verbs to show the librarian's role in this regard, the Hertfordshire description makes it clear that the librarian is not just 'responsible' (a more traditional word used in job descriptions) but has more active functions in ensuring that the best learning opportunities are available:

Role: Providing learning opportunities.
Responding to and working to support curriculum development, the head of library and information services:
Guides
Individual pupils in the selection and use of resources for curricular and leisure needs
Provides
Opportunities and activities which encourage independent learning skills
Motivates
And assists pupils to locate, retrieve, interpret, evaluate and present information, for example, through the teaching and assessment of information skills

Assesses
Pupils' library skills in line with accepted subject assessment techniques adopted in school
Promotes
An understanding of electronic information resources and other reference materials, leisure reading, etc.

It can be seen that the activities outlined above indicate a thoroughly rounded role as tutor, teacher and supporter in the curriculum process, relating the resources provided by the service for which the librarian is manager to ways in which pupils will and should use information. This in turn is related to wider aspects of school life, such as student assessment. The job description requires a librarian whose knowledge base spans the gamut of library materials, resources and educational issues. The skills required are those associated with teaching – instruction, guidance, assessment and motivation. Communication and a service-centred ethos are appropriate aptitudes for a librarian to fulfil such a job description.

The second main role for the librarian is that of management. As the Hertfordshire document specifies:

Role: Management
In partnership with the school management team, the librarian:
Determines
The aims and objectives of the library and information service
Produces
Clear policy on the role and use of the library and information service
Negotiates
Funding by managing finances and presenting budget proposals for school needs and for external services such as the Schools Library Service
Provides
A wide range of resources and information services which reflect the aims and objectives, the ethos and the curriculum of the school

Ensures

All pupils have access to learning resources required and that the quality of the stock is maintained through regular selection, maintenance and editing

Develops

Ways of communicating information about resources and services to staff, pupils and other users of the library and information service

Establishes

Systems which ensure the library operates efficiently on a daily basis

Evaluates

The library and information service, monitoring its performance

Promotes

Libraries to the whole school community

Trains

And supports the library assistant where one is appointed.

The job activities outlined above indicate a comprehensive management role that is necessary in order to offer a high-quality library and information service to the parent organization. It is a demanding job description in that the verbs used include 'ensure' and 'evaluate'; here it is not sufficient to merely 'provide'. If standards are to be set throughout the school's library and information service, it is important that the job description for the librarian reflects this fact – hence the use of words such as 'establish', 'determine' and 'negotiate'.

The third and last role is that of consultation, liaison or collaboration:

Role: Consultation

Maintaining

Effective partnership with teachers to identify their curricular requirements and match these to relevant resources

Establishing

Cooperative links with other libraries and information agencies, e.g. Schools Library Service, IT Advisory Service, museums, public and college library networks

Compiling

Databases, bibliographies and booklists

Collaborating

With teachers in the evaluation of learning resources and learning skills

Advising

On the availability of resources needed for curriculum development, for professional development of staff and for educational awareness of governors

Sharing

In-service opportunities with staff and other librarians, making full use of advisory services for own professional development

Developing

And maintaining links with feeder primary schools to ensure a coherent progression in resources and library skills.

These job functions identify in concrete terms the important role of consulting with others in order for the library and information service to meet its potential and therefore to enable others to reach their potential, too. They give firm instances about what constitutes liaison or collaboration, terms that can tend to be vague or inexact. The librarian therefore needs to be an effective and well-organized communicator.

The main headings for this job description – learning, management and consultation – identify the main thrusts of the purpose of the post of school librarian. They can be expressed in other ways of course, so that another job description for the post of a school librarian, for instance, might use three different, but complementary, headings: vision leadership and planning, communication and delivery (Ashcroft, 2000, 10). In Australia, one job description for a teacher librarian again details duties and responsibilities under three headings: curriculum leader, information specialist and information service manager (Australian School Library Association, 2001, 61).

While the terminology varies, a common pattern emerges. It is therefore possible to sum up the roles of the librarian succinctly by saying that this person is 'responsible for providing and managing resources, instigating programmes which facilitate the use of resources and integrating the library into the total life and work of the school' (Hertfordshire Schools Library Service, 1995).

A job description should indicate not only what the librarian is responsible *for* but also *to* whom the librarian is answerable: in this job description it is firmly stated that the librarian should report directly to the head teacher. This indicates not only that the librarian occupies a position that is regarded as a senior post but more importantly that the librarian should engage with all aspects of school life: curricular, pastoral and managerial. To place the librarian otherwise in most hierarchical structures in schools would be in effect to limit the potential of the library and information service. Indeed, a study of secondary school libraries in the UK (Sheffield Hallam University, 2000, 8) found that in nearly 38% of schools surveyed the librarian reported directly to the head teacher.

Negotiating

Negotiating sits uneasily in this list. Arguably, it is a core *management* skill. But it may not be regarded as a core *professional* skill, which is an important difference for individuals who consider themselves to be, and are classed, as professionally employed. In order to make progress with issues identified in this section, a school librarian needs to enter into a certain amount of negotiating with various individuals. It is therefore worthwhile for librarians to consider how much negotiating needs to take place within the organization to progress the role and post of the school librarian. Acceptance of this may help librarians think through the logic of their arguments and point of view and have more realistic expectations concerning likely outcomes from the negotiating process. A survey, undertaken by CILIP to identify employment features for solo librarians, found that school librarians were among those who sent in responses. The headings for this survey may provide starting points for a librarian who wishes to identify issues for negotiation in a school. The survey may be found at Appendix F.

Knowledge base for librarians

The next issue to be examined in terms of elements in the make-up of the effective school librarian is the range of knowledge such a post-holder is expected to attain. Areas of knowledge could be divided into the following three areas:

- educational knowledge
- librarianship knowledge
- technological knowledge.

The use of the term 'educational knowledge' is deliberate. Formal knowledge gained through a teacher training programme or from another educational course of study is one method, but knowledge of education can also be built up in a practical manner: through questioning, observation, practice, reading and so on. Unless validated or formally recognized, however, such knowledge is rarely known about, understood or appreciated (except perhaps through a staff appraisal/development system). Nevertheless, such knowledge can be very real and helpful to a librarian in a school.

Again, knowledge of librarianship as far as it is perceived to apply to libraries in schools is difficult to identify, unless formally validated or assessed. Knowledge of librarianship should rise above procedures and routines to include knowledge of the principles of classifying, cataloguing and indexing, resource search strategies, methods of resource acquisition, exploitation of library networks (both in the physical and electronic senses), and resources knowledge itself.

Currently, professional literature (both educational and the more specific for library science) has a common mantra: the future is technology. From everyday tasks to large-scale developments, the ability to effectively use and know how to exploit technology is basic to library provision in the 21st century. Whether it is a knowledge base, skill area or aptitude – or all three – must be a matter for personal debate. However, in this area at least, it is possible to demonstrate (and have validated and assessed) technological knowledge and abilities.

Professional development needs and opportunities

Apart from being involved in general professional development for the school staff as a whole and being aware of specific educational issues, the librarian in a school will have a need to identify their own professional development needs for updating and refreshing knowledge of and skills in library science. Training offered by professional groups goes beyond the traditional areas of librarianship and also features curriculum awareness, teaching skills (for information literacy) and aspects of management, ranging from finance to behaviour.

There are a number of issues in terms of professional development for professionals who may be characterized as operating as solo librarians, including access, funding, opportunity and time. Basically, it is difficult for a librarian to close the service in order to seek professional development. Alternatives should be identified if possible, although it may be appropriate for the school to decide as occasion dictates that its librarian's training has priority over other needs. Nevertheless, it is likely that a school librarian's professional development may be progressed through private reading, networking and using web-based listservs, attending weekend conferences and meetings outside the school day or during school holiday periods.

With a growing appreciation of the need for lifelong learning and methods such as distance learning, e-learning and other developments, there may be more options available that are suited to the needs of school librarians. This will be an issue for providers of professional development opportunities, whether initial (tertiary) education of librarians or indeed continuing education/vocational support.

On a practical level, it is important for the librarian in a school to identify the need for particular professional development and how that might be met. Although – encouragingly – there are indications that central funding for training of librarians in technology is available in parts of the United Kingdom (Streatfield, 1999, 17–18), nevertheless it is largely true that funding for training will need to be identified within the institution. In some schools, funding requirements for training purposes need to be identified within the library department budget. In terms of inclusiveness, it is preferable that the needs of the librarian be considered alongside those of other colleagues in the school.

It will be helpful to indicate, after the event, how valuable specific (school) librarianship training has been to the individual. Rather than relate the detail of training detail, any feedback on training received should focus on the benefit to the school through improvement or enhanced services in the school library.

Qualifications and experience of librarians

If we hold that the above knowledge bases are relevant for school librarians, it should be possible to identify appropriate qualifications and measure experience.

First of all, it is helpful to identify the range of staff who typically may staff and manage school libraries in the UK:

- *Dually qualified teacher and librarian*. The number of people employed in schools who are qualified both as a teacher and a librarian is still small, though growing. This category, however, was considered to be the ideal qualification for a school librarian in a major report on school libraries in the UK (Office of Arts and Libraries, 1986).
- *Chartered/qualified librarian*. In the UK, a chartered librarian is a professional librarian, who through experience and qualifications in library and information studies has become registered as a chartered member of the Chartered Institute of Library and Information Professionals. A qualified librarian is one who has either a professional qualification or successfully followed a course in library and information studies in a higher education institution.
- *Teacher*. A teacher from a range of different disciplines may be appointed to manage the library in a school. The teacher either may or may not undertake in-service training in running a library. Many teachers 'i/c of the library' do this in addition to existing (subject) teaching/pastoral commitments. The actual time allowed and devoted to do this job may

be very small indeed, although there may be other support in the library on a daily basis. As such, the post can be seen as one of liaison with teaching staff or simply taking responsibility for the allocation of the library budget.

- *Teacher-librarian*. A teacher-librarian is technically different from a teacher in charge of a library (described above) in that a teaching timetable may be reduced or not be relevant as the teacher's main job is to run the library. The post-holder may have some training for the job (again, possibly via in-service opportunities). In Australia, however, it should be noted, a teacher-librarian is the norm in state schools where a teacher from any discipline may become a teacher-librarian, having been seconded to follow a postgraduate course in school librarianship (Todd, 2001, 10).

- *Other*. This category will include perhaps retired people, volunteers or people employed on a non-teaching basis in the school. At any rate this is the largest group of people running school libraries in the UK, though there are considerable differences in the home countries – for instance, secondary or high school libraries in Scotland are staffed mainly by qualified librarians. There are probably many motives for people in this group to undertake such tasks: loyalty to the school, interest, suitable conditions and location for work, luck and 'being in the right place at the right time'. A position may have come about by personal recommendation or knowledge on the part of senior management, a useful solution perhaps when there is little understanding about how to recruit a librarian or perhaps when the field identified from advertising is considered to be small or unsuitable.

(It should be noted that pupil or student assistance is commonly found in schools. However, this group is not relevant at this time as we are looking at the variety of groups who may be *responsible* for libraries in schools.)

The overall ratio of chartered librarians to UK pupils was found to be one to 2220 (Sheffield Hallam University, 2000, 62). This compares with one qualified librarian for 1941 students for the state of Rhode Island in the USA: not a great deal of difference. However, there is a dramatic change when the British ratio is compared with that found for the state of California: one to 6361. It should be noted that these states were ranked 49th and 50th respectively out of 50 US states, in terms of provision of librarians in public or state schools (Hones, 1997, 165). Disparity of provision is therefore not isolated to the UK. The point is that the provision of qualified librarian posts in schools is not universal.

According to a survey of secondary school libraries (Sheffield Hallam University, 2000), categories of staffing in UK school libraries were as follows:

Full-time chartered librarian	29.3%
Part-time chartered librarian	7.3%
Full-time teacher librarian	2.4%
Part-time teacher librarian	1.2%
Full-time teacher	12.8%
Part-time teacher	1.2%
Other	46.8%

On the basis of this survey (one in three sample), it can be seen that in nearly half of the secondary schools in the UK, libraries were not managed by a person qualified in either librarianship or teaching. School libraries, however, are staffed by chartered librarians in 36.6% of cases and teachers in 17.6%.

From these statistics it is easy to identify those who hold a formal qualification in librarianship. It is, however, almost impossible to identify just who has a formal teaching or educational qualification as some of the chartered librarians may indeed also have an educational qualification (perhaps as a result of self-evaluation of their continuing professional development needs).

As far as dually qualified personnel are concerned – and indeed those persons who are qualified/experienced in educational matters and librarianship – Loertscher (1999, 9) asserts that the librarian 'holds a unique position' in a school because such a person has:

- Knowledge of the curriculum

- Education [as librarians in the USA additionally hold teaching qualifications]
- Experience
- Tools and materials expertise
- Knowledge of . . . technology to enhance learning
- A repertoire of successful practices with a wide variety of teachers, students and technologies – thus serving as an idea fountain
- Knowledge of student achievement over time.

The experience-base for librarians may be multi-faceted. Experience as a school librarian is one aspect but experience may be gained in other forums too. Many non-teacher school librarians in the UK come to the specialism with experience from other library and information science sectors, such as public library services or from other branches of the academic sector – colleges and universities. A number of librarians have moved from the special sector, including legal, commercial and industrial information sectors. Indeed, personnel may have moved to school librarianship from a number of fields, such as business, graphic design, accountancy and so on.

There is a view that to be a school librarian, experience from a background as a children's specialist in a public library service is necessary or at least beneficial. As can be seen, this is a misconception. There are links of course, and it may be helpful background, but librarians successfully bring their very individual experiences from a variety of backgrounds. This is because the inter-personal nature of the job and the need for significant self-motivation (without perhaps the support and help of a dedicated team) will be best fed by experience of the working world and in particular from interacting with other professional adults.

Some would argue that to be a librarian in a secondary school is not a suitable first professional post for newly qualified librarians, because of the factors identified above. However, at least one higher education institute in the UK that offers courses in librarianship has a programme to place students in secondary schools in a given area as part of the student's course. Students may have had experience of the working world prior to commencing a course of study in library science and the placement exercise at any rate provides an experience-base. Support has been available from the university concerned as well as the local schools library service. It has been seen as successful, so much so that a number of placements have led to permanent appointment as school librarian for the individual concerned upon graduation.

One aspect of experience that may be helpful in supporting the librarian is that of coping with stress. One librarian considers that 'many school libraries are staffed by only one person but have developed beyond the person's ability to cope with the mental, physical and emotional demands made on them' (Spink, 2000, 175). Work experience may provide some basis for analysis and strategies for negotiating improvements in both working conditions and development of the library service.

Trainee positions

As has been pointed out above, there is a concern that experience of the working world is helpful in order to be a school librarian, so that the post is not suitable for new entrants to the specialism. However, in addition to the placement scheme operated by one university referred to above, a small number of schools offer trainee or assistant librarian positions. This can be helpful for new entrants as support and a small team framework are available to enable professional development to occur. It also provides an element of a career structure.

Status, position and role of the librarian in the school

While it is advocated that the school librarian reports directly to the head teacher and – by implication, at least – has a firm position in the school, it does not necessarily follow that such a situation invariably comes about. Indeed, there may well be considerable misunderstanding of the role of the librarian, sometimes even leading to tension between various groups of staff in the organization.

For instance, the question 'Are librarians teachers?', headlined on the website of the American Association of School Librarians (Small, [2002]), is answered there by a review of the literature. In this, Small comments that a survey in the USA in the early 1990s 'indicated that more than one-quarter of a [librarian's] time is spent in class instruction and teacher training. This amounted to more than 13 hours per week in which the LMS [librarian] is involved in teaching activities.' This issue is further discussed in Chapter 4 on curriculum management and while it may readily be accepted that librarians teach, the question may still stand: are librarians teach*ers*? The question is therefore not so much about the function of the job, but rather the conditions for the post, in other words, employment conditions.

So, a librarian teaches and the issue is more related to the perception of that role by colleagues in the school. The status of the librarian in the school, especially regarding employment conditions, may not be clear. For instance, a librarian who is involved with developing the library in the curriculum may be invited to a departmental meeting. Such a meeting may take place after the school day. The librarian may be employed on a part-time basis. Attending such a meeting may be outside the employed hours of the individual. Does the librarian go to the meeting? Professionalism may 'rule the day' but what if attending such meetings in order to collaborate with colleagues (identified elsewhere in this book – especially Chapter 3 – as a key aspect of the job) becomes a regular event? When does it become imperative to argue that the job demands more than the time and conditions allowed?

In the UK, surveys (not least Sheffield Hallam University, 2000) have found that the employment conditions of librarians employed in schools vary considerably. In particular, this concerns salary, holiday entitlement, hours worked (generally full time or part time during the school term only), insurance cover and so on.

In order to avoid tensions such as those identified above which – on a daily basis – dilute the effectiveness of basic job functions, a librarian should therefore be employed on library duties in school on a full-time basis. In addition, the librarian's job description should be clear and the status of the post-holder unambiguous and recorded in appropriate school documentation. Librarians in schools may have used missionary-like zeal to develop the role of the library and the post of librarian but to embed significant development requires an overall understanding of the role that should not only be subject to the efforts of individuals. This of course is a huge issue that needs not only to be addressed by the library community or profession but also even more so by teacher-training programmes and professional bodies of teachers and (prospective) head teachers. Awareness raising and promoting an understanding of roles with the teaching profession will do more to set standards and raise expectations than lobbying by the library community, even though it is accepted that the latter is an important strategy and activity.

An ambiguous status in a hierarchical organization makes for unclear lines of communication and imprecise expectations. As has been established, a librarian in a school needs to communicate effectively and collaborate with a wide range of individuals, so a clearly understood role is important if the library is to make significant and sustained development.

Compromise is usually possible. For instance, it may occur that a librarian takes on further responsibilities, perhaps to become a full-time member of staff, e.g. examinations officer. Indeed, it tends to happen that many if not all staff in a school undertake extra duties and accept further responsibilities in return for allowances or increments in salary progression. So it is not very different for a librarian to take on other duties, though perhaps not traditionally associated with the role of librarian. It is possibly a question of balance – to do other things in a school may be perceived as a normal part of the school culture and of the conditions of being employed in a school. However, if taken out of balance there may be a dilution in the understanding of or lack of clear perception about the role of the librarian.

It should not be forgotten too that success as a librarian may bring promotion within the organization. Promotion as a school librarian tends to be limited in both scope and opportunity, so a school may reward good service by promotion through adding a range of responsibilities to the portfolio of duties of the librarian. When these duties are accompanied by appropriate salary, condition and status benefits, it could be argued that it would be churlish of a librarian to deny advancement!

Relationship with the school's board of governors or trustees

The relationship may be formal and distant. Anecdotally at least, it was certainly true in the past that librarians only saw governors at meetings of the governing body where the meetings were held in the library (the library having been closed to the school for the purpose or to prepare the room for the meeting). In a number of schools the link is strong, perhaps through a governor taking an interest in and responsibility for reporting about the school library to fellow governors. In others, an annual report or other communication that summarizes the position of the library over a given period may be required. A librarian may be familiar with various sub-groupings of the governing body (e.g. a committee that is concerned with finance). However, the library should also be represented in all relevant school documentation, curriculum reports, etc. Some school librarians are indeed members of governing bodies, being elected or appointed to be a representative of the school staff. Clearly, a link of some real sort is useful with a body that has considerable responsibility for the development of the school.

As a staff governor, I represent the non-teaching staff of the school on the governing body. This also involves being involved with various sub-groups, so I am a member of the Pupil and Personnel Committee. I'm also Governor Training Representative . . . and so am organizing an ICT evening for governors to show them what kind of work the pupils are doing with technology, such as word processing, Powerpoint, database use and construction, and so on. As a governor, I'm also on the panel responsible for selecting our new Head. Being a member of these bodies has been of great benefit to my continuing professional development as I feel as though I have learnt a lot from observing senior management in these situations. It has also been helpful in that governors get to know who you are, rather than a name on a staff list, and that personal interaction probably counts for a lot.

Sue Ward, school librarian, Nottinghamshire, UK

Pastoral role of the school librarian

This is something of an unappreciated role. As with perhaps any member of staff in a school, there is an implication that the librarian will relate to students, understand and empathize with them as an individual. Formally, of course, the library resources can support a personal and social education programme by ensuring that access to relevant personal information is available in various formats. (Indeed, the role of resources as bibliotherapy has been recognized for many years in librarianship.) A librarian may also be a tutor in a school that operates a group tutee system (a member of staff acts as tutor to a group rather than a whole class of students).

Close liaison with relevant staff concerning sensitive personal issues that may be covered in the curriculum will be especially helpful, for instance, sex education and bullying. The librarian may also be aware of specialized information services in the community that would be helpful to both specialized staff and students.

Support staff

For a facility that requires order to be efficient, procedures and routines are important. They are also time consuming. These job activities need to be carried out, but it is arguable whether the school gains the most benefit if the librarian, as perhaps the sole worker in the library, is solely or largely employed on servicing basic functions. There is a case for some form of support in the library, whether through dedicated or shared clerical staff or volunteers. (A job description for a library assistant is reproduced in Appendix C.)

Who is the best person to manage the library?

The UK Library Association (now CILIP)'s *Guidelines for secondary school libraries* recommends a chartered librarian as the most suitable post-holder in secondary schools (Tilke, 1998a, 30). However, a more pragmatic view should also be considered. This may be based on a concern that there would not be enough librarians to fill posts were such a recommendation acted upon. In the absence of any national directive about this issue, local conditions apply so that chartered librarians are employed in some areas but not others, but it can also vary between neighbouring schools. Scotland, however, is a notable exception, where it is usual for chartered librarians to manage high school libraries.

One factor in this issue has been the role of schools library services (SLS), the centrally organized support services in many local education authorities, who have had a firm advisory role concerning local development of library provision in schools. Some SLS successfully argued for local policies and funding so that qualified librarians should be appointed to each secondary school. As a result, in a number of areas in the UK, there were secondary schools with qualified librarians, often with common job descriptions, conditions of service, salary levels and support. However, for a variety of local reasons, this did not happen everywhere and the political climate has now changed in terms of the role of education authorities and support services (to more of a client-customer base) (Heeks and Kinnell, 1992; Lowe, 1992). As a result, the employment of chartered librarians is still fragmented across the country.

Case studies in professional journals attest to the developing role of qualified librarians, though in a number of cases such reports are anecdotal and articles may not be refereed or supported by research. Nevertheless, it can be seen that qualified librarians enable libraries in schools to engage in the learning process and effectively support the needs of students and teachers (e.g. Howard and Hopkins, 1988). However, it does not automatically follow that a developed and effective library will always managed by a qualified librarian. Whether it is a case of 'exceptions to prove the rule' or perhaps variable local factors (e.g. support from schools library services) must remain a moot point. It perhaps can only be said that – logically speaking – it is more likely (and easier to achieve) that qualified librarians will make sustained development possible than other groups of staff.

The ideal person to manage the school library has been regarded as a dually qualified teacher and librarian (Office of Arts and Libraries, 1986). As noted above, it is considered that only relatively few posts for a school librarian in the UK are filled by individuals who are qualified in such a manner. A number of librarians hold degrees in education (usually at master level), but that could be regarded as being subtly different from the concept as developed by the LISC report, as the OAL report is commonly known. The survey quoted above (Sheffield Hallam University, 2000) does not identify post-holders who are dually qualified. It does identify teacher-librarians but such posts (in the UK) do not require the holder to hold a qualification in librarianship. In this, it is different from the situation in Australia, where teachers in charge of secondary school libraries must have completed a course and hold a qualification in school librarianship.[1]

While in practice the lack of dually qualified librarians in UK schools may be due to limited employment and remuneration opportunities, the advantage of librarians so qualified is to promote and interact with the curriculum with the status, skills and experience of a teacher. However, a survey by Todd (2001) lists tensions identified by teacher-librarians in Australia that are similar to those experienced by librarians in the UK and USA (Bush and Kwielford, 2001, 10). Indeed, one Canadian teacher-librarian (Branch, 2000, 5) indicated that 'teacher-librarians are often assigned teaching duties, or other administrative duties such as . . . Guidance Counsellor'. In the UK, the issue for teachers and teacher-librarians is probably more one of being assigned substitution or relief duties to cover for absent colleagues. In a similar way to school libraries being used for other purposes when necessity dictates, teachers, when undertaking non-teaching duties, may be susceptible to being seconded to other teaching duties.

However qualified, what is important is that the librarian has a range of competencies, skills, knowledge and experience to fulfil the role effectively. Irrespective of the holder's qualifications and experience, it is vital that the post is a full-time appointment, otherwise impact will be marginalized. Managerial skills and outlook will further help in finding ways of furthering the role of the library, by identifying and working with the decision-making and managerial processes that are subtly different in each school. Furthermore, these attributes should be able to be assessed and evaluated by others. This could be done by means of job assessment or evaluation.

Role of head teachers and senior management teams in the library

Appraisal

Which leads us to the role of head teachers, rectors or principals and senior management teams in the role and development of the school's library.

It is not helpful or logical for the manager of a facility that may consume a proportion of annual funding and which is, in accountancy terms alone, a financial asset to the school, to be excluded from job assessment and evaluation procedures for school staff. Such an occurence will again give rise to uncertainty and ambiguity. However, it is not difficult to see why such a situation occurs. A librarian's job is different from teaching per se and technical aspects of the job may dominate the image senior management have. Naturally, because of unfamiliarity with these duties, management may be reluctant to appraise. As a result, a librarian may not be appraised or assessed in the same way as teaching colleagues. However, there should be enough common ground for the librarian to be fully involved because a librarian

- contributes to the learning process and curriculum development;
- is a manager of resources, staff and money in a similar way to others in the school – including heads of academic/subject departments (Jones, Jenkin and Kirkham, 1996).

Librarians in schools may be concerned that there is no one who can effectively appraise or assess the post-holder's level of skill in and knowledge of librarianship (and perhaps who can empathize with the tensions and difficulties that may have been encountered). One solution might be to allow another person to be also involved as appraiser, for instance, a representative from a schools library service who would typically have a relevant background and experience, including that of assisting with job appraisals on a regular basis.

Integration of the library

Loertscher (1999, 17) advocates an active role for head teachers or principals in the role of the library in the school. His checklist includes the following suggestions for head teachers so that they:

- provide in-service updates on library matters for staff or faculty on a regular basis, whether through short sessions or regular announcements or items at staff meetings
- place librarians 'on major governing councils and at curriculum meetings so they are included in curriculum decision making'
- ensure that teaching staff and librarian have time to plan, including providing 'incentives for collaboration to occur' (perhaps by making collaboration contribute to the annual evaluation for both teacher and librarian) and celebrating successful initiatives
- view documentation about planning and evaluation forms for projects to develop curricular-focused library use in order to monitor progress
- evaluate, after the event, in terms of more effective learning, as well as efficient use of resources and technology; in addition, expect an improvement or different learning in a curriculum area where collaboration is taking or has taken place.

Appointing librarians

But perhaps the most important job that a head teacher has is in selecting and appointing a librarian to the school. It is vital that the head teacher and others are clear about what they are looking for in a librarian. As school employees, librarians are appointed fairly irregularly. For instance, if a librarian has worked at a school for ten years, it is possible that a head teacher may never have thought about the selection or even appointed a librarian to the staff of the school. As there are about 25,000 members of the library profession in the UK compared with over a quarter of a million teaching staff, it is even possible to make a mathematical equation of the likelihood of head teachers appointing librarians!

Advice is available in a variety of forms. There are several professional organizations concerned with school libraries. In addition, school library services in most local education authorities provide help, support, advice and resources. Finally, there are independent consultants. Head teachers and senior management team members may use various networks and visit other schools to see libraries and librarians in action.

Advice to head teachers on appointing a school librarian from a schools library service

---

As a library plays such a pivotal role in ensuring sustained development and enhancement of learning and teaching for all members of the school community, not least students and staff, it is essential that the librarian has both professional and personal qualities to allow him/her to make a full contribution to the ethos of the school. Our specialist training in information management, reader development and relevant ICT applications makes us uniquely qualified to meet the demands of the curriculum, to support lifelong learning and to encourage the reading habit. As well as professional qualifications and experience – I don't think this is a first professional post – head teachers need to appoint someone with excellent inter-personal skills, an appreciation of the education world and a flexible approach in order to deal with ever changing demands. Above all, librarians should have an empathy with young people.

Sue Jones, former school librarian and
Head of the Hertfordshire Schools Library Service, England

Because librarians are appointed relatively infrequently, it is vital that the school can articulate and agree the main elements about the job the librarian is required to do. It is also important to draw up a person specification, identifying the skills and competencies, qualities and experience that will be most successful in a school.

It can be concluded that the head teacher or 'principal is also the key to the quality of school library media programs within schools' (Morris, 1995). What then is the benefit for the head teacher and the school for all

this activity? Morris, again: 'The Principal gains a school that is coopera-
tively functioning to provide quality education for students.'

Other issues for librarians in schools

A number of other issues remain to be discussed in relation to the role of
the librarian in the secondary or high school.

However, a role may develop in relation to the library as a haven or
refuge. As Primrose (1993), writing in the higher education sector, explained,
'the function of library staff is often misunderstood: some see us as too remote
or exalted to approach at all; others see us as menials . . . others again see us
as universal aunts'. The understanding of the overall role of a librarian may
be unclear, thus the image of the school librarian is ambivalent and this can
be a help to some students who may find secondary school life daunting.

Using the library, especially during free time (e.g. break or lunch) may
of course be a 'staging post' until students feel confident enough to make
friends and use other parts of the school. Others find a role in the library
as a volunteer or student assistant (pupils should never be called librarians).
But if the library is used as a place of refuge for too long, pupils may find
it difficult to integrate with their peers, so advice should be obtained from
specialist support staff in the school. One school librarian helped to assist
with the pastoral development of students in such a way and researchers
noted that the librarian has 'a unique position in being able to observe pupils
during recreation time and this might give an insight into both behaviour
and possible courses of action' (Williams and Wavell, 2001, 120).

A school librarian may be also aware of students who are extremely
concerned about their academic progress. Such students may spend all
their time in apparent study but may also confide in the librarian about their
fears. Without breaking a confidence, the librarian may provide some coun-
selling about studying (as a tangent of study skill development) and, if
appropriate, encourage the student to talk about her/his progress to specific
teachers, tutors or specialist support in the school.

The librarian should also be aware of bullying and anti-social behaviour occurring in the library, itself. For this reason alone, it is useful for the librarian to be included in communication to staff concerning pastoral, social, personal and health education needs of individual students.

Employment issues for school librarians

The variability of employment conditions for librarians in schools has been discussed (under Status, position and role of the librarian in the school) earlier in this chapter and elsewhere (e.g. Sheffield Hallam University, 2000; Tilke, 1998b). While there are a number of aspects of such situations, the most important are that librarians should:

- Identify particular concerns and whether they are unique to the school or shared by other, similarly placed individuals (perhaps in the locality). Be clear about the method of improving the situation – it may be in the power of the school to alter conditions, or, if applicable, perhaps the local education authority or board. The librarian should also ascertain whether s/he needs to alert appropriate trade union and/or legal representation. As an information professional and teacher of learning skills, the librarian will be adept at gathering and assessing information, before acting.
- Consider health and safety implications. As a service-focused facility, the librarian may need to be aware of specific health and safety implications for the employee. (As a manager, the librarian will be aware of implications for users of the library and information service.) This can include consideration of safe and healthy use of technology and ways of coping with natural disasters. At the other extreme, it will also involve a review of personal safety, perhaps from individuals within or without the organization, even, sadly, human disasters, whether one thinks of specific weapon-related incidents involving schools in countries as far apart as the UK, the USA and Japan.

Conclusion

'Conflict management; stress management; media presentation; prioritizing and learning to say "no"; leadership; management of change'. These were some of the conclusions reached by a committee looking at the training needs of a particular group of professional people, as reported in one national newspaper. There is perhaps nothing in this list that is startling, indeed it applies to a number of groups of workers. However, it made the pages of a national newspaper because of the professional group to which it applied: Anglican bishops. If proof were needed, this indicates that changing roles and adapting professional direction to new needs applies to all groups of professional people in society.

As school librarianship comes of age and moves from missionary work to developing flexible, focused services and managing a central facility of relevance to the curriculum, librarians in schools will be as aware of this trend as any other group. Yet, in developing an overt educational role and coming to terms with – even embracing – technological functions it is important to provide balance with the core skills and competencies of library science.

> Of course librarians must be responsive to the needs of their community be that an academic, private or public setting. However, as professionals, they also need to be guided by a set of core values. They must be flexible enough to deal with a changing world, but be strong enough to resist the latest fads and the seductive voices of populist commentators, who neither know nor care for the library service.
>
> Usherwood, 2002

Librarians' main skills will still be their best assets, but it is important to enhance rather than replace competencies with new skills and knowledge.

Note

1   A job description for the post of a teacher librarian is reproduced in guidelines for school libraries in Australia (Australian School Library Association, 2001, 60–2).

3
CONDITIONS FOR LEARNING

> The focus of [the] school library . . . has moved from resources to students to creating a community of lifelong learners. Students and their learning remain at the core of library . . . services, shaping the functions of school library media specialists [librarians].
>
> American Association of School Librarians, 1998b

Without learning, the library in a school would be nothing, as the need to learn is often the driving force that brings students to use the library. By using the library well students are learning. The product of schools is learning. Yet there is sometimes a contradiction between the phenomena outlined above and the perception of the library and its manager among those concerned with academic development in the school. In other words the library may be seen as a support facility in the school but one whose role is passive, so that interaction with the development of the curriculum is minimized.

In addition to such inaccurate views by the librarian's co-workers in the institution there may be a lack of knowledge and familiarity, on the part of the librarian, with educational theory, and in particular with that for learning. Finding out what students need to learn and know is one aspect of the job of a librarian, but understanding how they learn and how students could learn is an important mindset for the librarian to acquire.

This chapter looks at the contribution of the library to learning in the school, by focusing on major research in the area of secondary and high school libraries. The chapter also identifies other factors that school librarians need to consider if they are to provide effective learning conditions so that students may engage in real learning in the school library. However, this chapter will not attempt to explain educational theory or discuss the merits of Piaget, Dewey, Bloom and others (there are sufficient books, people and training courses for that). Rather, the aim is to identify some new issues in educational thinking as an introduction to discovering implications for the school library regarding effective learning.

Effective learning: the role of the school library

A question that is perhaps left unsaid more often than not refers to the effectiveness of the school library in terms of teaching and learning in the school. When asked to justify the library or to give an account of its performance, statistics and other output or quantitative measures could be supplied, but these go little way to identifying the effectiveness of the library as regards learning. Research into this area provides the librarian and others with findings to aid thought about how their library can better work to effectively support learning in the school.

For instance, research conducted by Streatfield and Markless (1994) for the British Library, to identify the effect on teaching and learning by school libraries, has looked holistically at the school as a teaching and learning organism. By looking at the roles of students, teachers and librarians, researchers analysed four models of learning:

- A school that may be characterized as offering a traditional or didactic teaching model. In this type of school, the focus is on direct teaching, even for topic or project work (where it exists) and is controlled by the teacher who typically does not involve the librarian. There is 'limited' involvement on the part of the teacher with the library. The teacher, however, expects the librarian to be organized and to respond to requests. In this type of school, as researchers found, teachers do not have a clear view or image of the library. Student use of the library is 'constrained': the librarian tends to be asked where things are and the main exercise of research is at sixth form or grade 11–12 level.

- A school that is 'nominally flexible'. Teaching and some 'independent work' are hallmarks of the teaching style in this sort of school. Where topic work exists, the theme is 'notified' to the librarian and specific resources requested. Teachers use the library as a source of information and resources. Their view of both library and librarian is as a 'good thing' but with little expectation (or views) beyond that. Students' use of the library is largely when sent by teachers and then they tend to ask the librarian for answers to the assignments set, rather than research themselves.

- A school described by the researchers as 'developmental'. Teaching, in this sort of school, is matched by a number of project assignments, where the theme and approach are discussed with the librarian, whose support is 'requested'. Teachers use the library as a source of support and help and their expectations of the librarian are the same. In addition, they consider that use of the library is important for students. Student use is characterized by class use. Students ask the librarian for help and advice when they encounter difficulties.

- A school where resource-based learning takes place. In such a model, there is an emphasis on learning. Project or topic work is 'planned and delivered' with the librarian and teachers' use of the library is regarded as 'central to learning'. Teachers' expectations of the librarian is as a 'colleague and ally' and of the library as an important resource for learning. Students (who are adept at using the library) see the librarian as a 'point of access beyond the library', enabling them to use specific resources that exist elsewhere.

Given such models for learning in schools, it is useful for secondary school librarians to work out where they think their facility is placed in the learning continuum. It is not only possible to use the overview described above but also a range of performance indicators and targets identified by Streatfield and Markless (1994) which centred on:

- whole school level – including policy, school development plans, library development plans, budget, access, librarian liaison
- departmental or faculty level – including curriculum knowledge, reference in programmes of study to resources, library induction courses
- classes or year groups use of the library – effective and consistent use of resources, information skills courses
- teachers – use of library, liaison with librarian, preparation of students for library-based assignments, curriculum development and liaison involving the library
- students – homework, class and recreational reading (using library resources); use, ability and 'confidence' in use of library resources; voluntary use of the library.

In addition to the research outlined above, two other main research findings are available to enable school librarians to identify their library's role in learning in the school.

The state government of Colorado, in the USA, has undertaken research to identify how the school librarian and school library enable students to achieve given educational standards. Irrespective of school, economic or societal factors, it was found that individual reading scores in the state's student assessment programme improved because of *increases* in a number of features of school library development. In particular, the research (Lance, Rodney and Hamilton-Pennell, 2000) found the following contributed to improved scores:

- *Increases in library provision* (per student/100 students). This included the opening hours of the library and the number of hours that library staff were employed. It also identified resources, including books, periodical subscriptions and electronic reference titles and overall library expenditure.
- *Increases in information and communication technology.* Computer networks, linking libraries with other areas of learning in a school, also individual resources, licensed/subscribed databases and internet access.

- *Collaboration.* Effective liaison between librarians and teachers was found to be a factor in helping students, together with the time librarians spent as 'in-service trainers of other teachers, acquainting them with the rapidly changing world of information'. Also relevant was time spent planning co-operatively with teachers, teaching information handling or information-literacy skills and managing a computer network enabling library resources and facilities to be used beyond the physical area of the library.
- *Flexible scheduling.* A factor was also the ability of students to visit and use library resources on an individual and group basis (rather than formal class use) on a need-to-use basis.
- *Indirect effects.* A number of other factors were also identified, including the level of engagement by the librarian(s) with school management and school-wide issues (which often led to a more direct result of collaboration, as identified above). In particular, indicators were found to be:

— regular meetings with school management and administration
— membership of curriculum and other committees and working groups in the school
— involvement in whole school and faculty/departmental meetings.

Interestingly, the Colorado research is entitled *How school librarians help kids achieve standards*, thus not merely throwing the accent on resource provision but highlighting the role of the librarian, working with other colleagues to develop the curriculum and being a partner in the learning process.

Recent research in Scotland (Williams and Wavell, 2001) looked at the impact of the school library on learning through case studies and focus groups. Two main client groups, teaching staff and students, were featured together with interviews with librarians. It is true that the views of teachers in particular 'were based on broad expectations of what the impact might be' but, altogether, the perceptions of impact were found in the following areas:

- acquiring information and knowledge
- developing information-handling, technology and reading skills
- 'higher achievement in school work'
- greater independence in working derived from developing study and reading habits
- ability to use study skills 'confidently and independently' and – importantly – to transfer these skills 'across the curriculum and beyond school'
- greater motivation
- development of interpersonal skills.

Case studies looked at broader educational areas of student motivation, progression, independence and interaction, and found indicators that are useful for librarians and others to use to assess the impact of the school library on learning processes and outcomes. For instance, motivation:

> Evidence of motivation was seen . . . by pupil enjoyment and participation and absorption in the tasks set . . . [such as] a project [or] looking for reading material. The indicators were identified as
>
> - Verbal and written expression of enthusiasm by pupils
> - Pupil willingness to participate in the activity set
> - Pupil application and absorption in the task
> - Willingness of pupils to continue their work either by returning to the [library] or at home
> - A change in attitude towards work over a period of time.

The report identified some fundamental issues that are essential in order to develop real learning experiences through use of the library. These were found to be:

- collaboration and liaison between librarians and teachers
- acceptance that effects are not easily identifiable or rather 'visible', but are certainly there in the wider context; arising out of the point above,

the report hints at a useful role for the librarian in formal networks, committees and groups debating and developing the curriculum in a school

- acceptance too – and understanding and use – of information-handling skills in the curriculum.

Collaboration and liaison

From research outlined above, it is clear that the over-riding common factor in ensuring that the school library has an impact on learning is through collaboration and liaison between teachers and the librarian. This may be achieved through:

- whole school meetings and projects
- departmental liaison and initiatives
- relationships with individual teachers.

Ideally, a mix of all three levels is best in order for relationships and motivation to be sustained.

Whole school involvement

The librarian should be entitled – as a matter of course – to attend meetings of the whole school teaching staff and to be able to do so. Whether matters are of direct relevance to the library or not is in itself irrelevant. The library is a part of the school and in order to play a full part, the librarian needs to know about curriculum and pastoral matters. (As this book aims to show, if a library is working effectively, it is relating to many areas of school life.) At these meetings, the librarian can make helpful comments about various issues and highlight the role of the library. Periodically library issues may be raised at such a whole school meeting. Where the school is organized in terms of upper, middle or lower school or other large groupings, again it is relevant for the librarian to be able to attend various meetings.

Departmental liaison

Working with departments in the secondary school should be a major strategy for the librarian. Attending heads of departments meetings is a useful job function as specific issues will be discussed, perhaps still in a whole-school manner, but nevertheless in some detail, and it will be important that the librarian is able both to attend (and listen) and to contribute. Specific detail could more effectively be discussed at meetings of individual departments.

In addition, the librarian should have a good relationship with senior curriculum managers or directors of studies. The library provides essential support to the curriculum and it is important to convince these individuals of the role of the library and potential contributions that can be made. It should be possible to ensure that the librarian receives departmental syllabuses, if not schemes of work, or a curriculum audit that may be copied by departments to the senior curriculum manager.

Nevertheless, it is important to be realistic about what the library can achieve, so it may be helpful to target individual departments at a particular time, rather than a general 'blanket' or 'scatter gun' approach. If such an unfocused approach were made, the result could be that either there may be little or no take-up or indeed too much at one time. It is preferable to focus on a department in each or perhaps only some of the disciplines: sciences, social sciences, arts, mathematics, languages and physical education.

Individual colleagues

A school librarian's ability to work successfully with a range of personalities in a school is a useful competence to develop. Arguably, for very practical reasons, working with individuals is a most effective approach for the librarian in a school to adopt.

The advantage of this method of liaison is that, if individuals are spread across subject departments, the library does not become over-associated with specific departments. Depending on the stage of development of the library, small, easily manageable projects with clear outcomes may be more helpful as a strategy to improve the effective role of the library in the school.

It may be too cynical to suggest that individuals may be targeted in individual departments in order to sow seeds for more whole-scale library/departmental development, but no doubt such an approach is possible. It is more likely that liaison will grow more naturally from informal contacts. However, it should be a strategy to target newly appointed members of staff, who should all (as a matter of course) visit the library at an early stage in order to become acquainted with the resources and services of the library.

Effective collaboration

Collaboration should be quite easy to achieve, but in practice it is relatively infrequent, as a survey of secondary school libraries in the UK (Sheffield Hallam University) in 2000, found. This may be due to lack of time, staff, status, opportunity, communication and/or motivation. These factors relate both to the librarian and others in the institution. However, such conditions can and should be overcome over time, at least in part. Strategies to overcome these limits to useful collaboration include:

- Identify or reason just why departments are not using the services of the library to support the curriculum. There could be practical reasons, e.g. physical distance of a department from the school library. Another common reason given is the length of individual lessons or periods in the timetable. But library resources could go to the department (as a bulk loan). Other possibilities include library subscription to web-based database services that could be networked to departments.
- Be aware of curriculum developments, both in general and in particular, as they impact on the school, and consider library implications. If a librarian does not have *entrée* to appropriate meetings where these matters are discussed, it may be helpful to compose a short report about library implications. This should be couched in positive language, and sent to the chair or convenor of the meeting, and, if appropriate, other colleagues

who will attend. Either ask for comments or suggest that the librarian could attend the meeting to listen and make helpful and appropriate comments.

- Alternatively, a librarian could obtain a copy of minutes of meetings and indicate, positively and pithily, how the library could help. When minutes are reviewed (i.e. matters arising) at a subsequent meeting, it may be possible to suggest that notes concerning library implications are communicated (preferably by the librarian).

- It may be helpful, when developing fruitful collaboration, to liaise with one department at a time, as identified above, as it will be more practical to visit individual departmental meetings as a special invitation (i.e. a one-off attendance). Alternatively, a librarian could accommodate a meeting in the library, the better to show just how the library may be involved in concrete curriculum development.

- Targeted communication should be varied in medium (i.e. by means of printed report, newsletter, e-mail and intranet) and use the language of departments and curriculum initiatives. This may heighten the profile and encourage the customer to ask (which is always better) for collaboration, with a view to working together or using the services of the library.

- Focus on individual students who may be motivated, efficient and effective users of the library and information service. This may be more interesting if the student habitually adopts different behaviour patterns between the library and classroom. In another way, students who may be causing concern could be another way to develop liaison. The library, for instance, may be able to assist with supporting the student, not by being a place to isolate them but a place for them to work on a curricular basis.

Figure 3.1 shows the flow process for collaboration with colleagues. It shows the role of each individual or group, the processes and outcomes that should occur when effectively collaborating together.

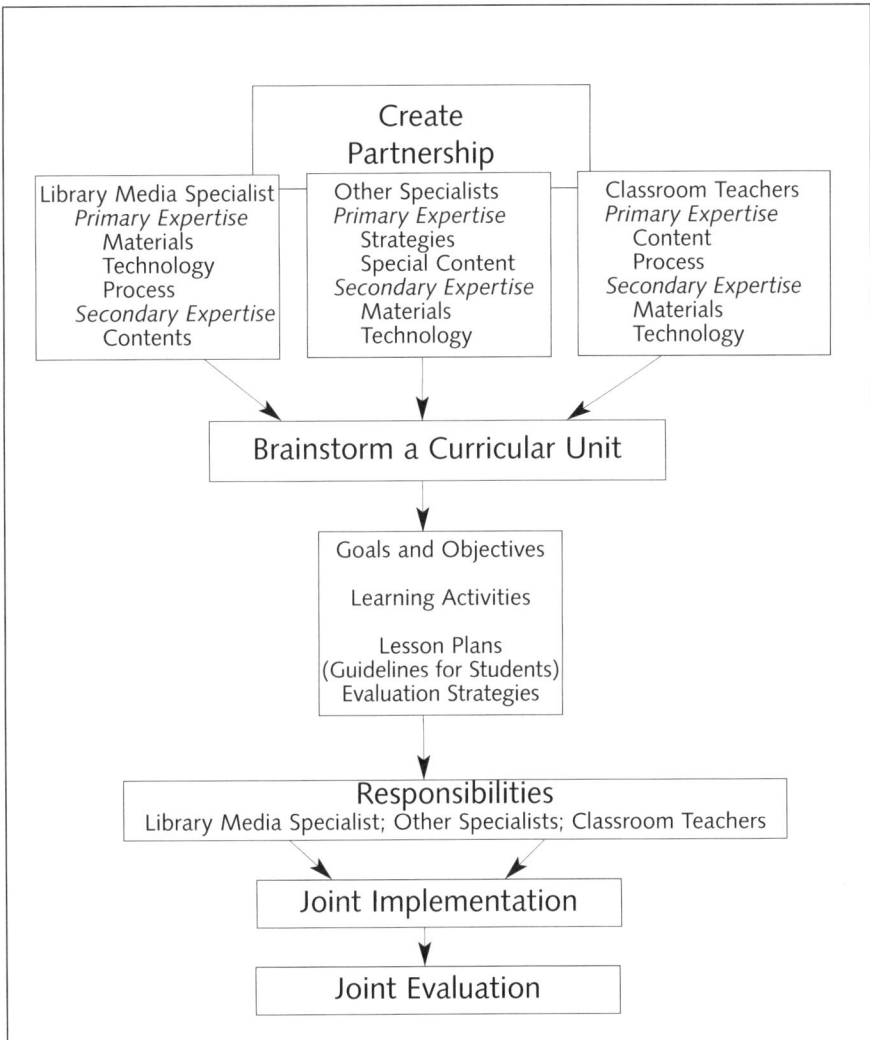

Fig. 3.1 *Curriculum planning with teachers: flow chart*

Reproduced, with permission, from Loertscher, David V. (1999) *Reinvent your school's library in the age of technology: a guide for principals and superintendents*, San José, Ca., Hi Willow Research and Publishing, 10.

Librarians will be liaising with . . . teachers to improve the literacy skills of their pupils. Ensuring progression in pupils' information handling skills will be a key objective.

Secondary Link Inspector (English),
Nottinghamshire LEA, UK (Powell, 1999, 8)

Projects are co-planned by the teachers . . . and the librarian and (projects) must contribute to students' content knowledge of the subject as well as their skills base to be considered a success.

Secondary school librarian, Bradford, England (Barrett, 1999, 5)

The student's conditions for learning – implications for the school library

There are a number of other conditions that students need to be able to learn effectively. Some, such as information skills or information literacy, are familiar to school librarians, but other aspects may not be so well perceived.

Biological needs of students

While educational matters are generally at the forefront of political life, social policy and current issues, focus may at times have concentrated on the organization of educational structures and formal curricula and examinations. But there has been a shift in educational thinking over the last decade, taking on board arguments and views of biologists, such as Thomas Czerner (2001) who, in his influential book *What makes you tick*, said of teenagers that 'at about the age of twelve' changes to the brain produce a result 'to markedly reduce your capacity to remember and learn'.

A neurologist (Thompson, 2001) further outlined this phenomenon (interestingly in a syndicated article in general newspapers – further indicating the more widespread interest in this area):

But what really caught our eye was a massive loss of brain tissue that occurs in the teenage years. The loss was like a wildfire, and you could see it in every teenager. Gray matter, which brain researchers believe supports all our thinking and emotions, is purged at a rate of 1 percent to 2 percent a year during this period. Stranger still, brain cells and connections are only being lost in the areas controlling impulses, risk-taking and self-control. These frontal lobels, which inhibit our violent passions, rash actions and regulate our emotions, are vastly immature throughout the teenage years.

However, there is unease about such conclusions. Caution has been advocated by a number of educationalists until further research is available, not least by Prof. Michael Barber (2001, 21) on behalf of the British government. Barber considers that while 'we in education will watch and learn from science . . . the implications for educational policy and practice are just beginning to emerge'. Again, the 'jury is out' on another aspect of research into the way the brain works, that of emotional intelligence or emotional literacy; nevertheless 'there can be no doubt that an individual's emotional state and ability to deal with their feelings can impact on their educational performance' (Bartlett, Burton and Peim, 2001, 156). What seems to be clear is that findings about brain research now and in the future are an educational issue that schools will need to address.

A related issue is research into sleep patterns and habits of teenagers, particularly the identification of important biological functions. Although evidence is limited, the National Sleep Foundation (2000) in the USA found that 'sleep researchers believe that insufficient sleep in teens and young adults is linked to . . . low grades and poor school performance . . . negative moods . . . increased likelihood of stimulant use'. The foundation has lobbied for 'sleep-friendly schools'. This involves educating school staff about the effects of sleep loss and how to identify it, also promoting an awareness of the necessity of good sleep habits among young people themselves, perhaps through curriculum programmes. The Foundation also considered there was a need to 'structure the school schedule and related activities to accommodate adolescents' sleep needs and behaviors' such as adopting later starting times for schools (which a number of schools in the USA and elsewhere have in fact done).

Understanding these conditions for learning will be important for a school and in particular, as far as this book is concerned at least, the school librarian. It is acknowledged that to move from a discussion about a tightly focused topic such as effective learning in the library to biological needs of teenagers may appear frivolous. However, it is an example of the school library relating to overall school and student needs, and can have very practical implications for the school library. For instance, there may be implications for the arrangement of the library, together with a consideration of the atmosphere to be promoted. Consider the need for the library – as is traditional – to be a quiet place. There is research to suggest that absolute quiet does not aid study but that this is in fact helped by the presence of low noise. Perhaps, then, low-volume piped music should be played in the library, possibly with the provision of beverages and snack food. A review of furniture may be appropriate if one wishes to take on board the more relaxed seating preferences of teenagers. The library could be divided up into rooms to cater for differing learning styles. In addition, there may be a need to reconsider what is appropriate behaviour for users in the library. Possibly thought needs to be given to the opening hours of the library: do they reflect the learning habits of teenagers?

Or is it useful to have a more formal atmosphere, with all the implications that that entails, and firmly focusing on study and research? Is this debate about engaging in feng shui or about creating optimum conditions for learning in the library? As with so much else, it is for the school that sees its library as integral to learning to decide for itself, for the questions raised above affect not only the library but the school as a whole.

But, for a whole host of practical, pedagogical and philosophical reasons, the library cannot and should not be radically different (in its aims, codes and regulations) from facilities and other areas in the school without a great deal of thought (with the possible exception of dual-use (public) libraries). At the very least, for a school library to be different, there needs to be distinct evidence in the library policy to that effect, and that in itself indicates that the school has made a clear choice about how the library should aim to be effective. There are therefore implications for school libraries – as for other areas and aspects of school life – from the more important educational, biological and other aspects of learning that are currently being discussed and developed.

Social and personal education

The library is a facility in the school that could be well placed for students to practise their personal and social education (PSE) skills. A simple example should suffice to demonstrate this aspect of learning in the school. Students may select resources from the library. By doing so, they are exercising choice. When borrowing material from the library, they take responsibility for its care and safe return. They also interact with an adult in a service setting, providing opportunities for the exchange of simple courtesies. Such a straightforward and common example of the library supporting learning should not be decried: 'student responsibility and behaviour are an integral part of growth and development; they dramatically affect the academic climate of a school' (Schmoker, 1996, 97). PSE may be observed informally in the library, that is, outside of formal lessons times. This can be a role that is unappreciated, so needs to be highlighted by the librarian. It can be marked though, for instance to 'enhance self-esteem by enabling pupils to have their work recognised in some way, for instance through awards or displays' (Williams and Wavell, 2001, 110).

Behaviour management

A young person's brain, biorhythms and learning styles may have identifiable behavioural bi-products. This may be manifested in schools by adverse or inappropriate behaviour on the part of students. The library may be a forum for the exhibition of such behaviour, which may range from mild intransigence to violence.

Awareness of and strategies for managing alternative behaviour should be considered as a condition for effective learning, as found in research discussed earlier in this chapter. 'The policy in school A encouraged a respect for the needs of others while working in the [library] and this calm, studious atmosphere was reflected in the pupils' behaviour when compared with the classroom and other schools where there was not the same emphasis' (Williams and Wavell, 2001).

In Chapter 2, the pastoral role of the school librarian was identified. Skills and knowledge associated with this role may be seen in the librarian's management of student behaviour in the library. There may be occasions, e.g. breaks from formal lessons and outside of the formal school day, when the librarian deals with or accepts that behavioural standards may be different from that expected within formal tuition time – in other words, students may need to relax or 'let off steam'. If this is the case, the librarian should consider just how far behavioural differences may go and ensure that students and staff understand such nuances.

At least one school librarian considers that 'the best approach for the librarian to adopt is the behaviourist approach, which recognises that good behaviour is a skill that can be taught' (Spink, 2000, 176). It is a skill that can be developed, in part, by modelling behaviour through observing adult users of a school library.

On the other hand, there may be occasions when individual pupils behave in the school library in a manner that contradicts school rules and expectations, perhaps showing little respect for the library and its manager. It is essential that a librarian is perceived as having an unambigious status with regard to monitoring and setting appropriate standards of behaviour in a library that is clearly understood by students, staff and others. This means that a librarian needs both to be aware of relevant school policies and to be included in them and the procedures for dealing with behavioural issues and problems. On a practical level, it also means that the librarian should be privy to information and communication about individual students, so attendance at relevant meetings is again helpful. In the final analysis, as Spink observes, 'the librarian has to manage behaviour in the library for the benefit of the whole school community'.

Information literacy and plagiarism

Whether defined as study skills, information-handling skills, information literacy or any other term, there is a significant role for the school library in teaching and progressing students' skills. Guidelines for school libraries insist that 'Good information skills which contribute to effective learning are essential' (Tilke, 1998a, 61). A skills curriculum will encompass library, technology and revision or reviewing skills, together with those of reading (e.g. skimming and scanning) and writing skills, such as note-taking and essay writing. While an induction session or programme may often be found in schools, a progressive curriculum, based on an audit of skills and the curriculum, may be less common and therefore may be an issue addressed by library development plans. Skill development certainly provides students with a framework for effective learning.

On the other hand, plagiarism could be regarded as a result of insufficient study skills teaching and learning. At worst, it could be a manifestation of adverse behavioural patterns. Especially when the internet is used, plagiarism may be a result of a casual attitude to learning and a low awareness of the concept of original thought. Nevertheless it is an identifiable by-product of learning and the library should have a particular role in ensuring that adequate procedures and strategies are in place for dealing with plagiarism.

Conclusion

So, not all schools are the same. Curricula may vary but learning styles certainly will. Therefore all libraries in schools will be different, and rightly so. Nevertheless, in the recent past, there has been a common goal, which has been described as the 'Holy Grail Model . . . the "all singing, all dancing" learning resource centre dedicated to supporting independent learning – fine, if that is what the school is really trying to do' (Streatfield and Markless, 2001, 3). This universal goal has caused many libraries and librarians excessive effort to attain an inappropriate purpose. It is far better for the library to effectively support the school where it is, educationally speaking (and where it is going); hence the need for a relevant policy and development process and plan for the library (see Chapter 5). An understanding of learning and conditions to optimize learning in the school is therefore essential to the process of linking the library to the curriculum. This chapter has aimed to provide options for identifying effective learning in and through school libraries and raised a number of issues about how pupils approach learning. If factors and conditions outlined in this chapter are not considered, it is highly unlikely that the school library and information service will be in a position to meet the challenges of change which inevitably affect schools.

As an agent for change, the library and information service could be slightly in advance of practice (teaching and learning styles) in a particular school. If the library is established at a radically different point from the rest of the school, it will not fully engage with colleagues so that collaboration is ineffective or non-existent. It is vital therefore that the library is placed at an accessible point on the learning continuum of a school but nevertheless that the librarian is poised for library-curriculum development when change occurs.

4
MANAGING THE CURRICULUM-RELATED ROLE

A curricular leader and a full participant on the instructional team, the library media specialist [librarian] constantly updates personal skills and knowledge in order to work effectively with teachers, administrators, and other staff.

American Association of School Librarians, 1998a, 4

Guidelines, publications, conferences and training courses for school librarians all continually link the school library and the curriculum. Keeping up to date with developments in school librarianship necessitates a focus on the curricular role of the school library. It can be said that a school library exists through and for the school curriculum. This chapter therefore looks at aspects of the management of the curriculum as regards the school library, particularly highlighting the skills users need to access in order to benefit from using resources and information.

But why should there be such an accent on the curriculum or rather why does it have to be continually referred to and articulated? Perhaps it is because such thoughts may be 'honoured more in the breach' than otherwise. Just refer to an index or contents page for books on educational matters and identify how many entries there may be for libraries or similar terms, such as resources. It is sadly probable that there are very few such entries. Hence the need to focus the thoughts of educationalists – when they thought or think of libraries in schools – away from a vague feeling that they are 'a good thing' to something more focused and relevant to mainstream school life. This was certainly how educationalists tended to think in the past.

After all, this may have been a reason behind the establishment of a government working party in the 1980s which produced an important report known to British school librarians simply as the 'LISC report' but whose full title is *School libraries: the foundations of the curriculum* (Office of Arts and Libraries, 1986). This report aimed to focus the mind of government and the educational community, indeed many groups other than purely the library community, on the importance and function of library services in schools, especially in relation to the curriculum. It was a formative document and although it applied to England only, it was a catalyst for similar initiatives elsewhere. Working parties and reports subsequently appeared for other home countries in the UK (Northern Ireland, Scotland and Wales). It made many recommendations concerning libraries in schools and schools library services (SLS), not least advocating national and regional policy for school library provision, appointment of qualified librarians in secondary schools and the focusing of school library resources on the needs of the curriculum.

However, it is one thing to talk about resourcing or supporting the curriculum and another to actually do so. For any librarian contemplating this huge task, it is advisable first to be absolutely sure just what the curriculum is, in other words, identify just what the librarian is letting her or himself in for!

Identifying the school curriculum

'The curriculum is often referred to as though it were a collection of subjects that appear on the timetable of schools, but another way of looking at the curriculum is as all the experiences that the school provides' (Bartlett, Burton and Peim, 2001, 72). It may be held, therefore, that the school curriculum can be divided into three broad areas: a formal, stated curriculum, an emotional, behavioural and social curriculum, together with a wider or hidden curriculum.

- *Formal stated curriculum*. This curriculum and its content in terms of subject coverage may be easily identifiable, especially if there is a state or legislated codified curriculum that governs all schools in a given area. But even here there may be variations and options, perhaps to do with several educational bodies offering syllabi for public examinations. Therefore identifying just exactly what is included in an individual school's curriculum may still take some work. School documentation should be used to supplement official documents. It may be that official documents form the basis of a librarian's survey of the school's own curriculum, followed by general school documents, supplemented by detail that may be found in departmental data and handbooks.

- *Emotional, behavioural and social curriculum*. The basis for personal and social education (PSE), or an emotional curriculum, may also be found in official information. Again, options or particular applications for the individual school will mean that the librarian needs to consult a school's own documentation for supplementary, specific information, and talk to colleagues in the school. 'There can be no doubt that an individual's emotional state and ability to deal with their feelings can impact on their educational performance' (ibid., 156), so an understanding of the elements of this curriculum will assist librarians in their exercise of behaviour management in the library. It will also assist with providing resources to enable students to develop an understanding of acceptable bounds of behaviour, together with resources that deal with, for instance, peer pressure and bullying, death and bereavement, sex education and drug abuse.

- *Wider or hidden curriculum*. Finally, a wider curriculum will exist in schools but information on or about 'it' may not be forthcoming, at least in detail. To gather helpful information about what it is will involve the librarian in using advanced information-handling skills (akin to those of a private detective, perhaps), identifying, observing and piecing together information from many and varied sources. This aspect of the curriculum is related to the values, morality and ethos of the school, so consideration of the importance of students being truthful, honest and principled may be regarded as examples of a wider or hidden curriculum.

In addition to the above, which is really focused on content, it is helpful if the librarian is aware that there are two other important aspects of the curriculum: pedagogy and assessment. Pedagogy is the science of teaching, and styles of learning prevalent in a school are an important aspect for the school librarian to bear in mind, as discussed in the previous chapter. Assessment is concerned with the formal measurement or testing of learning and again it is essential that a librarian accepts and appreciates that assessment of library involvement in the curriculum should occur in order for the involvement to be valid (Bartlett, Burton and Peim, 2001, 73).

The library's role in supporting the curriculum

Having arrived at an understanding of the school's curriculum, it is sensible to identify potential library support or involvement. The following basic functions should be identified in the school library policy. They should also be the corner-stones or foundations for planned library development and be the focus of liaison with and publicity to subject teaching staff.

Resources

Resources will typically be in a variety of formats. They could be cross-curricular in nature or entirely focused on the needs of one subject, grade area or age range. Resources may be permanently owned by the school, available for a period of time through a paid subscription to another organization or borrowed from a central service, such as a schools library service. The relevance, ability range, quality and quantity of resources the library can offer will be key to supporting the curriculum.

Services and products

As well as resources per se, a school library can provide a range of value-added services. The library's catalogue is a service to users, allowing individuals to access the school library's collections through a variety of access terms. Particular equipment may be required in the library in order for users to interrogate data contained in some resources. In addition, the library may publicize recent acquisitions, offer a reservation service and provide current awareness services, e.g. for periodicals. The library may also be involved directly in supplying a reprographic service to teachers.

Information literacy, research and study skills

Resources and products provided by the library and information service require and demand skills in order to effectively select, evaluate and use information and data in the library's collections. As identified in the previous chapter, the librarian can offer courses and practice in information literacy skills to students.

Study facilities

Opportunities for private, individual, quiet study should be valued by the school and associated with the library. Study facilities may be provided throughout the library and/or focused on a particular area of the facility. In addition, the library may offer facilities such as a smaller room off the main library area for group work and for seminar purposes.

Getting the library's role across

Through an understanding of the learning style(s) of the school – discussed in Chapter 3 – the librarian may better identify curriculum areas and tailor potentially useful library functions to further and enhance the school curriculum. Then well-understood school policy about the library should be used as the basic plan for the development of the library.

As identified in Chapter 3, close liaison or collaboration with individual subject teachers and departments is vital in order to embed and progress the concept that the library will usefully engage with learning and the curriculum in the school. However, the librarian will need to work with a range of other employees who also work in the organization in order to develop the curricular role of the library. These groups and individuals include:

- *Information and communication technology staff.* While technical expertise is vital in the modern secondary school library, it is important to understand the limits of an individual's technical skills. Where an individual librarian's skills and experience with technology and its applications are extensive, it is useful to work out just what is appropriate for the librarian to do in terms of technical support and development. In other words, is it more productive for the librarian to interact more with the user and the information available through technology or to spend time on making technological products work? It is important therefore to relate to the ICT department and benefit from their skills and expertise. Technology teachers should perceive that the library uses technology in a real way. In addition, there is common ground in use and teaching of ICT skills, so collaboration is helpful too.
- *Support and office staff.* Specialist support in other areas of the school, such as science departments, may be useful contacts in order to further stronger links with departments. On a practical level, good links with office staff may be helpful as they may facilitate access to senior management.
- *Special educational needs and other counsellors.* The professional literature indicates a growing awareness of the role of special educational needs teaching staff, health educators and others in relation to a burgeoning role for the library, be it a question of a contribution to life skills, emotional literacy, information skills or knowledge for citizenship. Indeed resources may have a 'bibliotherapic' function, where use of appropriate materials may provide explanation and empathy for a particular medical, psychological or social condition. Librarians will typically be experienced in catering for the library needs of individuals and can offer this aptitude as a service to other specialists in the school.
- *Senior management or administrators.* One school librarian suggests that librarians should 'persuade even one major administrator, who sets classroom schedules, that your programme is worthwhile, and you are off to a fly-

ing start. The rest requires little else but hard work' and also suggests that 'it helps to start at the top. And start big' (MacDonell, 2001, 15).

 It is important that the school librarian understands other people's agendas and is sensitive to the overall needs of the school. However, good foundations, through policy and development and on-going liaison with individual teachers, *should* over time develop an understanding that the school librarian is concerned with supporting the curriculum, students and the teaching staff.

It must be accepted, however, that this does not happen all the time. For some librarians, at least, it can be depressing. One wrote a letter to an educational magazine (in response to an article that outlined the different groups of people who work in schools and neglected to include librarians) which concluded 'I know for sure that I, and many others in my profession, do not exist at all'. As this is not necessarily an isolated or extreme view, it can be concluded that getting the curricular role and function of the library and its manager understood and appreciated is simply not easy, nor is it inevitable that change will occur. One expert on educational change noted that 'not every situation is alterable, especially at certain periods of time but . . . successful change is possible in the real world, even under difficult conditions' (Fullan, 1991, 101).

Given such untenable or depressing situations, a natural consequence is to lose heart, become cynical or possibly negative. A librarian may be so focused on problems for the library in a school that it may be understandably difficult to consider the relative problems of other departments and areas of life in the school. Taking a wider view may not only reduce feelings of lack of motivation but could offer a way through. Teachers, too, may have similar concerns: for instance, a feeling that their subject is on the fringe of and not important to the curriculum, a perception that the students they teach do not achieve good enough results in public examinations or that they are not able to offer high-status courses. It is often salutory for the librarian to realize that other colleagues in the school may have similar experiences or rather have similar perceptions about their place and status in the organization.

It is therefore advisable for a library manager to firmly relate to individuals within the school. However, because the librarian in a school may be 'solo' with no peer or someone with a similar background to talk to, it is also helpful to use networks or other support outside the school. For example, listservs for school librarians exist and can provide a means of information and advice (information about several relevant listservs is provided in Appendix H). Professional organizations are important resources too.[1] Local networks of school librarians may offer solace, support and co-operative ways of working. Local advisory services, such as schools library services (common in many local education authorities in some countries) offer a valuable – and sometimes largely unperceived – advisory and support service. So a school librarian can seek practical help, advice and empathy from a team of librarians, who are experienced in supporting school libraries and may have held a similar post themselves (Tilke, 1997, 11). In the management of change, which is by definition uncertain, it is important for a school librarian to build up helpful support networks.

Dependency on the library

Sadly, occasionally a secondary school library may be used – ostensibly in a curricular fashion – with more dependency than is desirable, rather than as a support. This may happen as a 'one off' but when it occurs more regularly, the school librarian should be concerned about the library learning experience and attitude of students. A librarian will be able to identify it because typically a class will just appear in the library without notice, possibly without a teacher, students have no clear idea why they are there or what to do and no liaison with the teacher concerned has occurred.

It is possible to salvage the position there and then by briefly giving students some tips about researching and by trying to make the experience positive. After the event, it would be helpful to feed back to the absent teacher and by trying to generate positive reactions to what is really an unsatisfactory experience. Where this practice occurs repeatedly and the above strategies do not work, then it is advisable to take advice from a network of librarians or the Schools Library Service, but certainly also from a departmental head and others in the school. In addition, strengthen and re-issue guidelines to staff concerning the use of the library (not forgetting to include safety implications, i.e. if an emergency evacuation occurred while the class was in the library, who is responsible for registering them?). In the final analysis, a class could be returned back to the teacher and the classroom. At the end of the day, it is important that teaching colleagues can count on the library as a positive experience and that they and their students do not associate the library with a 'sink' or negative and ill-focused situation.

Curriculum involvement for the school librarian – getting started

Rather than starting with resources and considerations about staff involvement, it may be helpful to consider how students cope with the need to research and find real information. The following case study of a real enquiry may illustrate this point.

Case study of a student coping with real information

Why is February a shorter month than other months in the year?

A question asked of a Grade 7 student, who had several options in the library to research, i.e.:

- reference (print) sources
- non-fiction titles
- internet/world wide web.

In order to provide a full answer, the student found that one source was not sufficient. He had to extract and use information from a variety of sources. For instance, he could usefully use information on solar and lunar aspects, but also needed knowledge about the position of the axis of the earth at the beginning of the calendar year. In addition he found that Roman names for months could yield an answer. The student was dealing with a real enquiry and using real information that, in the nature of things, is very untidy.

The student also needed to:

- understand a variety of search terms, e.g. 'February', 'calendar', 'months'; some sources provided cross references, but such prompts were not always in evidence
- use several sources which could be best accessed in the time available through use of particular reading skills, such as skimming and scanning
- identify relevant resources from a larger number of possible tools and this involved judgement, keeping to task and confidence.

Once relevant resources were accessed and used, the student found that he needed note-taking skills, together with those of reviewing and evaluation.

The above is an example of a 'simple enquiry' that should only have taken ten minutes, or so the student (and his parent) understood. There may indeed be other aspects to the exercise that are not identified above; however it illustrates the point that high expectations, together with an unarticulated assumption that students possess certain skills, exist. Analysis of homework results may provide part of the answer concerning the level of expertise in the process, but the librarian may usefully suggest that library involvement may assist in raising academic achievement in very practical ways.

Case study of a senior student searching for specific material in general books

'Do you have any books on puddings and desserts?'

This was an enquiry from a student who was six months away from attending university. The student had looked in the school library a few days previously as the librarian concerned had, on request, directed her to the cookery and food section in the library. The student came back two days later to look again and not having found specific books on puddings and desserts, asked the librarian for help. It was found that the student did not need detailed information but some photographs of puddings to give her ideas for a collage as part of an art portfolio for an advanced course. By looking inside a number of general cookery books, sufficient stimulus material for the student in the form of photographs and illustrations was found.

Again, a 'simple enquiry'. Again, the librarian assumed that a student possessed the skills to locate the necessary material. In this example, causes for concern were:

- A student in the final year of school life was unfamiliar with the principle of how materials were organized in the library and unable to use aids (subject index and catalogue) to locate material.
- There was limited awareness of how material might be available, e.g. the student could not find any books with the words 'dessert' or 'puddings' in the title so assumed that the library did not contain any relevant information.
- Analysis skills were not used, so logical thinking skills were under-utilized, i.e. the thought process: desserts are parts of meals so 'dessert > meal > general cookery' was not gone through.

However, there were some positive aspects in that the student:

- thought about using the library (or perhaps was encouraged by the teacher to do so)
- asked the librarian for help

- did not give up at the first attempt but returned hoping or thinking that more material might be available.

Overall, some implications for the librarian could be:

- *User education*. The student joined the school from a nearby school in order to follow an advanced course of study, so user education needed to be provided at such a stage in the student's school career.
- *Curricular use of the library*. It could be concluded that skills learnt earlier in school (even at primary or elementary education levels) were not practised. (This is especially an issue when students change from a largely formal taught curriculum in their middle secondary school years to more of an individual approach in their final years at secondary school.)
- *Organization*. The library needed better guiding and needed to promote use of its locational aids.

These simple case studies show the sort of enquiries that school libraries experience every day, yet they indicate the need for being involved in the curriculum. Helping to set assignments and assisting with thinking skills, even before a student has moved from his or her seat in the classroom, the librarian can provide support to students and teachers, enabling more successful learning experiences to occur.

Many practitioners would argue that, in addition to focusing on students' needs, a school librarian needs to start by liaising with the teaching staff. As one librarian commented: 'Many teachers, though reluctant to admit it, have never felt comfortable in libraries, are untrained in research, and afraid of looking lost during a lesson with their own students'(Macdonell, 2001, 15). It is difficult in practice to confront this directly in individual schools. However, some school librarians and schools library services have developed in-service programmes whereby teachers are presented with questions (often real enquiries, collected and recorded by librarians over a period of time) and asked to use library resources in order to find the answers. More particularly, teachers may be asked to record how they found the answer, what they considered were their strengths and weaknesses and what their feelings were in undertaking such tasks. This approach enables a school librarian to simulate the experience of students for subject-teaching colleagues.

It must be noted that that some school librarians are reluctant to take on or develop a role as 'instructional consultant' (Turner, 1993, 11–12). Perhaps they sense a tension between the traditional service of a resource provider and consultant, and a role that advises teachers on teaching methods and learning outcomes as much as anything else. However, the learning needs of students are a prime concern of a librarian, so the role is a legitimate one. It is of course one that needs powers of persuasion, diplomacy and tact in liaising with colleagues. However, the real issue may be one of time management. Prioritizing what is important for a school library to achieve should indicate the importance of liaising with colleagues. Turner suggests using 'attending skills' (ibid., 49) so that, even if the time for liaising with a colleague is not ideal, other needs in the library are put on one side, so that a colleague has the librarian's attention, both mentally and in terms of body language. The interview should be summarized and action identified, rather than leaving outcomes vague.

Two options are therefore available to a school librarian. As Macdonell advised (see above), it is possible to work on a macro scale and prepare a large programme of activities designed to improve learning through the school by utilizing the resources of the school library. This can involve:

- awareness-raising session for the whole teaching staff
- presentations to departmental staff
- information and documentation provided in a range of policy and planning documents, as well as handbooks and other school information – whether aimed at teachers or others (such as governors or trustees and parents)
- a time-frame with the aim of leading to understanding and acceptance of a whole-school policy on learning skills, etc.
- timetabled programmes of induction or information skills
- audit to establish regular progression and reinforcement of skills across

the curriculum and through the age ranges
• evaluation of programmes, skill development and competencies.

Or, conversely, 'think small' and operate on a micro scale. This will involve looking at learning styles undertaken in a librarian's school and identifying the state of policy and development for the school library (as will be discussed in Chapter 5). From this, a librarian and others (including perhaps a curriculum manager or a library steering committee) may consider that it is more effective to work in a very focused or small-scale way. Options here include working with individual colleagues, specific year groups and/or particular subject or phase areas of the school. Such a method of development could be an end in itself or it could lead to assessment and evaluation in order to prove that such a way of proceeding is effective. It is an incremental way of development, requiring time in order to embed itself in the psyche of the school's teaching and learning styles.[2]

Curriculum involvement: progression of the library's role

Again, this depends on the method undertaken to establish the role of the school library in the learning life of the school. Nevertheless, irrespective of the method undertaken, management skills of observation and reflection are needed to assess and evaluate the library's role, whether effected through the provision and promotion of resources or through a programme of user education.

If a large programme has been undertaken, there is no guarantee that it will have an infinite life. Even if all other things are equal, so that pressures and priorities of the moment do not make an impact on the programme, it may need to be developed in particular areas, in the light of evaluation by teachers, students and the librarian.

If the programme operates at the micro scale, there may be considerable scope for development, providing that evaluation has identified that such initiatives are helpful to learning in the school.

If this is the case, individual exercises could be expanded to be a mixture of separate courses within different subject departments or other areas of the curriculum. In seeking to develop the practice of particular skills it may be helpful to just take a small element (skill) and work in detail. Clearly this will vary with the skills in question. For instance, locational skills may not need as much attention over a period of time, but the more complex skill of note taking will require on-going development over time. However, it is important to vary the programme so that students do not become bored.

Orientation courses are sometimes all that can be readily accomplished by the school librarian. This is basic or standard user education and should not be decried in the pursuit of integrated information skill programmes. There may well be a firm place for such courses, as they are often seen as useful for a new intake of students. Such courses therefore are seen as natural events for initial familiarization with the school and its ways. However, orientation courses may also have a useful role for students of advanced courses, especially if students are changing from largely class-taught ways of working to managing subject options and individual study commitments. Orientation exercises will both remind students of resources, services and support and help equip them for the pressures of a new way of working, not least as preparation for life in institutions of higher education.

Guidelines (Tilke, 1998a, 57) indicate that several models for implementing the learning skills curriculum in schools exist:

- separate information skills course
- mini information skills course followed by specific curricular work that expands and reinforces the skills learnt
- integrated cross-curricular approach based on a whole school policy for learning skills provision.

It is relatively straightforward to ensure that specific areas of skills are covered in an entirely separate information skills course; however, it is possible that pupils will not transfer the skills to other subject or curricular areas. In the second model, a measure of curricular involvement means that skills are reinforced and developed, though again transferance of skills may only extend to the areas of the curriculum that are supporting the information skills programme. The final model however 'requires a high degree of cooperation and planning between departments and the librarian, and strong senior management support. Pupils will be provided with a systematic development of information skills in all subject areas and across the age range'[3] (Tilke, 1998a).

A librarian may well expect that incremental use of the library over time will lead to a whole-school policy on information/learning skills. This may happen; on the other hand, it may not. It will be important to realize that change will occur in its own way and at its own pace. In practice, change may be slow and incremental. If only for the self-development and motivation of the librarian, it is important to develop the managerial skills of reflection and assessment, otherwise the practitioner may not recognize a whole-school use of information and learning skills when and if it happens. (Management skills of presenting arguments and suggesting appropriate action by others too may be required of a school librarian to turn a current de facto situation into a formal and recognized position, e.g. 'We now have a clear information skill programme'.)

The teaching role of the librarian

In providing courses, classes, sessions and support to improve learning, the librarian acts as a teacher or tutor. Indeed, US information literacy standards state that 'As teacher, the library media specialist collaborates with students and other members of the learning community to analyze learning and information needs, to locate and use resources that will meet those needs, and to understand and communicate the information the resources provide' (American Association of School Librarians, 1998a, 4). Such a role of mediation is more traditional for librarians as it is firmly part of a service ethos.

This teaching role may be unperceived and owes its development as much to interpersonal and management skills as to anything else. Teaching duties may not be stated in a librarian's job description nor may much be made of them in school documentation. However, for a librarian to engage meaningfully with students and their learning needs, teaching is undoubtedly needed, as an aptly titled research report called *Sneaky teaching* (Valentine and Nelson) identified as long ago as 1988. Indeed, a plethora of published reports have discussed and highlighted the librarian's role in the teaching process (such as British Library, 1990; Streatfield and Markless, 1994; research in the United States noted by Small, [2002]). They identify a common characteristic: that the school librarian has a teaching role that is under-appreciated. Reasons for this may be many and varied. However, this aspect of the job needs careful handling. If it is emphasized too much, the individual experiences and professional skills of a school librarian may be undervalued. If understated, a perception may result that the librarian does not meaningfully engage with students and teachers and their needs.

The school librarian's teaching role may consist of:

- formal class or group teaching
- team-teaching with a subject or class teacher
- small group support
- support and guidance to individual students

and, as with all teaching, preparation and assessment of teaching and learning. Teaching may take place wholly in the library or in other areas of the school, such as introducing assignments with the subject teacher in a classroom or laboratory.

I'm still surprised when teachers and administrators underestimate the amount, level, and importance of the library media specialist's teaching role . . . . You have probably found, as I have, that teaching activities often consume a significant portion of the [librarian's] day, ranging from one-to-one individualized instruction to group training offered to a variety of learning audiences including students, teachers, administrators, library staff, parents, community groups and school boards.

Prof. Ruth V. Small, lecturer in librarianship and information studies, Syracuse University, USA (Small, [2002])

Assessment of the role of the school library in the learning process

Assessment and evaluation will be dealt with in detail in Chapter 11, but it is worth identifying here what assessment looks like in relation to the educational role of the library and its impact on learning in the school. Again, the management skills of observation and reflection come to the fore. As much can be gained from observation and assessment about the *quality* of use of the library by students and teachers as from statistics of library use. Clearly, it will be necessary to agree criteria with teaching colleagues so meaningful conclusions may be reached. Assessment may range from small scale and regular to a large-scale, special exercise.

Lynn Barrett, Librarian at Dixons City Technology College, Bradford, UK, writes:

In preparation for research undertaken for management consultants who were looking at innovations in CTCs (City Technology Colleges), I undertook a survey of staff [which is reproduced in Appendix A] as I was asked to report on our Information Handling Skills Project. I talked with staff who had been actively involved – one or two from most departments. We looked at the following areas and found that as a result of the project the six-year, whole-school project has had a very positive impact.

Impact on pupil achievement
Teachers feel that students use the library and books more effectively. They use the internet with greater confidence and are aware of its inherent problems. Students work independently more effectively and are more selective about the resources they use, using a wide range of skills which are progressed year by year.

Impact on the quality of teaching
Information-handling skills underpin the National Literacy Strategy for Key Stage 3 and thus our work has enabled teachers across the curriculum to actively support the Strategy. Also, teachers are better able to differentiate research

---

assignments and are more aware of what they are asking students to do. Teachers are required to think about the explicit teaching of information skills and to recognize the importance of checking that resources match the requirements of assignments as well as the individual needs of their students.

Impact on teacher workload

There is mainly a different focus to the workload in that skills are constantly being built into any research work planned. The work of research and independent learning is positively shared with the librarians. Teachers find planning easier because of the baseline assessments of information skills that are carried out in Year 7.

Impact on teacher morale

Teachers are more confident in setting research assignments. Teachers have the support and the resources to experiment with different styles of teaching and learning. They feel rewarded when they see that students are more able to cope with the demands and expectations put upon them and, therefore, able to achieve a higher degree of success.

What are information skills?

Once a librarian or indeed others begin to talk about information skills there is already ground for misunderstanding. Just what are information skills? Are study skills, research skills, library skills and information literacy the same? There are so many different definitions of these terms, which of course are not co-terminous. Therefore, in the same way that it is important for a school to agree core functions for its library and express this in its own policy for the facility, it is best that a school comes to an understanding about just what the terminology means and what skills actually are. This should diminish any confusion that in turn may lead to a mismatch of expectations. For instance, a librarian may use the term and really equate it with locational skills, together with those of evaluation, while teaching colleagues may be more focused on the term as meaning meta-cognitive skills, or skills associated with note taking and so on. With a clear understanding of the skills involved, teachers and librarians can effectively identify aims and productively plan for effective teaching and learning of various skills.

Figure 4.1 helpfully shows a grouping of various skills and the progression involved. It can be seen that technology, as much as library skills, acts as a root determinant and starting point for skill development.

Although there are many models of groups of information skills, it is accepted that they are based on a common process that comprise the following:

- planning
- locating and gathering
- selecting and appraising

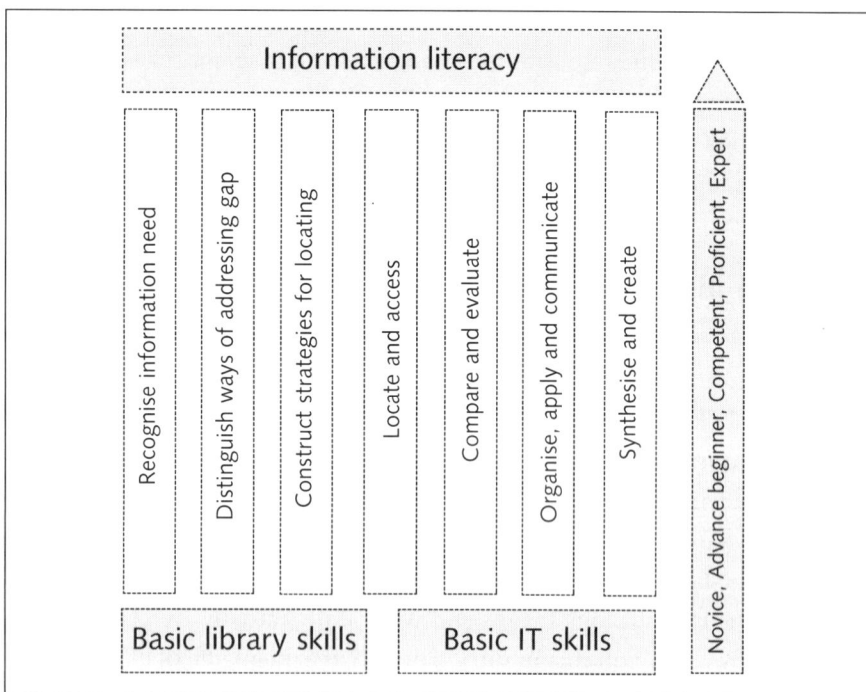

Fig. 4.1 *Skills development flow chart*

Reproduced, with permission, from *Library Association Record*, **103** (12) (December 2001), 753.

- organizing and recording
- communicating and realizing
- evaluating (Herring, 1996; Tilke, 1998a, 56).

The Trinity Grammar School Library seeks to serve the information needs of the students by giving them the skills, knowledge and understandings to help them:

- find their way confidently and efficiently to the information they are seeking
- know the value of competing sources of information and choose accordingly
- evaluate the validity of information found
- transform information into knowledge
- transform information into wisdom.

Darelyn Dawson and Lee FitzGerald. Trinity Grammar School, Sydney, Australia

---

In order to arrive at a realistic understanding with colleagues in a school, it is necessary for the librarian to analyse each of the elements of the common process (above) to identify specific skills. For instance, a very detailed listing of various skill groups comprising 'information literacy' by Markuson (1999, 82–4) includes the following:

Personal management skills
Pupils should be able to:

- understand and analyse assignments
- set realistic goals
- manage time effectively
- participate in group work
- understand the role of resource facilities in the school, including the library and the computer technology centre

- appreciate and follow procedures, rules and conventions, policies and services relating to such facilities
- 'understand the role of the library in a free society'
- 'know ethical, legal responsibilities for reproduction of library materials'.

These skills are wide ranging in extent and demand a great deal from students. The skills may be conceptual in nature and will be developed over considerable time, as much by example, role model and experience as by direct teaching.

Study skills

Pupils should:

- appreciate that skills are related to specific subject areas
- use a range of focused reading skills, including skimming and scanning
- be able to use a range of writing skills and understand the need to write for particular purposes and for different audiences
- listen effectively and be able to frame appropriate questions
- understand the nature of revision or reviewing for tests and examinations, including preparing in good time, use memorizing techniques (perhaps from keyword notes in list form), understand the nature of anxiety and the ability to read an examination paper effectively.

This is a useful interpretation of study skills in which the key activity is metacognitive. Students need to be able to think clearly and logically in order to successfully develop study skills.

Information retrieval skills

Pupils will be able to:

- identify, locate, retrieve, use and evaluate library materials available in physical form within the library, including books, reference material, periodicals, newspapers, videos and discs

- similarly access material on CD-ROMs, intranet databases and the internet (including subscription-based services)
- understand and effectively use a library classification system
- use the library's catalogue effectively, searching under a range of terms, i.e. author, title, keyword or subject
- prepare a list of alternative (or similar) search terms or keywords, relevant to the assignment or enquiry
- combine terms and keywords and search the catalogue in an advanced manner, having regard to Boolean logic.

Although in truth skills tend to be inter-related, these can be characterized as more functional in nature and direct teaching is more appropriate to this set than other groupings. However, thinking is still very much required.

Research skills
Pupils should have the ability to:

- take notes from a variety of verbal, written and audiovisual presentations and resources
- use notes to create helpful original material, e.g. outlines, mind maps, spider-graphs, full written report or other piece of writing or presentation
- analyse and organize material, and evaluate such material/information
- identify authorship and original work and desist from plagiarism
- prepare a bibliography and cite references according to a preferred format
- understand the nature of different formats and use research tools contained within media, e.g. bibliographies and contents pages in books, cumulated indexes to several issues of a periodical
- evaluate sources accessed in a research exercise, together with the ability to identify 'hard data' and 'soft data'.

Again, these skills are linked and work best if progressed and reinforced over time, especially as building blocks to avoid plagiarizing material.

As the list above is clearly comprehensive and possibly daunting for both learner and teacher, it is necessary to be quite clear in discussion and planning stages about the skills that will be introduced and/or developed for a particular group of students. To successfully introduce and develop these skills requires time, practice and a variety of approaches and learning experiences. This may best be developed through a written scheme of work – a library curriculum. However, it will be most effectively developed if applied through the whole curriculum. The benefit of a library curriculum is to express the skills base as an entity, ensure that the skills are not overlooked and to identify the library's role in the process.

Our aim has been to improve the teaching and learning of information skills in a progressive way throughout the school. One problematic area was DT (Design and Technology), but three years ago a research project for Year 9 was devised that has had great success. It involves researching a culture, identifying an image with that culture and then making something incorporating the image. It is a 16-week project, approximately one-half of which is spent on research. It begins with a brainstorming session about what makes up a culture, ancient or modern, and then input from the librarian about where to look and how to organize their findings. The students then choose a culture and do a literature search for appropriate sources. This is followed by having them construct a series of questions, the answers to which will help them form a picture of their culture. There is an emphasis on identifying images. They then do their research, keeping notes and bibliographies. This is followed by design sheets and then on to the making process with jewellery, boxes, bags, etc. as the products.

It is a long process and valuable because it is the *process* of research that is paramount in the first phase. Also, it is constructed so that students cannot just copy and paste a lot of facts together and turn it in.

The project grew out of a concern for the way Year 10 students were unable to research effectively for their GCSE course. The teachers all agree now that the Year 10s are able to research much more effectively because of having had the experience of the extended Year 9 project.

Lynn Barrett, Librarian, Dixons City Technology College, Bradford, UK

Conclusion

In order to promote and fulfil the library's role in the curriculum, the librarian needs to use a variety of managerial principles and practices. Factors to ensure successful involvement of the library in the school curriculum include:

- a librarian with appropriate status, support and time to focus on the learning skills curriculum vis-à-vis the library, involving close co-operation with teaching colleague in planning, teaching and assessing skills teaching and learning
- significant whole school and senior management support for the development of learning skills throughout the school, together with the acceptance of the need for continual assessment of the school's effectiveness in this regard (Tilke, 1998a, 60).

There may be some potential areas of tension over the development of information skills, generally with regard to teacher workload, morale and the quality of teaching. But they do not have to be tensions. Rather, the contribution of school library, subject departments and individual teachers may enable learning to progress more effectively, thus creating a change for the better for those involved in teaching, as well as the learners.

The role of the school library and librarian as an active partner in the curriculum can be well identified. However, it is not and should not be the sole focus for information-skill development in the school because this would isolate and limit effective information-skill learning. Information-skills teaching needs also to take place in the classroom, laboratory and other teaching places in a school. To blend class and library teaching and learning, and to work in co-operation and collaboration with teaching colleagues is essential for successful management of the library role in the school curriculum.

Notes

1   An extensive list of organizations in the UK who can assist school librarians is provided in the resource list in *On-the-job sourcebook for school librarians* (Library Association Publishing, 1998) by the same author.

2   Strategies and tips may be found in *On-the-job sourcebook for school librarians* (Library Association Publishing, 1998) by the same author, 95–101.

3   Library Association (now CILIP) guidelines were developed by a number of practitioners across the UK, who drew on evidence in a variety of formats, not least reports and monographs. In this connection, the guideline acknowledged the following source: Herring, James (1996) *Teaching information skills in schools*, Library Association Publishing.

5

POLICY AND DEVELOPMENT

Muri ga toreba, dori ga hikkomu.
(When irrationality passes [by], reason withdraws.)

Japanese proverb

Policy and development determine our everyday working lives, that of the
users of the library and of the institution itself. How many times do we hear
each day 'Our policy on this is . . .' or 'We need to consider our policy on
. . .'? This chapter looks at the reality of policy and development for the secondary school library and how they are both management functions and tools
for the school librarian.

What is policy and policy making?

Though policy is so all-pervasive, when we as librarians consider 'policy'
in the formal sense, we may think of something that is divorced from
reality or at least everyday events, and is codified and possibly fossilized in
a written document. We may also consider that policy is developed or
approved by others. This can be seen, for instance, in the general
development of school policies on discipline, attendance and staff regulations.

Bureaucrats make decisions by processing information with reference to appropriate rules. Strategic managers make decisions by developing policies and

plans that then provide a point of reference for the information processing and decision making of others.

Morgan, 1998

Surely policy making is purely theoretical? It is theoretical, as issues need to be thought through and considered and ideas have to be communicated. The more complex or detailed a concept is, the more written communication is important, in order to aid reflection and clear understanding.

The mission statement and aims of a school should be basic concepts for inclusion in the library policy. If the library does not relate to these basic tenets of the organization, it shows it is divorced from the main business of the school. They are starting points. Of course, the library policy can and should develop these, and have particular or more detailed aims.

When developing library mission statements:

the school librarian should look to the statements of the parent body. . . . The library's mission statement follows from the school's . . . statement and has been approved. . . . It includes a concrete, attainable and understandable set of parameters for the library in the context of the overall school vision and philosophy.

School librarian, Australia (Yates, 1997, 176)

Ways of getting the organization interested in the library policy

In practice, who, in the organization, is interested in policy *for the library*? Should they, and should librarians and library managers expect them to be? Are librarians interested in policies affecting other parts of the school? Policy is a two-way process. Librarians should be aware of policies in other areas of school and reflect relevant aspects in the library policy and vice versa. Because the library is a central school resource and facility, it is logical to expect that the policy for the school library will be of interest to the school community at large.

A number of strategies to involve members of the school in developing library policy are possible:

- Ask faculties or departments to consider their own policy areas and suggest elements that the library needs to consider for the latter's policy.
- Involve relevant senior managers and governing body.
- Get advice from external contacts, such as schools library services.
- Relate to curriculum documents, perhaps issued by agencies on behalf of central government.
- Consider principles and standards advocated in published guidelines on library and information services in secondary or high schools, either those produced nationally or reflecting a local situation, e.g. those developed by schools library services.

The focus for the Trinity Grammar School Library is on the enhancement of the learning outcomes for all of the students. Because our focus is clear, it was relatively easy to develop the Vision and Mission statements for the Library policy. The Vision statement for the Trinity Grammar School Library is *to create a Library that is the learning and teaching centre of the school.* Add this to the Mission statement that says that *the Library aims to provide a learning environment that values the individual as a lifelong learner who possesses a repertoire of independent learning skills as well as a love of literature.*

The Purpose statements were then developed around the Vision and Mission statements. At all times in this process we were in consultation with the all of the Key Learning Areas in the school.

We want the students at Trinity Grammar School who use the library to:

- value the search for truth and the disciplines of scholarship
- understand that learning is a lifelong process
- possess a love for learning and literature
- value information skills as a tool in learning
- apply knowledge and skills through a set of key competencies

- value creative and critical thinking through the information skills process
- recognize their own learning styles
- be autonomous learners
- celebrate collaborative learning
- be confident in the use of a range of technologies.

Darelyn Dawson and Lee FitzGerald,
Trinity Grammar School, Sydney, Australia

The policy's central tenet: the place of the school library in the school

A policy is absolutely crucial in helping to establish just what is the purpose and function of a library in a school. For library functions, there are many options, such as:

- academic support through a policy of centralized location of resources
- a study centre
- contribution to the school's social inclusion and equal opportunities policies
- a place for the 'sick and unruly' – a place for discipline and to locate pupils who are ill, to withdraw disruptive pupils from classes, a place for the exercise of detention
- an examination room
- a place for meetings of the governing body
- exclusive study place (and informal social area) for senior students, e.g. sixth form
- extra (timetabled) classroom.

Though the list above includes just a few of the possible functions or activities for a school library, there will be some that may cause librarians and others some disquiet, while they agree with others. Some are general, worthy aims, others express specific use – and abuse. For instance, a quiet place seems the ideal place to send a pupil who is sick and cannot work in the classroom. But is it the best place from the pupil's point of view? It may be that s/he would prefer to see a nurse and to be under the supervision of an appropriately qualified and experienced person. The expediency in using the library for this function is surely not relevant in a health and safety conscious world. Once it is used in such a way, other variations on a theme follow.

Another example: it is logical for the governing body to want somewhere quiet to meet for meetings and it seems sensible to use the library facility for such a purpose outside of the school's operating hours. However, is the preparation of the library for the meeting done outside the normal opening period of the library and is it all cleared up in time for the normal time when the library opens again? If the answer is 'No', does this show a regard for an academic role for the library, or indeed a clear understanding of the library's function in a school?

But it is possible to take the list of functions further:

- a place to send classes when teaching personnel cover is not available
- a focus for the school's cultural values
- a place for research
- a centre for technological support
- a facility with intranet management and inputting functions
- support for teaching, team teaching, resource-based learning
- facility to support the school's teaching of literacy
- homework centre
- a place for parent–teacher meetings
- stock cupboard for resources and unwanted furniture.

Again, the list includes functions and roles that seem in keeping with the tenor of policy and the direction a particular school wishes to pursue. But it should be noted that there are other features above that individuals may have reservations about, if not downright disagreement with. Also, general statements of intent are mixed with specific, practical uses. The examples given above range from those that are occasional and can be accommodated or accepted to those that occur regularly and constitute an abuse of the facility. But the list is by no means complete, for it is possible that the school library could also be an:

- archive and museum
- waiting room for visitors
- reprographic facilities centre
- a place for recreational reading
- venue for library-related after-school activities
- centralized (learning resources) ordering facility
- place to be photographed and to conduct interviews
- focus for learning skills teaching and learning.

There may indeed be more functions. It will be apparent that these activities and functions are listed in no real logical order. This is deliberate. From the list above, it can be concluded that there are several functions that most people would agree that a library *should* undertake. It will likewise be agreed that there are aspects that a library *should not* be expected to undertake. It may be admitted that the library is used for less relevant functions regularly or perhaps only from time to time. The point is that, over time, the library will be used and possibly abused.

How acceptable might such a state of affairs be? Let us explore one small example. Look in the educational or even general press to find photographs of head teachers or perhaps smiling students clutching certificates and awards. What can be seen in the background? Possibly, shelves of books. Look closely and it may be seen that they bear the hallmark of library-organized shelves and stock. Such an 'academic' background is considered appropriate for the image that the school wants to be portrayed. Did such a photographic session cause any disruption in the library? Was it an appropriate function for the library?

Multi-functional library facility

In reality, a school library serves a multitude of functions. As in any organization, there are times when library managers have no choice but to accept other people's wishes and orders. So, how will a policy for the library affect such uses and abuses of the role of the library?

A library policy is not a universal panacea. It is simply a management tool. It communicates ideas and values. What a policy can do is help others into a growing understanding about the function of the library in general terms. It will not and cannot be a safeguard for all eventualities.

In the small example given above, what would be the response of the librarian who has been asked or told that the library would be the venue for photographs? Intuitively, the librarian – as a manager – understands the situation. There may even be benefits that accrue to the library upon co-operation and other reasons for agreeing. In this situation, the library, by being a venue, may be taking part in the wider life of the school. It is all a question of balance. As Mortimore (1992, 154) noted, when looking at school effectiveness projects, 'there is no such thing as a free lunch' as there is always an agenda to be addressed.

Why does the school library exist?

The general aim is surely to maintain the library as a foundation for the curriculum, perhaps therefore moving it from the periphery of school life to be something of relevance to students and staff. Rather than asking what the library does and what the library functions are, is it not more appropriate to consider what the library is there for? Why does it exist? Addressing this question may narrow the options identified in the large list above to perhaps include the following statements, that a school library:

- supports the teaching and learning of the institution
- provides research opportunities for senior students
- offers a place for quiet, individual study
- is a facility for individual choice in selection of learning resources

- provides resources to support the formal and 'hidden' curriculum
- enables a school to provide a cultural focus
- appears as an imposing and impressive facility for the benefit of visitors.

A study about the impact of the school library on learning considered that:

the mission and goals of any SLRC [school library resource centre] indicate that support for the learning process is seen as central to the development of information and library services. SLRCs aim not only to provide a rich learning environment in terms of an appropriate range of resources but also in terms of developing the learning skills of pupils.

Williams and Wavell, 2001

How to arrive at an agreed statement about the library's function

First of all, a central idea or concept needs to be developed and stated. The ideal is to arrive at a concept agreed to by the whole school community. Although this seems straightforward, practically speaking, however, it may be quite difficult to achieve. The most democratic and quickest means may be to invite the whole staff to suggest ideas, perhaps at a general staff meeting. However, if you are launching 'cold' or without advance notice, possibly the worst thing to do is to ask a whole-school staff meeting for ideas. Progress of the idea will be limited by this means because of too many different perceptions in what is inevitably a large group of people. In addition, individual or sectional (hidden) agendas may exist so that it may be difficult to synthesize views on a single occasion. If using such a method, however, the issue being discussed needs to be tightly focused, both in terms of time allowed and the object of the exercise. Ideally, colleagues should receive some notice before the meeting, so that they are aware that comments and thoughts about the role of the library will be required.

Far more helpful will be for the school librarian to explore the following options:

- Arrive at a definition and circulate a statement to staff for discussion and comment.
- Invite all areas of school to separately contribute comments and views, which are then discussed, collated and synthesized.
- Encourage a library steering committee to consider the issue and agree a draft definition.
- Ask for the issue to be considered by senior managers, perhaps also providing a briefing paper for their information and guidance.
- Promote the need for an agreed and formalized policy to be ratified by governors or trustees of the school, as should be standard practice for whole school policies.

These options require time as consultation and communication are involved – perhaps through questionnaires or meetings – but arguably are more effective in the long term. Once it is clear why the library exists (and for whom), it is then possible to communicate this idea and effectively work towards the ideal.

Aspects of a school library policy

Once a basic understanding of the role of the library has been established, it is important to develop policy for different aspects of the function of the facility. Significant statements about the library should be made in the policy. These may include:

- *Access*. This may seem straightforward enough, but there may be implications to be highlighted. Not only should access to the facility in a physical sense be identified, but by implication, the security that exists for the facility and its resources. Also to be considered will be whether the same levels of access to resources will be offered to all users of the facility. It may be useful to identify policy guidance regarding any sensitive materials and the needs of adolescent users vis-à-vis pre-adolescent users. Particular examples would be access to use of the internet and sex education materials.

- *Censorship*. This is more of an issue in the USA as, for instance, perusal of US school librarianship journals shows. Nevertheless, a statement about the freedom of access for individuals in a school setting may be a valuable aspect to include in a school library policy. (See also Appendix I).
- *Services*. The library and information *service* is more than a static collection of resources that miraculously opens its doors at the beginning of the day and closes them again at the end. An identification of core services may be helpful. (These services are discussed throughout the book.)
- *Stock development*. This will follow on from and develop a basic understanding of the role of the library. Users may well benefit from knowledge of the strengths of the library and how collections are selected, maintained and edited.
- *Learning inputs and outputs*. Here, it may be appropriate to identify any teaching role taken by the school librarian and any learning outcomes/processes that students may expect from constructive use of the library.

We believe that free communication is essential to the preservation of a free society and a creative culture. We believe that these pressures towards conformity present the danger of limiting the range and variety of inquiry and expression on which our democracy and culture depend. We believe that every American community must jealously guard the freedom to publish and to circulate, in order to preserve its own freedom to read. We believe that publishers and librarians have a profound responsibility to give validity to that freedom to read by making it possible for the readers to choose freely from a variety of offerings.

From the American Library Association statement: *The Freedom to Read,* American Association of School Librarians, 1998b, 157

How detailed should policy be?

A policy should be comprehensive, though it is impossible to cover everything. Indeed, the longer a policy document becomes, the more difficult it is to communicate effectively its main tenets. It is useful to consider just what it is necessary to communicate. That, and that alone, should be the content of the policy. If there is a need to provide more detail, such 'subsidiary' policy could be relegated to a manual of practice. For instance, when outlining the main elements of stock selection, this could be done in a sentence in the main policy statement, with a rider that further information could be found in a manual. Other examples may include a policy for donations to the library (an example of which may be found at Appendix D) and one for dealing with complaints (see Appendix I). It may be sufficient to say in the policy that these exist, and place the detail somewhere elsewhere. Naturally, any such manual should be kept up to date and be available in several places where it may be consulted freely (perhaps even on a school library's web page).

Is there a blueprint policy?

Policy writing may appear a cumbersome process and possibly tedious. However, while the product, i.e. the written policy, is important, the process of communication, debate and dialogue that should occur during the preparation period are even more so. It is tempting to reproduce a policy document from another institution that looks helpful, but it is impossible to replicate the process of arriving at a *relevant* policy that is suited to the needs of the *individual* school.

However, it is possible to utilize good practice so it is not necessary to start entirely from scratch. National, professional and other school library guidelines have been produced and may be helpful starting points. Indeed, the UNESCO School Library Manifesto, reproduced in abridged form below, should engender much thought and debate, as it has been developed after much thought and consultation among groups and organizations in a number of countries. Support for school librarians may also be available from focus groups of colleagues, listservs and organizations such as schools library services. In fact, there will be so many stimulating ideas and so much material available that the issue will be more to select what is relevant, realistic and aspirational, rather than to hunt for concepts.

In addition it may also be possible to work together with school librarians in a given area, or from like-minded schools, to work on 'subsidiary' policy. The ideas and text that result then could be taken back to individual schools for comment and amendment, as may be appropriate. A good example of such co-operative working might be policy for stock selection or that for donations to the school library.

This is an abridged version of the UNESCO School Library Manifesto:

The School library in teaching and learning for all: IFLA/UNESCO School Library Manifesto

The school library provides information and ideas that are fundamental to functioning successfully in today's information and knowledge-based society. The school library equips students with lifelong learning skills and develops the imagination, enabling them to live as responsible citizens.

The Mission of the school library

The school library offers learning services, books and resources that enable all members of the school community to become critical thinkers and effective users of information in all formats and media. School libraries link to the wider library and information network in accord with the principles in the UNESCO Public Library Manifesto.

Library staff support the use of books and other information sources, ranging from the fictional to the documentary, from print to electronic, both on-site and remote. Materials complement and enrich textbooks, teaching materials and methodologies.

It has been demonstrated that, when librarians and teachers work together, students achieve higher levels of literacy, reading, learning, problem solving and information and communication technology skills.

Library services must be provided equally to all members of the school community, regardless of age, race, gender, religion, nationality, language, professional or social status. Specific services and materials must be provided for those who are unable to use mainstream library services and materials.

Access to services and collections should be based on the United Nations Universal Declaration of Rights and Freedoms, and should not be subject to any form of ideological, political or religious censorship, or to commercial pressures.

Funding legislation and networks

The school library is essential to every long-term strategy for literacy, education, information provision and economic, social and cultural development. School libraries must have adequate and sustained funding for trained staff, materials, technologies and facilities and be free of charge.

The school library is an essential partner in the local, regional and national library and information network. Where the school library shares facilities and/or resources with another type of library, such as a public library, the unique aims of the school library must be acknowledged and maintained.

Goals of the school library

The school library is integral to the educational process. The following core services are essential to the development of literacy, information literacy, teaching, learning and culture:

- Supporting and enhancing educational goals as outlined in the school's mission and curriculum;
- Developing and sustaining in children the habit and enjoyment of reading and learning, and the use of libraries throughout their lives;
- Offering opportunities for experiences in creating and using information for knowledge, understanding, imagination and enjoyment and in learning and practising skills for evaluating and using information;
- Providing access to global resources that expose learners to diverse ideas and experiences;
- Working with students, teachers, administrators and parents to achieve the school's mission;

- Proclaiming the concept that intellectual freedom and access to information are essential to effective and responsible citizenship and participation in a democracy;
- Promoting reading to the whole school community and beyond.

The school library in teaching and learning for all [2001]

On-going review of policy

The process of policy making is, as indicated above, important and valuable. As the process itself is intangible and needs to be experienced, the value gained from it – i.e. a widespread common understanding of the role and potential of the library – may become diluted over time. (This may be because of significant changes in staffing personnel and new pressures and initiatives. Also the passage of time makes us all forget, to a certain extent.)

In order to counter such an eventuality, a librarian will be able to develop other strategies to promote common understanding about the role of the library, as policy is only one instrument in management. Nevertheless, it may be useful to re-visit policy from time to time, looking for continued relevance or the need for adjustment, and again an appropriate process (not perhaps to the same extent as at first) may provide motivation and common understanding among the collegiate body of the school staff.

Development of the school library and information service

If a policy identifies what a library in a school exists for, a development plan formulates the means of achieving the goal and maintaining or improving yet further the standard of service.

We all make lists – things to do, things not to forget. We may prioritize these lists. A development plan may be thought of just as a (albeit big or sophisticated) list. A list reminds us to do things. A development plan does the same. It reminds us to take action. It also indicates to others the sort of action required in order to achieve a goal. For this reason alone, it is important that a library development plan, just like a policy, is communicated to others in the school community. Therefore a library development plan should be couched in the language of the school: by this is meant expressing outcomes in terms understood by and of relevance to the school as an organization.

For example, an item in a library development plan may be the installation of a computerized library management system. The benefit is not to make it easier to lend or issue library resources or send out reminders about items that have been kept past the date for return, or even that a system will show that a library is technologically advanced. Rather, benefits should be expressed in the following manner:

- Pupils experience real use of technology in their everyday school lives.
- Pupils develop useful IT skills through searching an automated catalogue.
- Compilation of a catalogue may maximize use of a school's existing resources.

This therefore continually relates the library to the aims and service of the school as a whole, by identifying a benefit to the school community.

UK secondary school guidelines (Tilke, 1998a, 14) have succinctly identified the salient points when development planning:

- The plan must relate to the policy for the school library.
- The plan needs to relate to the school's overall development plan.
- The process will involve auditing present resources and then looking at the library's list of priorities in the light of the audit; setting targets with deadlines; identifying relevant costs; implementation; evaluation.
- Typically, any such plan will cover a period of time between three and five years. It is helpful to identify short-, medium- and long-term developments, i.e. something that can be achieved within the present academic year, a project necessitating one to two years and an aim that may only be partially met during the period of the development plan.
- It may be useful to set up or reconvene a library steering committee to help with this process.

Justification of development funding

The days when Gervase Phinn, a local authority inspector who had responsibility for school libraries, could be told 'The head wants me to develop the library and has persuaded the Governors to release some capital to improve things' (Phinn, 1999) may be long gone. There is more likely to be an expectation that bids for development funds need to be justified, with advantages being clearly identified. A development plan allows that to occur. Far from being a bureaucratic exercise, a development plan can crystallize thinking and enable the librarian and others to prioritize development so that it is realistically planned. It is helpful to involve others in the planning and it is certainly necessary to communicate the contents of the development plan to staff and others in the school in order for realistic expectations to be made.

Planning ahead

Development plans may be cyclical and have a life-span of several years. It may be easy to identify development for the first year, often in some detail, but may be progressively harder for further years. Rather than seek to add detail for the future, it is better to edit detail in the first year, so that the overall plan and action required is clear and comprehensive.

Indeed, the school may have an overall procedure that heads of department need to work to. This may involve a written audit of the past year to aid thinking and support development plans, targets and priorities for the future. Areas for an annual departmental audit (Jones, Jenkin and Kirkham, 1996, 8) include:

- curriculum
- assessment and achievement
- resources
- staffing and staff development
- public examinations
- organization
- liaison and communication.

The areas identified about relate to a subject department but there is no reason why the library and information service should not use the same headings. The benefit in so doing is that the library works more and more as an academic department. That can be important, as one reason why the library is sometimes left out of or at least not fully integrated into the planning and development cycle is because it does not easily fit into the way that things are done in a school.

Does a plan deny flexibility?

It is important that a school library relates to its users effectively and efficiently. In a changing arena such as education, that means that a librarian needs to be flexible. Not only may educational policy (with its own priorities and time-scales) change, but local conditions alter and the users change too. Resources emerge, change and improve, sometimes without much advance notice. The librarian needs to capitalize on current events and changing needs and priorities. Flexibility therefore needs to be built in or remembered in development planning, in terms of finance and (staff) time. In other words, carefully estimate the amount of time and resources needed to achieve stated goals, building flexibility (possibly for other things) into the planning.

Nevertheless, a library development plan needs to have targets that are:

- specific
- measurable
- achievable
- realistic
- timelined (Jones, Jenkin and Kirkham, 1996, 12).

Reduction of library provision

Development does not always mean expansion. Reduction in library provision may occur. In the same way as national economies ebb and flow, a library, or perhaps any facility in a school, cannot expect to always be apportioned funding for expansion. Maintenance is also development. Reduction is also development, unwelcome though it may be to the librarian and others. Management is about learning from such situations, understanding them and operating a service as efficiently and effectively as possible under new conditions.

Equally, a reduction in funding for the school library does not necessarily mean that it has to work 'adversely' for the library. The situation may have occurred for a number of reasons, some of which may not have anything to do directly with the library. However, if the library service in the school has been seen to be inadequate and the response from senior decision makers is in fact to continually reduce funding, re-apportion library accommodation to other uses or even to re-distribute resources among departments, it would be most advisable to reassess the situation.

This could be achieved by looking at the policy and/or development plan (or, more likely, the absence of these), assessing conditions, both pro and con. Indeed, analysis of such a situation is really the starting point for library development (in the long term) rather than the reverse. In this scenario of terminal decline, everything should be (re-)examined. For such a situation, what is needed is a catalyst: it is possible that circumstances have arisen because of the absence of a full-time, experienced and qualified librarian to manage the library. External agencies, such as schools library services, could suggest and encourage change, especially to concerned individuals in the school community, be they teachers, parents, governors (or trustees) and pupils. The catalyst could therefore be someone to reassess and revamp library provision in the school.

Role of a library steering committee

A useful method of debating library policy and examining library functions is a library steering committee (Tilke, 1998b, 37). Ideally, a committee should be representative of most if not all areas of school life – staff from different subject and pastoral areas of the school, as well as students and possibly parents – with appointments to the committee being made by the head teacher or principal of the school. Action of this sort by the head teacher indicates the seriousness of the exercise. For this reason, too, the brief for the committee should be outlined by the head teacher, who ideally should chair the committee. If this is not possible then a member of the inner senior management team should be appointed to this position.

Library committees sometimes suffer criticism because they are seen as not producing anything worthwhile or consistently engage in negative criticism. Indeed, it has been known for a library committee to concern itself with the day-to-day running of the school library and adjust administrative routines rather than concentrating on policy and overall direction. These concerns indicate the necessity of a good brief for a committee and also, perhaps, for a time-scale for such a group. With a clear focus and brief, a committee can produce meaningful results and be disbanded, with a job well done.

If a standing or on-going committee is preferred or needed, then its meetings should have clear focus and membership be refreshed from time to time. The minutes of the meetings – and minutes or at least a record of meetings should be kept – could be disseminated to the school community, in whole or at least in summarized form.

If, however, what is really wanted is some form of on-going voice or opinion about the library and its role in the school, it may be possible to do this by different means – a library steering or standing committee is after all only one option. Good practice can be replicated but it is not a good idea to institute a committee just because another school has found it useful. It should only be used if it suits the needs of the school in question. Nevertheless, perhaps the greatest contribution a library committee can make is by looking at library provision in a school that has suffered from inadequate library provision over a period of time. This is because a committee's membership should reflect users and provide a distinct viewpoint. From this, it may be concluded that a library steering committee has a useful role at a certain stage in the development of a secondary or high school library.

Conclusion

Developing policy for the school library is an essential step in progress. It is not a starting point, or rather, it is not *only* a starting point. It is a management tool that is on-going. A survey of secondary school libraries (Sheffield Hallam University, 2000, 78) indicates that a significant proportion of secondary schools in the UK (60%) have found it useful to formulate a library policy document. A similar number of schools have a library development plan, while 61% of libraries in the survey appeared in an overall school development plan.

Nevertheless, school libraries are not the same everywhere. As Mortimore (1992, 154) pointed out, 'It is tacitly assumed that all schools have an equal chance of improvement, the reality is that schools in all countries vary enormously in their conditions . . . . The acceptance of this reality is not to condone a defeatist attitude . . . but merely to note that judgements of school effectiveness have to be carried out in sensitive ways.' School library development in the UK alone has been found to be variable (Office of Arts and Libraries, 1986) and the same is true for other parts of the world. By development is meant the different ways that school libraries have changed in the last 50 years or so, whether in terms of funding, staffing, buildings, technology and information skills and even in terms of differing policy statements. Surveys (not least Sheffield Hallam University, 2000) have shown that libraries within the same country have evolved in different ways and at varying paces and this piecemeal development of school libraries is mirrored in other countries too.

If the starting points are not the same and – arguably – the (realistic) goals or aims are different, nevertheless the process for development is remarkably similar. In this process, the need for clear analysis and in particular an awareness of user needs is imperative, and the management tools of policy and development planning are essential for any meaningful development.

In order to cater the library to the needs of an individual school, it is important to have a good understanding of the school's development plan, any education initiatives being addressed by that plan, the curriculum, and any special interests of the school. The more the librarian can work to meet the needs of the users, the more indispensable the library will become to the school.

Anne-Marie Tarter, Librarian, Ripon Grammar School, Yorkshire, UK

6
Management principles and styles

It is vital that the school librarian is a good manager as the responsibilities of the post are financial, operational and curricular. Without good management skills and appropriate experience, these responsibilities could not be carried out effectively.

Finance Director, Dixons City Technology College, Bradford, UK

A school library and information service needs to be managed. Without the input of a librarian such a facility is generally under-utilized and does not meet its potential. The manager of the facility is and should be its librarian. This chapter will look at a range of management skills required by a successful school librarian and focus on some personal qualities that arise out of managerial experience that are distinct from the technical skills traditionally associated with librarianship.

Management skills and situations

Librarians tend to be service-orientated individuals and will be adept at carrying out specific tasks and projects. However, there are various general areas that school librarians need to focus on and Morris (1995) has identified a number of management principles:

- planning
- leading/leadership

- directing
- controlling (staff, including understanding a brief and evaluation)
- revising (in order to improve work output).

When there are so many tasks to undertake and few people or only one person to do the work, the natural reaction is to be active. Aspects of management may be a significant issue for school librarians or library managers, not least because the employment trend has been towards librarians working as single-person or solo units. Solo librarians who want their service to be used well will use almost messianic zeal in order to provide and promote the best possible service. Such a person has to rely upon her or himself and needs to know how to do everything. However, the art of management is as much about reflection, planning and prioritizing and this is as true for single-person units as it is for librarians who are in charge of other library personnel.

In the popular children's picture book story *Farmer Duck* (Waddell and Oxenbury, 1991), a duck is exploited by a lazy farmer. The duck does all the work on the farm. However, the duck's friends, the other animals on the farm, reflect on and assess the situation and devise a resolution. Then they act. Naturally, there is a moral and happy end to the story! But although some of Morris's attributes indicate an active role, other aspects – arguably underpinning all these principles – require more reflective aptitudes, involving observation and analysis. In the story, the duck was undoubtedly active and efficient, but it was the other animals who were reflective and effective. Merge the two and qualities emerge that reflect those of a school library manager.

Especially in the absence of a current and accurate job description (see Chapter 2 and Appendix C) which may helpfully provide focus and direction, an individual may be so busy on everyday activities that over-arching management functions are forgotten. Yet these skills and aptitudes are essential to support the policy and development plans discussed in the previous chapter, and actually help a librarian focus on everyday activities.

As with policy development, management skills are not purely theoretical but need to be practised, both those skills that indicate action and those requiring reflection. Guidance on management functions is fortunately given by a number of sources. The American Association of School Librarians, in the very comprehensive *Information power* (1998b, 114) guidelines, offer the following advice:

> *Goals for the School Library Media Specialist [librarian]*
> Strong management skills are required to orchestrate a wide variety of complex technologies and resources and to supervise the specialized staff required to support them . . .
> 1 Maintain expertise in strategies and techniques of budgeting, supervision, scheduling, and all other areas of management responsibility.
> 2 Serve on the school's management team, and collaborate regularly with teachers and administrators through other formal and informal mechanisms to maintain the visibility and quality of the [library] program's management.
> 3 Report regularly to administrators and others regarding the program's holdings, services, uses and finances.
> 4 Participate in hiring, training, and evaluating all program staff, and maintain responsibility for assigning and scheduling staff and volunteers.
> 5 Administer the program budget and oversee acquisition and use of space, furnishings, equipment, and resources.
> 6 Oversee all aspects of the daily operation of the library media program.

Working and reporting concurrently, but independently of the above, UK guidelines (Tilke, 1998a, 25) indicated that 'it is vital that . . . the whole library service to the school is managed effectively' and offered the following management foci:

- time and finance
- library staff
- the school day
- accommodation
- learning resources
- promotion
- monitoring and evaluation.

In these two models, there is significant overlap but also some individual aspects, so it is worth merging the two and briefly describing these features. The following points identify key areas of a school librarian's functions that will be treated in more detail later in this book.

Time management

It is essential to be able to manage time. Irrespective of whether the time is one's own or that of another member of the library and information service staff, the librarian or library manager needs to be aware of the amount of time spent on various jobs, relevant deadlines and other limits placed on each service task. Prioritizing tasks assists in managing time effectively. While selection of staff may happen relatively infrequently, the time required to select appropriate personnel should be recognized. Training of staff should be on-going, so again there will be time implications. The library manager will need to spend time planning daily activity tasks and setting regular work targets for any library staff. If the librarian has wider management responsibilities within the school, it is vital that the library and information service functions effectively when the librarian is occupied elsewhere and on other matters. Time to attend meetings where important school information is communicated is also time well spent.

Budgeting skills

The budget of the library may be a significant portion of the overall school budget. Inevitably, funding is a scarce resource therefore the library budget should be apportioned wisely and carefully. The AASL (American Association of School Librarians) advocates that 'aligning budgetary and instructional priorities is a sound practice that will win support for the library media program' (AASL, 2001). Indeed, even if the library does not have a significant budget, the same principle should apply. It is important that the librarian should be seen to be acting in such an overt managerial manner – this may be seen most clearly when presenting budget and other information at relevant meetings. 'Documentation of present needs and long-range planning for future needs should be an ongoing process' (ibid.), therefore budgetary management is a continuous process.

Managing the school day

A great deal of activity occurs in a school each and every day and probably school employees consider that they are governed by the timetable or schedule more than anything else. As an essential facility in the institution, a library, as a general rule, should offer continuous service throughout the school day. In addition to classes visiting the library, small groups and individuals may also visit the library at the same time. There will also be implications for service provision at break and lunch times. A library may be open after school has formally finished, perhaps for homework purposes. Indeed, for residential or boarding schools, the library may function during the evenings and at weekends. In addition to supervising academic work, there are implications for health and safety and child protection measures and behaviour management. Managing the school day may be further complicated, especially in a library with limited space, as it is important not to have too many users at once. Unless management of this sort occurs, the net result may be that students do not benefit from a high-quality experience. For example, a large number of students may all be looking for the same item or similar resources at one particular time and the effect on the desired (probably, quiet) atmosphere may be inappropriate. As a result, a booking system for class use may need to be operated.

Managing facilities

The accommodation allocated by the school for the library needs to be appropriate for the services to be able to function adequately. As it is not easy to alter accommodation provision at will or at least in the short term, considerable ingenuity, thought and management will be required on the part of the librarian in order to make the library work as well as possible. Again, there will be health and safety implications, not least with regard to various technologies and their applications. AASL recommend that 'the arrangement of facilities should create an environment that encourages the use of various media, motivates students to use materials and services necessary for learning, and provides the design flexibility needed to accommodate new technologies' (2001). No longer will a staid, unchanging arrangement of accommodation be always sufficient. Relating library accommodation to the needs of the curriculum and requirements of technological developments highlight the need to regularly reassess or manage the facility.

Managing resources

Learning resources are the stock-in-trade of the school library and information service. Resources need to be selected, acquired, organized, stored and promoted to the school community and be easily retrieved by users. 'Once school [librarians] collect and use meaningful data about their collections, they will be able to determine what a core collection for their library must consist of . . . versus what resources can be obtained from other libraries or online sources' (Kachel, 1997, 17). Collating data about learning resources is an almost automatic activity for school librarians, yet it is using that information that is a management challenge. Information on collections and stock performance, once matched against curricular knowledge, can help identify strengths and weaknesses in the library collections.

Managing the audience

As indicated above, the resources and services of the library and information service need to be promoted. The library service needs to be active and pro-active. In the final analysis, students are not required to use the library or if they are forced to do so, the benefit they gain will be minimal. The best use is therefore voluntary and is aided through liaising with colleagues: 'working with teachers . . . [librarians] will be able to demonstrate that library collections are critical to the delivery of the school's curriculum' (Kachel,

1997). Relevant audiences are not only teachers and students but also governors, trustees or a school board, school administration or senior management, teaching staff or faculty, students and parents. The target audience for the school library therefore is more easily identified *and* reached than say for a public library service. Nevertheless on-going promotion should be focused upon:

- resources
- facilities and services
- mission, aims and objectives of the library and information service
- *and* the benefit of the library and information service to users.

The advantage to the librarian is the cohesion of the target groups but they mostly have differing requirements, be that subject focused or ability dependent.

Monitoring and evaluation

Monitoring and evaluation may be regarded as the most reflective management aspect of the school librarian's role (especially if qualitative evaluation is wanted or desired). It is possible, over time, and is common practice, to collect performance or output data. But, they are valuable only if management skills are applied to tease out trends and identify particular issues. It may be thought that it is the job of others to do that – in the hurly-burly of the current educational world, it is probably unlikely you will find anyone, and the library manager needs to be adept at pointing out and explaining conclusions gleaned from monitoring and evaluation measures. It is therefore not sufficient merely to collect data, but to be able to utilize and promote it and advocate or propose relevant action. Kachel, again: 'They [librarians] will be able to articulate cogently and justify to administrators and community representatives what funds are needed to secure necessary resources. They will be able to represent better the interests and needs of their library users' (1997). However, relevant qualitative evaluation is harder to obtain and again the onus is on the library manager to point out its importance for the role of the school library and information service.

Wider management responsibilities

From the two sources it can be concluded that the librarian's place in the management structure of the school ought to be clear and unambiguous. As the roles (identified in the comment at the head of this chapter) are administrative and curricular, clarity of role is sometimes lost because one of the roles is less well perceived by the school community.

Management competencies are therefore useful, indeed essential, skills for school librarians at the beginning of the 21st century, for as Levacic (1999, 17) in a study of the management role of head teachers states, 'a rationally managed organization is one which has explicit goals against which it measures performance. It uses a rational planning process . . . objectives are agreed and then information is obtained on all the alternative means by which the objectives might be attained.' This planning model is now common in many schools, according to research carried out by a British government educational inspection agency (ibid.). It was found that use of resource costing was an important element of the planning process and that monitoring and evaluation consisted of 'use of educational outcomes; consistency of practice across departments; involvement of senior and middle management and governors'.

The implications are surely there for a secondary school librarian – educational outcomes will be measured and similar management methodology should occur in the various departments in the school, of which the library and information service is one. The challenge for a school librarian is in moving from a role where the modus operandi is a purely technical/professional one to more of an educationally focused role. Resources should not be apportioned to a library just because there is an historical precedent for doing so, but rather will be based on the perceived potential benefit to users and the focused role of library resources as support to the curriculum. Indeed, it would be helpful and possibly preferable if benefits from using the library could be expressed as educational outcomes (perhaps along the lines of the effective learning research discussed in Chapter 3).

As a result of a management drive of classroom observations . . . to look at a variety of teaching and learning styles with a view to initially adopting one across all departments . . . a cadre group was selected from a cross section of departments and hierarchy. ... I was asked to join the group and as a school librarian I was delighted that my contribution to school issues such as teaching and learning styles and my cross-curricular overview was to be recognised.

School librarian (resource centre manager),

Nottingham, UK (Pallett, 2000, 7)

Analysis of management aptitudes and skills needed by school librarians

In conclusion, it is helpful to analyse the core skills and aptitudes needed by librarians in secondary schools.

Prioritization

An ongoing ability to judge situations and identify a variety of pressing demands and looming deadlines is a helpful one to develop. Such an aptitude may be utilized daily in a secondary school library.

Flexibility

This aptitude relates closely to the above. If a school librarian is efficient through systems alone (à la 'Farmer Duck'), such a person will find it difficult to be truly effective. While efficiency is to be lauded, effectiveness results from an understanding of the user's needs and the overall requirements of the organization. In order to provide balance and judgement, a flexible attitude may be aided by thought and reflection. It can almost become instinctive or intuitive in nature.

Supervision

This skill could be divided into several aspects:

- *Behaviour management*. An understanding of adolescence, of school rules, policies and expectations, together with an appreciation that students may behave *differently* in the library from elsewhere in the school will be a valuable experience-base. Behaviour expectations may be a considerable element in the daily management style of the librarian.
- *Health and safety implications*. Apart from daily issues such as sensible and legal precautions for accidents due to fire and natural causes, a school librarian should be aware of necessary precautions for personal child safety and of the dangers associated with terrorism and weapon-related incidents, as well as personal security. Again, a librarian should have a very clear understanding of relevant school policies and practices.
- *Staff, functions and resources*. Supervision of library staff, work activities and library procedures and the security of library resources.

Personnel skills

It is a truism that a librarian is a person who enters the library profession because of a liking for literature, books and reading. Librarians in schools (and elsewhere), as service providers, need to continually interact with other human beings. Finely honed personnel skills are needed to relate to, empathize with and understand a range of individuals and groups, ranging from governors, senior management, faculty colleagues to students and parents (not least volunteers in the school library).

Pro-active aptitude and skills

There are many occasions when the saying 'Information is power' comes into its own for school librarians, as opportunities for educational and library development may be had if the library manager seeks involvement. Equally, there are times when the librarian needs to be pro-active in order to sustain a standard of provision and maintain the atmosphere of the library against inappropriate use of the facility. Finally, there are occasions when to be pro-active would be folly. Judgement, based upon local knowledge of issues and personalities, arrived at through reflection, will generally lead to the right course of action.

Individual librarians may also think of other (possibly personnel-related) skills which this author refers to as 'sixth sense' skills. The term is used here to describe an understanding of the need for patience and a sense of humour. Tension and stress will inevitably occur in all teams and individuals, so a sense of timing and of occasion will be helpful. These skills or aptitudes may be also expressed through the librarian developing the library in such a way that it has an appreciably different atmosphere from anywhere else in a particular school. In this case a library user, on entering a school library, has an aesthetic sense of being somewhere that should invoke and require respect and value, provide comfort and offer a sense of peace. There may also be a 'tingle' factor where the reader or user thinks they may make a personal discovery while browsing – perhaps something quirky, challenging, but ultimately interesting, enjoyable and rewarding. At any rate, the atmosphere needs to be right in order for this to occur.

The librarian in a school should become adept at judging balance in a range of everyday duties, not least in relation to links with colleagues. The art of involving colleagues in developments and decisions concerning the library is a fine one – basically one wishes to avoid colleagues feeling that the library and librarian lack direction and purpose; but it is helpful that other members of staff feel an involvement in, even 'ownership' of, their library.

Conclusion

A solo librarian experiencing problems in running a library and information service may be excused for thinking that management principles are irrelevant or simply not a priority in the job. But short of school managers undergoing a 'conversion on the road to Damascus', it is likely that management tools may provide the development that a library and librarian need. Large-scale or macro change is possible, but evolutionary, incremental change is more likely and can probably be better embedded, so that benefits for each change, over time, are seen and appreciated.

Management skills and competencies are needed in all facilities offering a service, not least a school library. Skills and competencies such as those outlined in this chapter may be under-valued compared with technical and professional (librarianship) skills and even disregarded by facility managers. Yet management skills and competencies will assist a school librarian to be a dynamic and professional individual, and the manager of a service within an individual school. The blend of theory and practice is one that will appeal to a service-oriented profession which is undergoing change, just as school librarians can be change agents in their own organization.

7

FINANCIAL MANAGEMENT

On the library budget: This considerable sum must be managed expertly to ensure alignment with institutional needs and value for money. Additionally, the school librarian is key to . . . the management of curricular [departmental] resources through . . . ensuring cost effective acquisition, access and issue systems are in place.   Finance manager, UK secondary school

Traditionally, there is an expectation that funds will be apportioned by a school to its library each year to purchase . . . well, 'nice' new books. However, should funding based on such an ill-defined 'need' be valid? Will it, in fact, be liable to sudden budgetary cuts? Perhaps library funding is safe because it is too small and insignificant in relation to the overall school budget to be used for other purposes. Whatever the situation and size of the library allocation, it and the librarian will benefit from fiscal awareness and basic financial management. This chapter looks at a librarian's skill in managing the finance associated with a school library in order to effectively support the service's policy and development planning. Ways of establishing an acceptable modus operandi for agreeing resourcing levels or standards in the individual school library will also be identified.

Aspects of financial management for school librarians

Among the variety of skills, aptitudes and competencies discussed earlier in this book, it is tempting to add the technical skill of accountancy. But it is unnecessary to have such a high level of aptitude in financial management. Nevertheless it is usual for the manager of the school's library and information service to manage a budget for the facility. However small or large the sum of money, it should be apportioned and spent wisely so that a school community, particularly students, may reap the maximum reward from allocated funds. Indeed, it is arguable that a smaller sum of money takes as much if not greater concentration of thought and management, in order to achieve maximum value for money, than does a larger sum. Whatever the size of library funding, however, it is necessary that a school librarian be aware that:

- Funding is finite.
- There are competing demands for available funding.
- Management of library funding needs to be practised and to be seen to be practised.
- The school should be able to perceive a benefit from apportioning funding to the library and information service.

As Levacic et al. (1999, 17), in a study of the role of the head teacher as a manager, concluded 'the selection of the most appropriate course of action then depends upon knowledge of the projected costs balanced against expected benefits . . . the budgetary planning process, because it identifies costs and relates them to anticipated benefits, is an essential part of rational planning'. Decisions will necessarily be made on the basis of evidence and in pursuit of identified goals. Even if a senior management team is sympathetic to a project or aspect of school provision in general, if it does not fit into the prevailing plan, funding will not be allocated.

Financial management will be guided by:

- Development plan and policy for a school library. As discussed in Chapter 5, these basic management tools govern and focus the life of the school library, in financial as in other aspects.
- School procedures, including the budgetary cycle, which may vary in detail between individual schools. If only in order to prioritize, it is helpful to

be aware of communication about such information on an organized and regular basis, though knowledge of organizational information about school financial matters will be more valuable than that.

Financial management will consist of:

- planning and research for a budget proposal
- working to deadlines in a budgetary cycle
- apportioning a library budget on the basis of needs, developments and on-going financial commitments
- ascertaining the best or optimum terms from suppliers of goods and providers of services.

School library guidelines recommend that a financial report for the library 'should be produced which establishes targets for the development and resourcing of the library in an organized and coherent way' (Tilke, 1998a, 27). Such an approach will be more likely to safeguard funding allocations throughout a financial year and enable a librarian to build budgetary proposals year on year.

Above all, 'the wise use of money must be examined continually. Every decision should consider these questions: How much will it cost? Is it worth it? What are the alternatives?' (Driessen and Smyth, 1995, 6). These are inevitably the questions that will be in the minds of those responsible for allocating a school budget.

It can be argued that the limits of a budget actually dictate or lead decisions about aspects of school library provision. Indeed, adequate funding enables a school to 'provide adequate space, staffing, shelving, equipment, materials, preservation, replacement and supplies' (Driessen and Smyth, 1995) These authors and Kachel (1997, 15) nevertheless indicate that it is necessary for a school library manager to argue successfully for optimum or even adequate funding, and it is generally assumed that this will be on an annual basis.

Why should there be an annual or on-going budget for the school library?

If nothing else, it is useful for the library manager to be clear about this basic question, especially in a debate or meeting about budget allocations. A regular budget for a school library is considered necessary because:

- Information changes, knowledge changes. New resources can update a library collection and enable users to have access to more current, relevant information.
- Curriculum changes may necessitate further development of sections of a library collection.
- Newly published resources may explain concepts in a better way. In addition, information may be available in new formats that may further assist individualized and resource-based learning approaches. For instance, for some students, the concept of mapping an area could be explained more helpfully by means of an interactive software package rather than by a book. Also, in order to understand trench warfare, a video with perhaps re-touched clips of battlefields and action, with readings of war poetry, might enable some students to empathize more successfully than studying another history text.
- A growing awareness of students' different ability ranges may result in an audit of resources, thus identifying weaknesses in certain areas. For dyslexic or text-challenged students, for instance, it may be seen that the examples given in the bullet point above will be of particular use, but text materials to support the needs of these students will also need to be provided.
- Psychological factors may play a part, the 'new wood replacing dead wood' scenario, where the importance of variety is recognized. Users may be stimulated by new items in a way that they are not by older resources – an emotional response, as it were. It may not be logical, but it exists. If it didn't, many retail outlets would do little business!

There will probably be pressure on a library budget, either limiting its extent or questioning the necessity of any further expenditure. Competing and urgent needs in other parts of a school are common reasons for such pressure. In addition, a librarian may wish to relate budget proposals to prevailing learning styles in a school, as identified in Chapter 3, where it was noted that a school library cannot really be too adrift from the learning styles, and this applies to resource provision, as much as approach. Of course, it will not be easily possible for a librarian to suggest other ways of learning, if s/he cannot show resources that could be used. So, a librarian will need to judge just how far 'sprat to catch a mackerel' funding can go – it is all a matter of balance.

But, once the principle of an on-going budget allocation for a library and information service is accepted or established in broad terms, it should be possible to provide a target or standard in order to quantify or provide measurement to support a general aim. It is also helpful that an annual budget should be on-going and have continuity, rather than have to experience an alternate 'feast or famine' situation. 'It is most important that a stable budget be built for the library programme' notes Markuson (1999, 25) as the alternative is 'sporadic budgets [which] result in large segments of the collection becoming outdated at once'. The latter will be inevitable in such a situation. It may also mean that funding is not available when the optimum choice of resources is available. In addition, a library may not receive regular issues of periodicals or be able to pay regular charges or fees to subscription services. Irregular funding is in effect little better than no funding at all, as a school library will be extremely limited in being able to relate to curricular needs.

Elements of a school library budget

Resources:
- Books (identify category, e.g. Reference)
- Audiovisual
- Compact disc
- DVD
- Video

- CD-ROM
- Posters
- Artefacts

Standings orders and subscriptions:
- Annual publications
- Periodicals/newspapers
- Databases/online services

Common services/cost centre:
- Caretaking
- Cleaning
- Power
- Copyright licence fees

Stationery and equipment:
- Photocopier maintenance
- Binding

Also: Staff costs and training

N.B. These costs could also be shown in relation to the library development plan.

It can be seen, therefore, that a budget for a school library can be all embracing, especially if a cost-centre management style is adopted within the organization. This is where common costs, such as electricity, cleaning services and online time, for example, are apportioned, perhaps by formula, to each budget head or element in the overall school budget. It can also be reflected in actual costs, for instance, by telephone calls from a library telephone extension or direct line and postal costs. Clearly, where this financial management model is practised, there are many calls on available funding. Central financial records are normally made available in the form of regular printouts from a computer system to advise the cost-centre manager of current and cumulated levels of expenditure.

The budget report

A financial budget report is an important document, process and job activity for a school librarian to complete. In particular, a report should:

- identify any income to the library and information service (which could be payments for items lost while on loan, fines and theoretical discounts on goods purchased from suppliers)
- estimate regular expenditure, such as subscriptions and standing orders
- estimate expenditure on new and replacement stock
- highlight any future developments with appropriate costings, which might need to be budgeted for on a rolling programme over a number of years (Tilke, 1998a, 27).

A number of strategies will be important for the process of developing a budget report, including:

- Strong arguments. Especially if a librarian needs to present the budget at a meeting, it is helpful to prepare beforehand so that a librarian has arrived at real and logical answers for individuals who are not wholly convinced of the reasoning or the case as identified in a library budget document.
- Stating average costs. This may be easier for some resources (e.g. books) than others, but estimates should if possible be given for other items, such as videos and CD-ROMs.
- Stating real and on-going costs. It is helpful to provide real costs, such as the cost of on-going and annual subscriptions for newspapers, magazines and online databases. As one librarian has noted, 'choosing between print and electronic formats means a whole new set of budgeting guidelines' (Yucht, 2001, 39). Databases and electronic services that attract on-going costs depending on daily use need to be costed, perhaps using an average daily cost, arrived at by monitoring use over a certain limited period of time.
- Stating non-resource costs. These are often small items, but can, over a

period of time, amount to considerable sums of money. Examples include paper for any computer printers and photocopiers.

- Never making assumptions. What is obvious to a library manager is not always clear to others. For instance, the question 'Why does the library always need new books, surely xxx thousand items are enough?' should be anticipated and should be given a firm answer, focused on the needs of the school and the curriculum.

'Justifying purchases to administrators has traditionally been an area in which school library media specialists have not done a good job' (Kachel, 1997, 15). In times of financial strictures especially, a librarian needs to present good arguments and demonstrate – in curricular terms – that a 'difference' can be made through provision of existing and/or future resources. As also indicated in Chapter 5, Kachel recommends formulating a 'long-range collection development plan' as one way of achieving this.

Formulae to quantify and cost a library budget

It may be helpful to look to a formula to quantify and cost a library budget. Once a formula has been agreed in principle, it militates against vagueness and the idea that the library is a 'good thing' (and a 'good thing' only). Where the latter situation occurs, the library budget may be more subject to cuts unless the costing for the budget is clear and the need to acquire new stock understood. Again, the budget report both feeds into and is supported by the library policy. A formula, if introduced, should be identified in a library budget report.

There are several methods of formulating the requirements of library resourcing and budgeting. Most are based on identifying an optimum size for a school's library collection, with the aim of both reaching and maintaining such a level of provision. However, it is possible to take other approaches. Possibilities include the following.

UK approach

The Library Association (now CILIP)'s guidelines provide a recommendation (Tilke, 1998a, Appendix 3) for secondary school library resourcing. This is based on one item per pupil for each subject in the prescribed or formal curriculum laid down by the central government. (Although now focused on the ten subjects in the (original) English national curriculum, thinking for this is based on that of school inspectors who arrived at a figure for library resources per pupil, prior to the introduction of the original national curriculum.) In addition, it was felt that another three items per pupil would reflect extra-curricular library needs, e.g. catering for personal reading needs. Therefore 13 items per pupil was to be the minimum effective standard. It was estimated that more effective provision would be achieved if the figures were increased by 20%, so an average stock figure of 15.6 per pupil was arrived at.

There is a rider to this formula in that the materials should be relevant, current and in good physical condition, and the guidelines supported earlier recommendations (Department of Education and Science, 1989) from central government school inspectors that 10% of the library's stock should be replaced each year.

Australian approach

While Australian school library guidelines (Australian School Library Association, 2001, 31) focus on the quality and relevance of resources, very specific advice is nevertheless provided concerning the size of a 'foundation' collection. A foundation collection is one 'that provides an acceptable resourcing level to meet learning outcomes'.

There are some differences from the British model, such as a sliding scale of recommended items per student. This model reflects differing sizes of school, so the number of items per pupil is on a decreasing scale as the size of a collection grows. It may be perceived that a certain collection size will provide a comprehensive range of resources so that a higher unit count (per pupil) is not absolutely necessary. The guidelines provide a detailed table of figures to support this principle, based on an actual survey of collection sizes in schools in one Australian state. A few examples from the table illustrate the point:

Pupils in school	Collection size	Access to electronic resources	Items per pupil
300	7,880	110	26
700	13,944	195	20
1,100	18,189	254	16
1,500	21,318	298	14

Australian guidance also indicates the importance of electronic resources and attempts to quantify a collection that includes CD-ROM, online database subscriptions and recommended websites. These figures were based on a selective survey of school library provision in Australia in 1992.

It should be noted that a similarity with the British model is found in the recommendation that 10% of items should be replaced each year. Therefore, the formula for annual funding in this model is:

Foundation collection size based on enrolment size	$\times$	10% (replacement)	$\times$	average price of resources

US approach

While the British model implicitly sees a value in providing a rounded collection and the Australian model also advocates some breadth in coverage, a trend in the USA is towards collection mapping, where the library collection is firmly focused on the curricular needs of students. Indeed, Kachel considers that 'the concept of a "well-rounded" collection, meaning a library that contains a few good titles on every subject, is an archaic philosophy of how to develop a school library collection' (1997, 20). Furthermore 'school libraries today need to rely on other types of libraries to provide . . . recreational and other materials of personal interest to their students and teachers'.

US guidelines recommend that a school library 'requires a level of funding that will give all students adequate opportunities' and a 'budget that supports the continuous collection of information in all formats' (American Association of School Librarians, 1998b, 109)

Possibly because of differing curricula in schools throughout the USA, a quantitative recommendation about the optimum or effective size of library collections and details about on-going funding are not relevant to the US situation. The importance of collaborative collection development policies is stressed in literature about US school library provision, which also includes extensive suggestions for in-house methods for assessing standards and performance of library collections.

A librarian's own model

A school librarian may prefer to blend the methods of quantifying and costing as outlined above so that the reality of an individual situation is better reflected. One school librarian analysed the stock of a school library and compared the findings against those identified in a survey of British school libraries (Sheffield Hallam University, 2000). This was felt to have 'more credibility' with school managers, bearing in mind the prevailing methodology of identifying value in local government services (Sykes, 2001, 118–21). Importantly, quantitative and qualitative evaluation was undertaken, thus reflecting differing scenarios:

- School libraries that in theory have sufficient items in the library collections, but in reality the stock largely consists of redundant, out-of-date materials that are irrelevant to the needs of the curriculum. Here a qualitative analysis will be of real value.
- School libraries that do not meet either comparative or recommended quantitative guidelines. Although the contents of the collection could be relevant and useful there simply is not enough material to meet the

needs of all students. A qualitative evaluation will be of less use in such a situation.

Again, the importance of a school library policy, together with development planning and management skills enabling a librarian to identify effectiveness and progress plans, is apparent. Relating funding criteria to the learning style(s) prevalent in a school is again helpful.

A weakness is that detailed standards generally emanate from organizations concerned with the development of school libraries, typically the library community and its professional organizations, and not government or specifically educational organizations per se. Using standards developed by library organizations may lack credibility or *realpolitik* with senior managers in the school, even though they may accept that standards are professionally relevant and would be helpful if they were applied in the school situation. Comparing your figures and projects with other people's may be a more successful strategy. At the end of the day, it is the judgement of a school librarian that will identify an acceptable or realistic solution to this issue.

Grants and sponsorship

Special funding may be available for particular purposes. This may occur within the school's budget, or be extra funding from the board or local authority, or perhaps central government. Such funding is more likely to be irregular or 'one-off', though it is always possible that more regular money could be available. It is also conceivable that other public/private bodies may provide ad-hoc, one-off funding opportunities.

Where such initiatives occur, no doubt senior management will provide detailed information and guidelines about how areas of the school may apply or 'make a case' for funding.

The proposal from a school library and information service for extra funding should:

- be accurate, precise and in accordance with the intention of the funding
- identify benefits
- outline time-scale for implementation
- indicate evaluation criteria (which may actually be required from funding information).

A library committee comes into its own for such an exercise. This is because a bid for extra funding will typically be a focused project that can enable the school library to directly benefit different parts of the organization. Clearly, a committee formed of representatives from different areas of a school should be a great fillip and endorsement of a project's viability.

Sponsorship may also be available. This method of funding is different from grants, as it is more likely to come from a commercial organization. From their point of view, sponsorship is provided to achieve several things, including the enhancement of the image of a company and the provision of positive local community links, as well as perhaps creating a philanthropic aspect to the commercial organization. When sponsorship is involved, at least on a large scale, it is best to work on a school-wide basis. It will be unhelpful to senior management – and possibly against school policy – for individual departments to engage in direct dialogue with an external organization.

Having said that, there is still a mistaken belief that librarians should be expected to approach publishers and other resource suppliers to ask for free materials in order to stock the school library. Publishers are extremely unlikely to be able to support such a strategy and the only tangible result will be a waste of the time of the librarian, plus the incurring of unnecessary stationery and postage costs.

Supply and value for money

Value is a term often used in relation to funding but may be imprecisely used, as cost may in fact be a more relevant word. Value could be interpreted as 'opportunity' cost, an economic term to indicate the cost a purchaser is willing to pay in order to acquire goods or services at a particular time, to a given standard. (The 'cost' could be in cash terms or relate to the time of library staff.) Value *for money* can be identified as a benefit received from goods or services. Senior managers may expect a school librarian, as a budget holder, to identify value from finance apportioned to a library. One practical way of identifying value for money is in the supply of resources to the school library. There are two main methods available to the librarian:

- *Direct ordering*. This is where library staff will be responsible for ordering directly from book and magazine publishers and other suppliers or specific or branded resources.
- *Use of suppliers and agents*. This is where a librarian places orders for materials with distributing organizations that deal directly with producers, whether it is book or magazine publishers or producers of audiovisual resources. It is an extension of the idea that one obtains a daily newspaper from a newsagent, rather than the original publisher. At the further end of this scale, companies exist that can provide anything from books to tractors to schools in other regions of the world from where the producers of such goods are located.

Whether it is better to order direct from publishers or deal with suppliers may be answered by taking into account the amount of time spent by library staff on completing different ordering procedures – involving perhaps purchase orders, handling invoices and coping with different methods of payment, with considerable shipping or postal costs – and an assessment of what could be usefully done with the time of the library staff that is *not* spent on the above. Here a decision may be related to the job description for the post-holder concerned, together with the school library policy and development plan.

In order to identify the most effective method for a school's library and information service to obtain selected and desired resources, it may be helpful to consider the timing of ordering: are orders placed at certain, perhaps fixed, times of the year? Alternatively, are orders placed regularly, perhaps in order to assist with a steady supply of material to keep the library collections relevant and useful? In addition it is worth identifying strategies to deal with any backlog of servicing (and storage) of library stock that may occur if too many items arrive in the library at the same time, and that may be exacerbated if large orders are placed at fixed times of the year.

Then it is useful to decide what are the preferred and more effective means of selection for the school library, which might typically include:

- visit of a representative showing new stock from a particular publisher or supplier
- direct mailing from particular suppliers, including catalogues
- use of journals containing reviews of children's literature
- considerable accent on retrospective collection development involving the librarian looking at specific areas of the library collections over a period of time in order to identify and fill in gaps in the stock
- availability of added services, made possible by contracting with or purchasing from 'library suppliers'. These services may include access to online databases, focused collection development listings of resources, current awareness services, showroom facilities, etc.

A librarian may, for instance, use the latter type of service by deciding to employ a subscription agent for periodicals and serial publications. There may be a financial gain in the process, depending on the amount of titles to which a library and information service needs to subscribe. However the real advantage may be in the ease of payment for library and school finance staff, i.e. one payment for all the subscriptions to the agent, rather than many payments to different periodical publishers during a given period of time. Another service that will be provided by a journal subscription agent is checking on non-received or late issues of periodicals, further freeing the time of library staff for more important duties.

Consideration of these aspects allows the manager of the library and information service to demonstrate that the school receives value for money from the act of ordering materials for the facility, together with any relevant opportunity cost. There are however, several other aspects that should be considered when reflecting on the best value for money for the school:

'Servicing' of library materials

Various processes are invariably carried out on materials purchased for a school library before the items are available for selection by users from the open shelves. This is because the items need to be methodically stored so that they can be found easily. A classification system is used to achieve this. The classification system code for the item needs to be easily seen on the outside of the resource in order for it to be filed appropriately.

In addition, the librarian anticipates that materials will be well used and need to be available in a good physical state for a certain amount of time. The librarian will in addition want to ensure that efficient records of loan transactions are kept so that assets are safeguarded. In detail therefore, a number of servicing aspects are typically undertaken to prepare a resource for use in the library, such as the addition of the following:

- label affixed to the spine or end of the item showing the classification mark for the resource
- stamp or label showing ownership of the item
- barcode showing that the item has been listed in the library's automated catalogue or record of the school library's assets
- date label showing the extent of the loan period for the item
- plastic cover, protective packaging or other binding to prolong the active life of the item.

It is possible to undertake all these servicing tasks in-house but again consideration should be given to the time taken by library staff in carrying out these tasks. In addition, the materials for servicing need to be purchased and stored. The alternative, both for opportunity cost and economies of scale, is to contract with a library supplier so that servicing is done prior to the delivery of the item.

Use of schools library services (SLS) resource collections

Another possibility is to use a local schools library service. Here an option could be: 'purchase or borrow'. In other words, a school may decide to subscribe to an organization that, through economies of scale, provides a wide range of resources that a school can borrow for its own library, either to supplement the resources it owns or indeed to form the nucleus of a school library collection. Within a school, a librarian can argue that it is more cost-effective to maintain a centralized resource collection rather than exclusively build up collections in individual departments. Extending this logic, there are items that may have a limited life in one school, but could be used in another school, so it is feasible to borrow books and other resources from an SLS and return them when no longer required.

Loan collection services are commonly provided by most SLS who 'may provide schools with the largest proportion of the total number of learning resources used in schools. SLS learning resources are selected by librarians knowledgeable about literature for children and young people and experienced in assessing other types of learning resources for their suitability within various teaching and learning situations' (Tilke, 1998a, 66). In addition, SLS assist school librarians with advice and services to purchase materials for individual school libraries. The advantages of using such services include the following:

- Breadth and variety may be included in library collections, especially in terms of age interest and subject coverage.
- There will be support for areas of stock in most demand as typically may occur where a class or whole year group is undertaking a study of a topic at the same time. Calling in extra resources from an SLS topic collection and then returning the resources once study of a particular topic has ended may be a useful way of supplementing a library's own resources on a given topic.
- Provision of resources for short-term or one-off needs is supported. Again, when there is a demand for a particular amount of resources on a particular topic or theme and that topic is not likely to be visited again for

some time, then it may be more cost-effective to use SLS resources.
• Availability in the locality of resources for suddenly expressed needs is also important. In spite of the most careful liaison and planning, there are likely to be demands that arise very quickly and the ability to call on, have delivered or go and get resources at short notice may be very helpful.

The many other services of SLS are discussed elsewhere in this book, as relevant to the topic in hand, and can be found in the index. These services may be available individually or as a package. Service specifications and agreements vary according to local conditions, as they depend on how funding for an SLS in a local education authority is arranged. But, overall use of SLS resource collections may be a factor in determining value for money in relation to the budget of the school library.

Note: There is an assumption that independent or privately run schools cannot use schools library services, as these latter were established to support publicly funded or state schools in the UK. With changes to funding mechanisms, more and more SLS operate as a 'business unit' of a local authority and schools 'buy into' the service. While local variations will inevitably apply, it may well be possible for independent schools to also purchase the services on offer from an SLS.

Discounts

Another aspect of value for money is a discount in price. This may occur for one-off orders but is possibly more likely for customers who contract over time or who have an account with a supplier. Indeed, a librarian may be under some pressure from a school to obtain discounts from suppliers.

In its most obvious form, discount may be seen as a reduction in the total cost for goods and services that is payable by a school. There may be sliding scales of discounts, more being given for larger sums spent with a particular supplier and to reward continuing customers. However, there are also other aspects that can be regarded as discounts, such as payment on monthly statement for account holders, rather than payment of individual invoices. In addition, delivery costs may be waived or reduced. The sort of servicing discussed above may be provided at a reduced or nil cost, perhaps depending on the level of commitment to the supplier from the customer. In other words, a greater amount of a school library's budget could be committed to a single supplier, as opposed to using a variety of suppliers. There may also be more direct benefit in terms of added services being provided by a single supplier at a discounted rate (though a librarian may consider that a wider range of publications may in fact be seen through using more than one supplier). However, it is important to bear in mind the scale or size of the library budget concerned – what might seem a considerable sum to an individual school can appear vastly different to an organization with a multi-million euro turnover. A recent trend for school librarians to group together to form consortia in order to negotiate reduced rates with specialist library (and other) firms may make discounts more realistic for individual schools (though this particular development may be more in evidence in the independent school sector).

Monitoring financial information

As a manager who is responsible for a budget-head or item in the overall accounts of a school, a librarian should receive information about expenditure to date in the current financial year that has been coded against the budget for the library. This information may be sufficient to enable a library manager to assess the progress of financial expenditure in a current financial year. If this is not the case, a librarian may wish to keep informal financial records so as to:

• Reconcile recorded expenditure with committed expenditure, in order to identify a total of available funding for spending. For some resources in particular, e.g. books, there can be a significant time period between the date the item has been ordered and the delivery date (let alone the date of the arrival of an invoice, requiring payment by a particular date). This may occur, for instance, because of delays in publication or supply.

Also, periodical subscription payments for a following year may need to be paid late in the current financial year (though it may be possible for payments to be coded against the next financial year's budget). Identifying true available funding figures may therefore take a little work by a library manager.

- Identify where exactly the expenditure has in fact been spent during a year. There may be a wish to show to departments how the library has committed expenditure to certain subject areas. In addition, it may be helpful to show how spending is progressing in terms of a development plan. On a more mundane level, it may assist with queries about payment or delivery of particular items. The aim is not to create detailed accounts that require significant time to maintain but rather – perhaps by means of a spreadsheet – to provide a simple management tool that is helpful to a librarian.

A survey noted that school librarians were not usually regarded as managers by their senior management teams (Shakeshaft, 1998, 31) and that financial information was not forthcoming to individual librarians. How widespread this may be in general is not currently known, but it is vital that school librarians are as pro-active as possible in obtaining information, however basic, that enables them to manage a library budget efficiently and effectively.

Inventory

An inventory is simply a listing of resources, equipment and things of value owned by an organization. It is an aspect of financial accounting and seeks to identify an organization's assets. In library terms, however, the word inventory is used more specifically to mean a stock-check, i.e. checking the catalogue of the library collection against the library's physical stock, both that on the shelves and that on loan.

There are several reasons for taking an inventory of the stock of a school library:

- The accuracy of the catalogue may be verified.
- Losses and missing items in the library catalogue may be identified.
- The process is a requirement of financial managers in the school (and any external auditors).
- Inventory acts as an impetus for the return of overdue items (this is especially effective when publicity announces when the inventory is to take place, perhaps with an amnesty on the after-effects of very outstanding non-returned library loans).
- It is also a stimulus for the return of items that have been borrowed but not recorded in the library's issue system.

Most of the above may act as advantages for undertaking such a task. Perhaps, though, there are some disadvantages to the procedure. Possibly an atmosphere of distrust may be engendered in a school community by such a procedure. More practically, as a library probably needs to be closed for the purpose of stock taking, there is the opportunity cost of closing a central curricular facility in a school in order to fulfil a routine, administrative function. One librarian at least considers it a 'stressful' job activity, and one that does not allow for other duties during the same time period (Smallwood, 1997, 11). Indeed, the time taken in inventorying by the library staff must be weighed in the balance against the usefulness of the task in hand. This is especially true when an inventory is taken each and every year. Other issues could include an assessment of the usefulness of the time be spent on this procedure. The library manager may wish to assess the productiveness of the time and the necessity for repeating such a procedure every year.

However, inventory taking may be a feature built into or available with automated library management systems and where it exists has certainly reduced the herculean efforts that were necessary to operate more manual systems in the past. It is also possible to take an inventory of a part of a school library's collection each year, rather than stock taking the whole collection. This is useful in order to highlight particularly well-used or popular areas of the collection or to cover the whole collection in systematic stages over a number of years.

Above all, the purpose of the undertaking needs to be considered. To provide management information about a part of the school's assets will be considered more worthy than merely to undertake an inventory because it is an annual exercise – a sort of tradition, as it were. Certainly to provide a better service to users, i.e. by providing an accurate catalogue, is a good aim, as is the use of data to assist with collection development, perhaps allied with a bid for extra funding. Indeed, in a situation where the security of library resources is considered ineffective, a library manager may wish to use data collected by means of an inventory in a bid for extra funding to enable a security system to be installed.

An electronic security system for the school library

A commercially produced electronic security system helps to provide greater security for library resources that are stored or made available to users in an open-access situation. Users who take items out of a library without having them recorded in the facility's issuing and loan system (when items will also be de-sensitized) will be reminded that this is the case – a noise is emitted when the user passes security gates placed at the exit of the library.

The details of different systems vary and a school librarian will need to research the different options carefully, but probably only after consideration of a number of questions, such as:

- What is the justification for a system? Has the case for installing a system been well made? Are there alternative strategies, perhaps to do with the arrangement of the library or education of users, that could be tried? Have they been tried, and failed?
- What will be the image of the library when security gates and/or barriers are fitted?
- Will such a feature of the library sit well with any school statement on the values and standards of behaviour expected of the institution's students, particularly as regards honesty, trust and responsibility?

- Will a system work with the physical configuration of the present library accommodation?
- Has the installation and maintenance workload for the library staff been taken into account? Are there sufficient staff to supervise such a system?
- Is there sufficient physical space at an entrance so that a system will not interfere with any computerized library management system?
- How many entrances/exits does the library have? Has the high cost of gates or barriers at each entrance been accounted for?

A security system may well be the best available option for a school's library and indeed be very beneficial. However, a library manager will no doubt realize that it is a technological system and is therefore not perfect. In addition, a number of procedures and sanctions may need to be applied once the system has been installed. These include the need for on-going specific servicing of library materials to enable a system to work, and deterrents to and ways of dealing with repeated or serious unauthorized 'borrowing' of library resources, which of course require human intervention and management.

Valuing library assets

As an alternative to an inventory, sometimes a library manager will be asked to identify the (cash) value of library assets. There are, sadly, occasions when this needs to be undertaken retrospectively, usually as the aftermath of a fire or water damage in the school library. However, this may also be an exercise required by financial managers (perhaps for insurance purposes).

As far as equipment is concerned, it should be relatively simple to identify the costs of particular items, perhaps by recording the purchase price in any inventory or listing of such items, and applying an annual allowance for depreciation (depending on the provision of insurance cover). Computers in the library may be covered by costs apportioned to the ICT department.

Valuing the book stock

Books, however – still arguably the largest part of the resources of a school library – need to be valued on a cost basis. It may be possible, if using a computer catalogue system that records the cost of a book in a specific data field, to provide a total amount for the purchase cost of items. The replacement costs, though, may be higher owing to inflation and increased publication costs.

If a computer management system does not provide this information, a methodology for working out the cost of a book stock should be formulated. A basic formula could be:

Number of books in the library x Current average price of books = ...

This formula may be made more complex. For instance, the ratio of hardback to paperback books in a library may be identified, in order to use differing price bands for these formats. This may be done perhaps by an automated library management system or simply by looking at a shelf of books and counting the number of books in each format. For greater balance, a shelf could be taken at random in different parts of the library. The numbers could be totalled and divided by the number of shelves. A mathematical calculation to identify the proportion of paperback to hardback books in stock may thus be arrived at.

It is possible to obtain or work out current average prices for categories or types of books, as various indices of prices are published by the book trade and may also be available from a library supplier. Thus:

1/3 of total book stock of the library in hardback format x current average price of hardback books = ...
Therefore, 2/3 of total book stock of the library in paperback format x current average price of paperback books = ...

It is also possible to calculate a cost according to the ratio of non-fiction to fiction books in a school library, and more specifically children's fiction and non-fiction, together with 'adult' fiction and non-fiction (as these categories

137

tend to have different average price ranges). Once a formula has been arrived at, it will just need to be refreshed on an annual basis with current price ranges.

The question of the depreciation of book stock may be anathema to some as books attract emotional responses and values from individuals. Indeed, an older book may have rarity value and therefore cost more, but this may mix cost and value in an unhelpful or impractical way. Indeed, others would argue that older books should be withdrawn from the library (as guidelines generally suggest), so a question of depreciation is best negotiated or dealt with on an individual school basis. The argument may be considered, of course, in the event of having to replace the entire stock at one time.

A formula, more or less detailed as a library manager and others require, may therefore be helpful in arriving at an accurate figure for the cost of replacing a school library in the event of fire or other disaster.

Conclusion

'School [libraries] are very expensive!' rightly insists one secondary school librarian. From the finance expended on them alone, it is necessary that school libraries make an impact and a difference. If they do not, 'they will in all probability be under funded and irrelevant to the curriculum as a whole and in the long term will probably be shut down' (Sykes, 2000, 16–18). This is a powerful argument by one librarian. In making an 'impact', librarians are exercising their knowledge, competencies and skills, not least that of financial management. Such an important aspect of a librarian's management role has been recognized in UK secondary school library guidelines (Tilke, 1998a, 27): 'good budgetary management skills will enable the library manager to be aware of financial commitments and expenditure'. These skills also enable a librarian 'to demonstrate to others the financial position of the library'. Nevertheless, no specific training in financial matters is required, rather it is utilizing numeracy skills, together with an outlook developed from core managerial aptitudes. As with other aspects of the librarian's role identified in this book, the qualities identified in this chapter will only be maximized by good communication, analytical and advocacy skills.

8
MANAGING THE BUILDING AND EQUIPMENT

School inspector Gervase Phinn was 'shown into a bare, cold, featureless room with a few ancient tomes and dog-eared textbooks scattered along the high wooden bookcases. The atmosphere carried a warm pervasive smell of dust, and the grey walls did not help. This was —— High School Library, the supposed central learning resource, the foundation of the curriculum, the place of academic study, reading and research.'   Phinn, 1999, 237

The purpose of this chapter is to show how active a librarian's role can be in terms of management of the premises, or physical space, that a school library occupies and the fixed or heavy equipment that is contained within library accommodation. An active librarian's role greatly reduces the chance of situations such as the one described above occurring.

There are two ways of looking at this role, firstly from a school library manager's point of view and secondly from that of the users. For the librarian, the role will consist of:

- responsibility for health and safety and other legal obligations in the school library
- safeguarding the school's fixed and moveable assets
- promoting the efficiency of the library and information service, through the way the accommodation is configured
- considering the aesthetic function, by creating an atmosphere and tone for the library.

From the point of view of users – students, staff, senior management, parents and visitors and library staff – there may be a range of expectations, needs and demands, some of which may be conflicting. For instance, students may wish for a school library that will enable them to relax during non-lesson times while staff may prefer that there is an area for silent study. Visitors need somewhere to wait for appointment times and parents may wish for a waiting area to collect children at the end of the school day. Library staff may need space to work on preparing stock for the library.

It is also useful to identify the management implications for the different stages of school library development. Therefore, strategies and skills will range from daily management skills to project management, depending on whether the library is:

- functioning in existing space that is sufficient for present and future needs, with reasonable furnishing and equipment, so that the librarian's role is involved more with regular maintenance
- housed in reasonable accommodation but where library functions are not working well enough; here the librarian is not anticipating expansion but rather looking for ways to alter configurations of furniture and equipment, aiming to build flexibility into a spatial plan
- housed in inadequate premises so that the librarian needs to advocate that a school provide increased, altered or improved accommodation
- unable to function because accommodation is not relevant or useful and new accommodation is required. With any development of a complete new facility, the librarian is exercising project management skills.

It is likely that a school librarian will encounter several of these scenarios during her or his career. Although guidelines concerning school library provision are available, these tend to be advisory and recommended rather than mandatory; library accommodation in secondary schools varies considerably. There is therefore a real challenge to librarians in terms of assessing provision, looking for ways to change and implement perceived improvements, advocate new investment in the school library facility and take part in managing building or refurbishment project development.

Why should accommodation be devoted in school for library purposes?

There may be a number of reasons why a library has developed in a school, ranging for instance from housing a collection of books donated by a significant local individual to utilizing historic rooms that are unsuitable for other school purposes. A centralized library may have been included in plans because a school simply should have one (historical reason). The reasons could be good, bad or indifferent in themselves, but they are at best subsidiary to the answer to the question which should be found in the school library policy. Unless this question is clearly answered, it is really impossible to truly justify the space, expense and effort involved in providing, developing and maintaining library provision.

In the real world, subsidiary and local reasons for developing school libraries will exist and that must be acknowledged. Furthermore, they can sit alongside an over-riding curricular reason, but if the latter is not identified and acknowledged, any library development, irrespective of size, will not meet its potential.

What should be included in library accommodation?

Having decided that centralized library facilities are useful to a school, there needs to be an identification of what exactly is needed within a library. Here, it is tempting to go off immediately and construct a list of features, furniture and equipment, though the next logical step is to again consult the functions of a school library as identified in a policy document.

So for instance, a function may be 'to provide study facilities'. This is simple enough to analyse, but how many study spaces should be provided? Where should they be provided – together in one place or located in small clusters throughout a library? How do teaching staff want students to study and how do students themselves want to study in a library?

Or, a function may be to support recreational and personal needs of students. This may be deconstructed to mean supplying a range of fiction materials, perhaps audio or music recordings, magazines and recreational non-fiction. More thought in interpreting this may be needed as far as space, furniture and equipment is concerned. A spatial allowance or estimate should be made for a sufficient amount of shelving and for displays (arguably vital in terms of promoting such stock to users). An appropriately furnished and sited reading area and indeed consideration of the whole aesthetic environment of the library, which is so important to this aspect of library provision, needs to be thought about.

Who can help with library accommodation development?

The role of a library steering committee was considered in Chapter 5; a committee can play a most helpful role in teasing out the implications for a library from stated and desired functions. A library committee can also assist in arriving at a range of functions and services that a school library can offer as well as having a vision of the future for such a centralized facility. It is preferable, though, that a committee is firmly focused on the overall aim and the benefit and usefulness to the school, rather than recommending individual pieces of furniture and colour schemes, tempting though that is.

It is possible to obtain detailed, technical help and advice from a range of sources, including:

- *Guidelines for school libraries*. There are several available, such as the Australian School Library Association (2001), Charlton (2002), Dewe (1996), Markuson (1999) and Tilke (1998a). They sometimes include complementary information about spatial requirements, furniture and fittings, lighting and air, aesthetics, and health and safety issues. Used as a checklist or for more detail, guidelines will be a good starting point for any consideration of development of the physical space of a school library.

- *Schools Library Services*. SLS may provide access to current guidelines and indeed offer specific advice and advocacy that can be used within an individual school. They will be aware of good examples of school libraries and can recommend suppliers. Some SLS have also published their own guidelines or manuals about school library premises.
- *Other schools*. Schools and colleges, either in the locality or further afield, may provide valuable information concerning accommodation for a school library. Because theirs will be a specific experience, it is arguable that it is more valuable to talk to individuals involved and ascertain what worked and (perhaps more importantly) what did not work, as this information could help prevent costly and time-wasting errors. If a visit is difficult to arrange, it may be possible to network electronically with schools, view school library websites (which may have photographs) and use listservs to obtain information.
- *Consultants*. Past school librarians or those formerly with a schools library service may provide a valuable in-depth service to individual schools, bringing extensive experience to support a valuable, expensive and one-off project for a particular school. National organizations may maintain a list of consultants and their areas of expertise (e.g. the UK School Library Association). Consultants are sometimes retained by or on the staff of suppliers of library furniture and equipment.
- *Architects*. A key professional in any large-scale building or significant alteration/extension project, an architect is an important ally. The architect's appreciation of the aims, functions and aspirations of the school's library and information service will be a key determinant in the success of a new school library building project. Managing communication with an architect (often through an intermediary, such as a member of the school administration or SMT or a local education authority) will be a significant role for a school librarian during the life of a particular project.
- *Users of a school library*. At appropriate stages in the project, it is helpful to consult with potential users of a 'new' library: students, staff and others. Using a library committee in the first instance perhaps, it is possible to obtain feedback and suggestions, but preferably related to specific plans

or possibilities. Therefore, it is important to be clear about what comments and feedback are required, so it is best to frame questions and present possibilities after research and costings have been done, in order that expectations are raised on realistic proposals.

Specific issues regarding school library provision

A number of issues associated with premises are common to most library situations. The following points are ones that the librarian will need to manage and evaluate. These issues are not one-off considerations but should be assessed and evaluated as an on-going job activity:

Aesthetic aspect of library provision

Go into a shop or someone's home and it is likely that you will have an instinctive view, impression or opinion of the space, whether it is based on décor, furnishings, atmosphere or ambience. This aspect of a school library has been touched on earlier in this book in relation to creating an ethos of use for the library and a statement of the school's value in its library and information service. However, such an intangible result can be built up from a range of very practical steps in library design, such as those identified by Hyams (2001, 420–1) who summarized the necessary elements of successful library design projects in Cambridgeshire, England:

- Ensure access for all, use the opportunity to build in access without compromising attractive design.
- Design a flexible layout to accommodate new services . . . for the future.
- Plan a simple layout with good sightlines and discrete zones.
- Provide effective signage and guiding for maximum use of services.
- Maximize space and light and avoid clutter to create a feeling of space and airiness.
- Select a colour scheme to give harmony and cohesion throughout the library.

- Purchase flexible shelving and furniture to reflect the style of the building and the needs of the customers.

Although some of these points are more relevant to setting up a new facility, a librarian should regularly monitor these features of a school library as they can deteriorate over time. For instance, items of furniture added over time could inhibit hitherto good sightlines. Signage and guiding may become out of date or tatty, worn or faded in appearance. Paint too can fade from the original colour. Aesthetic features of a library are therefore not just arrived at, they need to be maintained.

The library as archive

Archives in schools may be limited or sizeable in terms of physical objects and documents, so have obvious spatial implications. Electronic archives on the other hand could be extensive, but they may be aimed at preserving school documents for specific management and administration purposes. However, an archive made available through a school library will probably be for different purposes, e.g. for students to use as a curricular resource and for former students to visit and consult. A school archive could be included as part of a local studies collection (Southcombe, 1999, 13), which may be available in a school library.

For a school of more recent history and with, by implication, a more limited archive, a feature may be made in the school library, either through use of a small room or a corner of the (main) library room. Display boards for showing photographs could be a good way of promoting interest in the history of the school. It could be relatively inexpensively done, but does have a spatial implication.

In some schools, such as those established several hundred years ago, and which may be independent rather than funded by the state, archives may be considerable in terms of size and value. Whether modest or extensive in size, and especially if original documents and artefacts are included, there are implications for the care, preservation and storage of these items, that again have space implications. Archives tend to grow over time, so the situation is one that can be periodically reassessed by a library manager. Temperature control, lighting, security and access are other issues to be borne in mind in developing or monitoring important archival collections.

The cost of setting up or improving accommodation for a school archive collection will be considerable, as will be maintenance costs. Where rare and valuable items are concerned, it would be especially helpful to obtain specialist advice, e.g. from suppliers of archival equipment, other schools or institutions with small archive collections, or public, local or regional archive collections.

Cleaning

Especially if a library is carpeted (in order to deaden noise), it is important that the cleaning of a facility is done regularly and to an acceptable standard. Dust is also prevalent in libraries, and is circulated when resources are moved from shelves. For the benefit of the health of users as well as those who work in the library, a cleaning service specification should be available to and agreed by a school library's manager.

Display

Modern bookstores give a lot of attention to layout and the importance of display, for obvious reasons. This is true of public libraries too. The adage appears to be that 'a book spine does not sell a book'. Display as an aid to promoting resources is almost as much of a mind-set as a job activity. Clearly large set displays are effective (and take time and planning to achieve) but equally so will a small display of books displayed face-forward or even one book shown in such a manner at the end of a bookshelf. Therefore thought needs to be given to the amount of floor and shelf space allowed for display.

Equal opportunities and access

It is important to consider the needs of all users when planning and configuring library accommodation. This will apply particularly, for instance, when there is library provision on upper floors, or divided between two floors (perhaps with a mezzanine level). Lift facilities may be required. In addition, in calculating available floor space, the needs of users who move about with the aid of wheelchairs should be borne in mind. There is a range of special needs that may need to be accommodated in a school library. Some of these needs will be common to different sorts of facilities in general and may be identified in official documents. Other needs are specific to library situations, e.g. the height of shelves. Liaison with a local public library service would be valuable in this regard in particular as public libraries have considerable experience in planning and altering their premises to ensure that people of all abilities can access the facilities.

Functions

It is useful to allow for future development in the library. While it is not always possible to anticipate what extra services or resources may be required, there may be a school policy or expectation that enrolment will rise over a given period of time. This may well have implications for a library in terms of human traffic flow and the amount of study space accommodation needed.

- Study or seating spaces. For a number of years, there was government advice on the number of study or rather seating spaces to be allowed in secondary school libraries in England. This is now no longer the case. For effective estimates of how many study spaces to allow, it may be better for a librarian to base a figure on an analysis of learning styles prevalent in the school (as discussed in Chapter 3). This will also make a difference to whether seating is provided in class or group configurations, or individual study facilities, as well as seating spaces provided at computer terminals.

- To better cater for teaching and learning in the library (while still providing an appropriate overall atmosphere) a room or rooms may be set aside off the main library area to allow for teaching purposes, quiet or silent study and the use of specific types of media.

The use of technology in a school library makes more demands on available space as technology allows access to other resources, thus complementing existing resources rather than replacing them. Space to access monitors and OPACs is necessary. Added implications will be siting, not only for security and noise reasons, but to limit glare from direct sunlight.

Health and safety issues

These may be stated in law and appear in specific regulations, e.g. fire safety regulations. A school as an organization will be aware of these so information should be available in-house or electronically (perhaps from a local authority or utility). It would be useful to liaise with the member of staff nominated as a health and safety liaison officer for the school. Specific aspects may nevertheless need consideration from a librarian, such as ensuring that emergency exits in the library can be easily reached and that it is clearly understood how to reach a central place for registration of pupils who have been evacuated. In addition, fire extinguishers should be able to be quickly located and activated. There may be an inspection of school premises by various agencies, such as the fire service, and there will be a need for a librarian to know any outcome of or recommendations from such an inspection of school library facilities (Tilke, 1998b, 73).

Light, power and common services

Sufficient light, both natural and artificial, is required in a library. Library resources also need to be protected from excessive or strong light (for instance, because of potential fading on the spines of books and inability to read computer screens). Blinds should be at least allowed for in plans and costed for a budget, even if they are not actually ordered or fitted until a library has been running for a time, in order to identify where the exact need is. This could be seasonal, e.g. with low-lying winter sun in the northern hemisphere.

Artificial lighting levels could be looked at as improvements in these configurations that could enable a library to be used more effectively. For instance, too many overhead lights could make the overall library space light and bright, but may leave bays of shelves in shadow. Effective use of spotlights can help illuminate dark areas. Some flickering lightbulbs may cause illness, for instance, by triggering a migraine attack.

Power usage also needs to be identified – light, heat, air conditioning, technology and other usage make considerable demands on power supply. Depending on the location of a school, air conditioning may be helpful, if not essential, both for humans and the care of resources. Finally, water supply is helpful. Handling books and other resources means contact with a considerable amount of dust (and germs), so water supply is a useful hygiene facility in a school library.

Other uses of the library facility

The library accommodation in a school may be used for other purposes. In surveys (Sheffield Hallam University, 2000, 6; Shakeshaft, 1998, 32) it has been found that the facilities allocated to the library are used for other purposes in approximately 80% of schools. This use ranges from occasional meetings and events to regular use as a timetabled classroom for subject teaching. In cases where a library is unable to function at these times then clearly the situation is regrettable. However, on a practical level, a librarian needs to manage such use in terms of library functions, layout and security of stock. Where such other use coincides with no library staff being on duty, however, it is likely that the quality of the library will suffer, especially when the library is 'regularly used for an unsuitable purpose, such as a detention centre' (Shakeshaft, 1998, 32).

Noise policy

As a school librarian will be aware, 'a flourishing, effective school library is not necessarily a quiet place and it can be difficult for the librarian to create and maintain the desired learning atmosphere' (Spink, 2000, 175). However, it may be found that teaching staff – whether users or non-users of the library – have generally held expectations that quiet, even silence, is the desired atmosphere in a library, though the reasoning for this may be unclear (save for tradition). Nevertheless, a quiet environment aids concentration. Zoning activities in a school library according to noise levels may be a partial solution (as will be the creation of seminar rooms, identified above), together with the use of carpet, and grouping furniture to deaden noise. An expectation of universal quiet may become a tension in a library facility and it could be useful to identify this issue in any policy development process in order to help others understand the functions of a modern school library. Nevertheless, expectations of appropriate behaviour in the library should be explained to users, so misunderstandings are minimized.

Sightlines

A school library needs good sightlines for a number of reasons, not least because of security, safety and the monitoring of behaviour. Sightlines should relate to the area from which a school library is usually supervised and enable a library manager to readily see how the library is being used. Good sightlines should allow views to the end of a library and to corners, and are afforded as much by reasonable height as by layout of furniture and equipment. It is likely that a library manager will experience times in a school library 'when students need help, the printer is jammed, a teacher needs a video played, and you have an idea that the girl and boy you haven't seen for a few minutes behind the book cases are not looking for books. . . . If you have a say in designing a new library, be sure to keep these times in mind as far as saving steps, time, frustration' (Smallwood, 1997, 19). Clear sightlines will help to assist with the smooth running of a facility.

Space and layout

In addition to technology and study space implications, identified above, spatial considerations need to take account of an agreed or targeted stock or collection level. It is possible to calculate the amount of shelves required by arriving at an average number of resources that can comfortably (but not tightly) be fitted on to an individual shelf, for instance, 30 items per shelf. Divide this number by an agreed optimum collection size for a library (say, 15,000 items), to arrive at the number of shelves required. Other resource storage (e.g. for newspapers and magazines), office and workspace need to be also included. Careful thought should be given to a main entrance and exit, as a number of loan transactions will be made at this place. In addition, there may be issues of bag storage and security systems. The mounting and viewing of displays have space implications. Indeed, it could be helpful to plan more than one layout. Changing a layout, a strategy employed with success in the retail industry, can, either in whole or in part, provide new impetus and a 'fresh look' for users and potential users. Flexibility in using space and layout can be helpful as it will allow the librarian to 'shape the allocation of physical space in the library' (Todd, 2001, 23) according to the learning needs of students.

Solutions to problems of inadequate library provision

Once library accommodation has been evaluated – perhaps using guidelines as indicators – and found to be inadequate, solutions to the problem may be suggested by the librarian, library steering committee or the senior management team. These may include the following:

Dual purpose libraries

This category of library is very much the exception rather than the rule. In some areas with a strong, tightly located community, a joint school and public library is the optimum way of operating a library and information service. There are some highly publicized examples and variations on the theme, such as the community-resource-based learning project at St Ivo School, Cambridgeshire, whose librarian/project manager considered that 'co-ordination is the most important key word' (Ashcroft, 2000, 12). In some areas, such as South Ayrshire in Scotland, there is a policy of developing joint public and school libraries, where relevant. However, with or without celebrated examples, some librarians or others in a school may identify such a method of delivery as the way forward for library provision. It may be so, and a considerable number of partnerships, issues and negotiation will need to be entered into in order to progress such a project. Those involved in such an undertaking will no doubt have their own criteria for success, and these may include the following questions and issues:

- Will the needs of both local community and school be equally or appropriately covered?
- Is the school physically located in the centre of the community?
- Have safety, security, access and other issues been considered for all individuals concerned, including students, school staff, library staff and members of the public?
- Will the development impinge on or raise pressure for community use of other facilities in the school, for instance, a theatre or hall, swimming pool or other sports facilities, music recording facilities?
- Have legal, funding and employment implications been taken into account?
- Apart from facilities, what can the school offer to the community, and what can the community offer to the school? (Examples may be community service on the part of students, and oral history on the part of the community.)

As the reader will be aware, the point becomes not a (school) library–community issue but rather that of the school as a whole and community. There are so many issues associated purely with library provision, but in reality, community expectations will be much more than that. Library provision of this sort therefore needs to work equally for both school and wider (local) communities.

Siting

A good site is helpful for a central resource, such as a library. It is always possible that, with internal reajustment to school buildings, a more central site may become available for a library facility. In addition, a new entrance may provide access to better or more used thoroughfares, enabling the school community to use the facility more easily. Many guidelines specifically recommend that a school library be sited as centrally as possible, indicating that a library should be within a main building and/or adjacent to other services, such as a canteen or dining area, main teaching areas and administration centre. There is also the issue of which floor of the building a centralized library should be located. Logistically, the ground floor should be preferred, bearing in mind the concentration of load that a floor will need to take, also the need for regular deliveries and ultimately for access for users with disabilities. A tension arises when the centre of teaching is not on a ground or bottom floor – is it preferable that a library be located where access is easier for users (assuming a school is contained within one building) or do logistical aspects apply more?

Split-site library provision

Library provision ranging over more than one site in a secondary school is not very common. Indeed, a survey (Sheffield Hallam University, 2000, 21) found that only 12% of schools in the UK had two or more sites. However, school amalgamation on more than one site makes the situation possible. A school's management team too may accept that library provision is inadequate but that there is no way to improve this in a library's current location. A solution may be to operate a library service over more than one site. There are a number of issues associated with establishing such a project and a considerable number of management issues for the maintenance and development of a split-site operation, such as duplication of stock, equipment and staff, access, technology and (especially if both sites are not equally staffed) security. It could be a solution, but the many issues need to be thought through carefully, not least that of a central location.

Project management

This is usually associated with the process of developing new and altered premises as it features a specifically financed project, with an agreed time-span and involves a range of professions and services, such as architects, planners, surveyors, engineers, electrical and other service providers and commercial suppliers, including sub-contractors. Given the number of people involved in a building project, communication may be seen to be a particularly important aspect of project management. A library may be the sole facility in such a project, or can be one of a number of areas of school life that are affected. Especially in the latter case, it is necessary for the librarian to be aware of issues that will have implications for the library, such as the supply of common services and thoroughfares (Tilke, 1998b, 121). A lot of detailed work, involving consultation of technical drawings and plans, will be required over a considerable time-scale. Where the new project is a self-contained building, the library manager will need to accept that some space is required for plant and equipment to run common services, so is basically 'dead' space as far as library configuration is concerned. Again, it will be helpful to consult plans at an early stage in order to become familiar with 'fixed' details.

Furniture and equipment

Although the time spent on considering the space of a school library is valuable, it should not be forgotten that the area is designed to be used, and used heavily, so the placing and function of furniture and equipment are very important. Access to resources and equipment should be optimized and furniture and fittings should be capable of sustained, indeed heavy, use.

Furniture and fittings

A range of specialized library furniture will be required in a school library. Guidelines and advice will typically identify or list the sort of furniture to be considered. Library furniture suppliers, too, can offer advice and costing services. Although such purchases tend to be irregular in nature, a library manager should remember that individual pieces wear out or break. Therefore, it is useful to consider on-going supply needs when fitting out a school library, perhaps preferring mass-produced, modular units.

Flexibility, too, should be a firm feature. Library shelving with adjustable shelves is the most obvious example, but easily moveable, free-standing shelving units (on lockable castor-wheels) enable layouts to be altered quickly and safely. As part of health and safety management, the sturdiness and safety of furniture is an important consideration. Testing of various items of furniture, such as study carrels and chairs, by students and other users can be a useful monitoring tool for a librarian.

Equipment

With a number of developments in technology, a school library typically now houses a range of technological devices and equipment, all of which have storage and floor space implications. Associated with the use of technology and electrical equipment will be the need for an appropriate number of power outlets, cabling or a suitable environment for wireless communication. In particular, a library manager should consider the following:

Library management computer and security systems

Over 70% of schools surveyed by Sheffield Hallam University (2000, 11) operated an automated library management system. While the software itself has little accommodation implications, the hardware needed to run it has. This ranges from terminals to administer the system to a dedicated server, cabling and OPAC terminals. Installation of a system will have implications for the configuration and location of a library counter or reception desk area, especially if operated in conjunction with an automated security system. This is because a signal used in the latter may adversely affect the operation of an automated (library management) system. It is possible to avoid this by physically separating both systems by a particular distance (which can be advised by manufacturers and suppliers).

Audio facilities

To enable users to access websites and software products, it should be relatively simple to provide headphones attached to individual computers. However, for audio-tape listening stations or for listening to recorded music in a library, zoning of such activities or even listening booths should also be considered.

Photocopying and reproduction facilities

Typically, photocopying facilities are available in libraries. Given the amount of time that needs to be allowed for even low-grade maintenance work on these machines, appropriate siting of photocopiers should be considered carefully. Monitoring of photocopying may be required in order to comply with copyright laws. Therefore, siting a photocopier near to a staffed library reception desk may be both helpful and efficient. The storage of paper for a photocopier, any coin or card box to operate the system and display of photocopying and copyright regulations are other spatial implications.

A school library and information service may, in addition, offer more comprehensive reproduction facilities for staff. Where a large number of highly sophisticated machines are provided, it is hoped that a separate room would be provided, in order to satisfy issues such as noise, ventilation, security, storage and workspace for the operative concerned.

Case study: converting an existing facility into a modern school library

My remit was to transform an old 1940s out-of-date library into a 21st Century Learning Resource Centre.

I was appointed on 28 October 1996, and the Learning Resource Centre was to be opened and fully functional on 28 February 1997. The fiction area had already been redesigned when I arrived, and I was to redesign the non-fiction sections. The layout is important here . . . . The library was the length of four classrooms, and lent itself to three distinct areas. The middle and bottom areas (approximately three classrooms in length) were to be my design responsibility. The content consisted of twelve 6'6" x 6'6" double-sided oak shelving, mainly empty as three-quarters of the book stock had been weeded and withdrawn before I arrived, and the bottom section was mothballed as a storage area.

The library had been closed for six weeks prior to my arrival. As the fiction area was now usable, I opened the library to students and began six weeks of observing how the students used the library. I looked at what the physical needs were and how I could use the new design to change the current perception held by the school community that the library was irrelevant to learning, and not worth visiting!

In particular:

- I was fortunate to have a supportive and forward thinking Head Teacher, and full support from the governing body.
- Finance had been made available for redevelopment following the previous OFSTED inspection.
- I put forward a radical design, and following discussions with the Head Teacher and relevant Governors, it was accepted.
- The most difficult area was finding a library furniture supplier that would provide and fit new shelving in the allotted time.
- The project took eight weeks from start to finish, and the deadlines set by the Governing body were met.

The experience was a positive one for me. I viewed it as a challenge, and was determined to create a Learning Resource Centre that would be a centre for learning, its use being so ingrained into the life of the school community that it would be impossible to remove it! This was achieved, and the Learning Resource Centre is now a natural part of school life.

Lynn Winkworth, currently School Librarian at Headington School, Oxford, but describing a library project while employed in an other secondary school in Oxfordshire, UK.

Conclusion

It is helpful to imagine just what a good school library and information service will look and sound like. If a school librarian cannot imagine this, it will be difficult for others to appreciate it. Indeed, it is worth describing what happens in a school library and use this description in appropriate reports, whether an architect's brief or a report to an external inspectorial body. One librarian has described his 'library heaven':

> People fill the place. They are busy. Many are seated at tables, although some move from place to place. It is not particularly quiet. Students and adults in the room are engaged, working in all sorts of modes. Some work individually, perhaps reading and writing. Others are talking in small groups, and perhaps elsewhere in the facility one or two teachers are working with their entire class. People are reading books, newspapers and magazines. They are clicking away at computer keyboards, printing, using other learning tools and the copy machine. In library heaven, the copy machine works. Browsers comb the stacks. Kids are passing books back and forth to each other as they talk quietly in the paperback corner . . . . Arriving students often go to the computers and spend a few minutes using the catalog before going to the shelves to find their books . . . . Students use the library's computers to access the local public library's catalog and other online sources to obtain the information they need . . . . Gazing around the facility one can see students using the internet to write papers, create original multimedia projects . . . that they save into portfolios that will later be used for assessment of specific, locally developed and community supported learning objectives . . . . At the circulation desk, materials are quickly checked out . . . a parent volunteer is sorting and then reshelving books... teachers come and go throughout the day ... [one teacher consults] with the library media specialist about an upcoming unit of study for which she has scheduled time for her classes to use the library to prepare a research-based project.
>
> Shoemaker, 2001, 19–21

And so on. 'Library heaven', however, does not just happen. The valuable space allocated by the school to its library and information service requires and deserves careful thought and management. This will be a situation that applies to nearly all secondary and high schools in the UK, as a survey (Sheffield Hallam University, 2000, 6) found that just 2% of schools did not have a library site. A key aspect is flexibility, whether in the use of dedicated library accommodation, furniture and fittings or work practices of the library manager. Much is rightly made of a librarian's role in large projects, such as completely new or substantially altered library accommodation. However, as a manager of a site-based service, a librarian's responsibility on a daily basis, together with a quality assurance role, is considerable. Management of premises and equipment, therefore, is not an occasional role for the librarian, but an on-going one, requiring, as identified in this chapter, the application of specific and general knowledge, skills and awareness.

9

MANAGING RESOURCES AND COLLECTION DEVELOPMENT

From this:

The books on the shelf bore witness to the fact that there had not been a full audit or clear-out of the old and inappropriate material for some time. There were books entitled 'Wireless Studies for Beginners', 'Life in the Belgian Congo', 'Harmless Scientific Experiments for Girls' and 'Our King: George VI'.

Phinn, 1999, 237

to this from a school librarian:

The users must feel that it is their library. That it exists to provide them with relevant and interesting material that they want to borrow and use. That they have a say in what is stocked and what happens there.

Ecclestone, 2001, 62

Learning and information resources are key to a school library. This is so obvious a statement that it is a truism. However the real issues and questions are, are they the right resources, are they in sufficient quantities to cope with the demands placed on a library and information service and do they extend, satisfy and interest users? As we can see from the above comments, the wrong resources imply that school library provision serves no useful purpose at all while the right resources indicate users value what is and can be provided for them.

This chapter aims to identify management issues associated with resources and having a sense of direction and focus for a school library collection.

Types of resources for a secondary school library

It is helpful to identify the range or types of resources that a school library can supply and be expected to offer in its collections. This basic information can be included in a policy for the school library (see Chapter 5) and, as we have seen, that aids the acquisition of development funding for the library. As information and knowledge are available from a variety of formats, and it is likely that the range of media will expand over time, it is effective to identify what in fact the library will collect and make available.

Advice to heads of department in a secondary school states that a librarian's co-heads of department colleagues should ensure that 'the library contains books relating to [a] department's curricular area' (Jones, Jenkin and Kirkham, 1996, 80). But now learning resources include, as well as books, a variety of media, and a modern school library offers to users:

- online and interactive resources – internet, fee-based subscription services on the web, intranet
- media resources, including CD-ROMs, video and audio recordings ('talking books')
- hard-copy print-based resources, comprising books, periodicals and newspapers, maps
- artefacts and realia or objects.

While books are still very much the dominant media in school libraries, a survey (Sheffield Hallam University, 2000, 45) found that a variety of non-book resources were stocked in school libraries and that the most popular type of resource was CD-ROM. See Table 9.1 for a full popularity listing.

Table 9.1 *The popularity of non-book resources*

Resource/media	% of school libraries stocking
CD-ROM	87%
Talking books/audio cassettes	62%
Commercial videos	54%

Computer software	53%
Educational videos	39%
Music recordings	25%

Source: adapted from Sheffield Hallam University (2000) *Survey of secondary school libraries main findings: a report prepared for The Library Association*, Sheffield: Survey and Statistical Research Centre, Sheffield Hallam University, 45.

Note: Statistical figures from the survey have been rounded down to the next whole number in this table.

There are practical implications for many of the types of resource media discussed above, particularly funding, storage and access (not least with regard to the internet). Again, clear identification of what a library will collect will aid budgeting, development planning, storage, accommodation and promotion, among other aspects of library management.

School library collection management

Traditionally, it is customary to look at resources for the school library in terms of selection, maintenance and editing. Guidelines (Tilke, 1998a, 40) indicate that all these aspects of school library collection management are regular or on-going job activities and that, as a key aspect of policy, 'good quality stock and its regular use depend on the relationship between the librarian and teaching staff' (ibid.).

Selecting appropriate materials

Much attention is rightly given to selection of materials for a school library collection. However, on analysis, it may be found that acquisition should be distinguished from selection. Selection of materials involves the following general strategies:

- Consulting with and encouraging recommendations from teaching col-

163

leagues. This will allow the collections to develop a practical, sharper focus and local relevance. It is also helpful to consult with students in this regard too.

- Researching curriculum needs. In addition to asking colleagues, it is also useful to analyse curriculum documentation, and obtain advice from a schools library service and other advisory services.
- Including significant and new needs in the library development and action plans.

Analysing stock selection criteria

It is worth a librarian reflecting on how s/he actually selects stock. Even though criteria, skills and knowledge are utilized, for an experienced librarian, it may appear that stock appears to be selected almost automatically. There is nothing wrong with this in itself. This, after all, may be how expertise looks. For a librarian, it is worth running stock selection in slow motion just so as to identify the actual elements involved. On analysis, it may be that aspects fall into the following categories:

- *Academic and intellectual*, involving an analysis of content of the item under review. The results are then applied to the needs of the collection and a conclusion reached as to whether the item supports, extends or complements what is already available.
- *Language and communication*, identifying how well ideas and concepts are explained through text and the use of language, especially in works of imaginative literature.
- *Aesthetic*, involving a consideration of the look and attractiveness of the resource. Even if users have specific research needs, they need to be motivated to select an item and the physical appeal of an item should not be disregarded.
- *Practical*, including a review of indexes, list of contents, bibliography, print size, layout and illustrative material and other helpful means of extracting information effectively. An analysis of the physical qualities of the item

will be useful, including the robustness of packaging or binding, as it should be possible for the item to be used repeatedly and still be in a reasonably good condition.

It will be helpful to be aware of the elements of the process if only so that a librarian can explain to users and others in a school community that there are professional skills, knowledge and expertise involved in stock selection. This again raises the credibility of a library manager's role and indicates that there is a focused library and information service that is dedicated to a school's needs.

Acquisition of stock

Acquisition is really only a procedure. It is concerned with the process of procurement or purchase of an item. Acquisition occurs *after* a decision has been made that an item should be selected for a school library collection. Unfortunately, lay people think that acquisition is the same as selection. On a practical level, a library and information service benefits from colleagues being involved in the selection process, but, on the whole, it is impractical and inefficient for colleagues to procure items for a school library. As identified in Chapter 7, it is more efficient if a library manager deals with specific suppliers to obtain the best terms and added services. This will not happen if colleagues make private purchases, 'donate' them to the library (a euphemism for locating them there) and then reclaim the cost of the items from the school, as the cost will usually be coded to the budget for the library.

Maintenance and editing of items in library collections

Less attention may be given to maintaining a collection. This could be because it is labour intensive and may be a first casualty when staff time is at a premium. There is also a financial cost implication as a review of an item may indicate that it needs to be repaired or re-bound in some way. Therefore, the management of collections may tend to concentrate on selection followed (hopefully after good use) by editing or weeding items and with-drawing items from the circulating or main sequence. Maintenance could involve judicious use of a library store or reserve collection where items may be stored away from the main collection for occasional use.

Nevertheless, giving attention to maintenance of a collection as an on-going job activity may avoid the need to give significant time to major retrospective editing of the stock at certain periods. It also enables the quality of a collection to remain high. If irregular or considerable review or editing restores a stock to a high level of quality, it follows that, for a period of time at least, a lower level of quality was experienced by users of a library collection. In the real world, that is inevitable to a degree, but it is important that in the meantime users' perceptions of the collection are not negative, as it will take time and effort to reverse or improve such impres-sions, however inaccurate they may in fact be. It may be more helpful, therefore, to maintain even quality in a collection as much as possible.

Major editing, weeding or even culling of a school library stock is inevitable in a number of situations, not least to make up for a significant time of neglect. Logically it should be done at one time, so that a difference can be perceived and the material removed should be replaced by new stock (inevitably, over time). Development of policy and awareness raising of a need to withdraw stock should precede any actual operation of weeding. The amount of editing necessary may be considerable and this can come as a shock to members of the school community. Many people think books, in par-ticular among library resources, are almost sacrosanct, and consider that a book must be of use to someone and should be kept. However, individu-als with such views are generally not likely to use such books themselves: rather they find it difficult to accept that no one else is interested in them, and that the library is a living school facility, not a national deposit collec-tion.

However logical the argument is, though, emotions can 'rule the day', and opposition may be vigorous and determined. This can de-rail library progress and even affect relationships while a particular librarian is in post. The sight of a skip or bin full of books can start a whispering campaign against the school's library and information service and its manager. It can appear a big issue for a school community, which, after all, is a small world. If a librarian senses that the time is not right for a large-scale operation, the process of editing should be staged, and detailed in a development plan for the library. Ideally, editing should be a joint process with subject colleagues, and books could be offered to departments (at the risk of departmental libraries becoming bigger, or even that pupils could use items that are considered significantly inaccurate or unhelpful). Support from senior management is essential, but even this may not stop ill-feeling. The overriding long-term plan for a school library is the important thing. A short, sharp change can be accomplished, but if not, then compromise is the best strategy.

Fortunately, there are many anecdotal accounts of success stories following major editing. Advice should be sought (e.g. from a schools library service) before contemplating such drastic action. Severe editing could be staged over time, with the use of a store as a temporary measure (in order for 'valuable but unused' items to show their worth – or not, as the case may be).

It is vital that the school librarian is a good manager as the responsibilities of the post are financial, operational and curricular. At Dixons CTC, the annual book spend, college wide, approaches 5% of non-staffing government funding; the library figure for resources approaches 2%. This considerable sum must be managed expertly to ensure alignment with institutional needs and value for money. Operationally, the school librarian must manage the access to and use of over 20,000 resources in the collection as well as the many functions that support the 7000 to 8000 students and staff who use the facility every week. Additionally, the school librarian is key to helping with the management of curricular [departmental] resources through knowing the requirements of different areas and ensuring cost-effective acquisition, access and issue systems are in place.

Finance Director, Dixons City Technology College, Bradford, UK

Issues connected with managing collection development

There are a number of issues and features related to collection development that a school librarian needs to manage. Some current concerns, with implications for a library collection, may also need to be addressed. A number of these are listed below in alphabetical order.

Able readers

Able readers may be characterized as having reading abilities and tastes significantly beyond that of their cohort or year group. If it is held (for instance, in a library policy) that a library collection need to stimulate and stretch an individual student's faculties and imagination, then there will be implications for a library's collection. It may only be a matter of degree as a span of ability ranges for materials should be remembered in general when building up a collection. However, there may be cost, location and spatial implications in catering for such needs. It may be considered that borrowing and exchanging from schools library service stock may be more effective than purely purchasing material, in order to provide variety.

Archives

This issue was raised in the previous chapter as far as accommodation is concerned. In terms of collection development, it will be helpful to clarify the role of librarian vis-à-vis responsibility for school archives, especially regarding electronic archives. The aim and objective of an archive collection needs to be clear – for instance, whether an archive is concerned with the school only and is for student/curricular use – in order to avoid unnecessary and inappropriate materials being donated or lodged in the library. There may be other implications, as a school library could have built up or been donated a collection that is really more about the local area than the school per se. In order to maintain such a collection, there will be issues of physical maintenance as well as acquiring new material to develop the collection. Such a situation may also arise with a rare and valuable book collection.

Boys, reading and literacy development

The professional literature (for librarians) and the educational literature indicate a concern for boys' reading abilities and motivation. If this situation is a particular concern in an individual school, awareness of specific school policy and action plans is necessary. A librarian will then be able to effectively liaise with a number of departments and specialists (e.g. English department, special needs, counsellor support) and be able to indicate whether developmental work is needed in terms of providing relevant resources in the library to support specific needs. A new section could be compiled, culling items from elsewhere in a library's collection or indeed elsewhere in the school. This embryonic section could be supplemented by new additions to stock and borrowed resources from an SLS.

Co-operative collection schemes

A school library may be a member of a local interlibrary loan scheme, however informal. This may be limited, for instance, to a particular subject area or medium (e.g. periodicals). However, it may be formalized with a union catalogue or similar device. As Kachel (1997, 79) suggests, 'resource sharing, or interlibrary loan, is undoubtably the most widely instituted cooperative collection technique. Resource sharing involves sharing of existing resources, while many other collaborative collection activities will focus on the provision and purchase of future resources.'

So, there may be implications for future stock selection as well as administrative issues. A concern may be that a resource may be on loan to another school when required by the school that lent the item and that such schemes merely duplicate much less effectively the work of schools library services (which may themselves access public library regional interlibrary loan schemes).

Another aspect that may be of interest to a librarian is to purchase from a document supply service, perhaps from a national library service; this is especially valuable where the service's collection has digitized parts of its collection. The British Library scheme is a good example and periodical articles or other material may be supplied (at a cost) for specific and specialized research needs.

Departmental libraries

In theory, the idea that a school library should be *the* central access point for learning resources in a school is admirable but one that may be difficult to fully achieve in a physical sense. In most cases, it is impractical for school libraries to hold multiple copies of school texts, even though it may be desirable to loan them to students using a computerized library management system. (It may be more the case that university libraries hold multiple copies of essential texts for specific courses, hence the expectation that a school library will act likewise.) It is inevitable, therefore, that departmental libraries or stock cupboards will be built up. Multiple-copy departmental stock may be supplemented by a small number of copies or even single copies of supplementary or more advanced texts and therefore over time comprehensive departmental libraries are built up. Enthusiasm by an individual teacher or head of department, plus the distance of a teaching area from a school library, may also be contributing factors to this phenomenon. The real issue is that students may rely and be encouraged to rely wholly on these smaller and more limited collections to the detriment of learning and study skills (and, at the risk of making life in higher education more difficult for them). Their use of a school library is marginalized. This is a serious concern when this happens where students may be timetabled for private study or 'study hall' (sometimes called a 'free lesson'), but still not use a school library – particularly when a school has invested in school library resources for the benefit of students.

A librarian's strategy could be to encourage departmental heads to identify what is useful to keep in their department's collection and to transfer other materials (that are still relevant and useful to students) to the centralized library. It would be effective to record such decisions both in library and departmental policy (and/or manuals). An alternative could be to catalogue departmental resources in a computerized catalogue of all the school's resources and to have a terminal allowing access to this database available in the relevant department.

Donations

It is quite common for donations to be offered to a school library. While the principle is acceptable in itself, the size, regularity, quality and relevance of donations may be causes for concern. It should not matter who the donor is – teacher, department, parent, governor or trustee, influential person or organization in the local area – but in practice it does. Therefore, a school library manager will need to use tact and discretion in handling the issue. However, the library should not become the repository of materials that are not wanted by the original owners and are of no use to the users of the facility. A policy or guidance note could be drafted and agreed in school on this issue. It would be useful to have this information available at several places in the school (not least the reception and administration area and on the school website). Furthermore, it is important that senior managers are aware of the aim of the policy on donations for it is likely that it is they who will, in the first instance, be approached by prospective donors. An example of a policy for donations is included in Appendix D.

Duplication of stock

It is a tradition that a library usually holds only a single copy of a particular resource in a collection, principally in order to maximize variety and depth in available resources. Therefore, duplication of stock items may be seen in a negative way. However, it may be helpful in some circumstances, for instance in areas of the collection that experience heavy, concentrated use by students. In addition, duplication may be necessary because of split-site (centralized) libraries and collections held in subject departments. Nevertheless, over time, unhelpful duplication may arise (e.g. because of donations). Regular maintenance of the collections will identify and correct such situations.

Fiction and recreational reading

Where a library policy has indicated that a core function is to support users' recreational reading needs, collection development needs to support that policy with an appropriate selection of stock. This needs to be kept up to date so that it attracts readers, and extends their reading interests, for example by providing a wide selection from a number of genres. Schools library services loan collections (plus any current stock selection or reviewing service that may be available), review journals and library suppliers showroom stock (and published lists) can all help a school librarian to keep stock current.

Legal issues

Copyright, copying of non-book materials, photocopying, digital copying and legal access to internet sites will be some of the legal issues that a school librarian needs to manage. In addition, there are likely to be licence agreements for electronic products used in a school library. A school librarian will need to be aware of (and perhaps have responsibility for) licences for copying within an educational institution in general (Norman, 1999). This especially is a very real responsibility when a photocopying service is available in a school library.

Library web page

A school library web page can be a useful resource in its own right. Any in-house guides or lists and other information to promote library resources can be most valuable if available on a website, especially if it is kept up to date. A library web page could also host a computerized catalogue of library or school resources and be an access point to web-based magazines or other databases to which a library has a subscription.

Magazines and newspapers

Most secondary school libraries stock daily and weekly newspapers and magazines or periodicals. Current copies in hard copy are generally held in a school library for reading, while back issues (and some current issues) may be borrowed. However, the use and relevance of long files of previous issues of magazines and newspapers may need to be addressed by a school librarian. Recent past issues may be well used, e.g. for language translation and media studies purposes. However, with availability of previous issues on the internet, a librarian may wish to consider just how long it is helpful to keep back files. There may be issues of space. Additionally, decisions about the length of files may depend on individual periodical titles, e.g. a more academic title (perhaps with a printed cumulative index) may demand longer back files than a more ephemeral title.

In general it is useful to monitor continually the relevance of stocking titles as it is easy to just let a subscription 'ride' for another year. Monitoring and evaluation techniques (discussed in Chapter 11) could be used to identify the usefulness of newspapers and magazines to a school library.

New media represented in library collections

As an extension of the above point, new media may include back files of periodicals in CD-ROM format or available as a subscription on the internet. Another example might be graphic novels or manga (a Japanese term now increasingly used to refer to the medium) that may be stocked to cater for the reading needs of boys (as discussed above). Implications will not only be spatial and financial, but also how the collection can be developed so that a reasonable selection is available.

Professional collection

A library may house a collection of materials that support the professional development of the staff of a school. Resources may include books, videos and periodicals. There will be issues of cost, appropriate organization and storage, and finding ways of promoting use of these resources. The existence and development of such a collection in a library will be even more important with any significant training and education of new entrants to the teaching profession in school. Not least this is because a good impression of a relevant school library and information service should stay with colleagues through their careers and feed into their subsequent teaching practice.

Reference materials

Reference materials tend to be expensive to purchase, especially where related to a specific subject area, because they tend to have a more limited print run and thus the unit cost is higher. There may be a choice of format for a particular resource; also, a specific resource item may change its format because of the limited market it serves or because, in a new format, it becomes more efficient to produce. Examples of this are magazine and newspaper subscription services, together with general encyclopedias and subject-specific reference works, all available on the internet, but with a subscription charge. Monitoring use and identifying potential use of reference-type materials will be important management operations for a school librarian in order to gain the most benefit from expensive resources in a library collection. A physically large reference collection, possibly daunting in itself for users, may be increasingly more a thing of the past, replaced by electronic media.

Trends in resource production

Web-based products will be a dominant trend in the format of and access to specific resources. For other media, such as DVD, issues will be the amount of specific resources that are focused on the educational rather than the general or leisure market and – especially if material is available for loan – the availability of equipment at users' homes in order to view the item. Books are not sacrosanct either when it comes to production issues, whether thinking of production standards (with implications for durability of use), limited print-runs, titles with associated media (textbooks with CD-ROMs are common in some other countries) and the realistic future and potential of e-books. These issues demand not that the librarian can see the future clearly but can identify resource trends and plan accordingly for library collection development. This may involve making policy choices for long-term collection development.

Collection mapping and foundation collections

'The library collection is built with the school curriculum as a guide' (Markuson, 1999, 25). Collection development in many, if not most, secondary school libraries is focused on this aim. The broad sweep of this book is that a school library is a curricular resource and library collections need to accurately support the taught and wider curriculum of a school. Strategies to develop this were discussed earlier in Chapter 5, when policy and development planning were discussed. Collection planning was touched upon in Chapter 7 on finance where it was established that there are several options for a librarian in terms of identifying and reaching the optimum amount of resources for a school library collection.

In Australian secondary schools, it is felt that 'teaching and learning outcomes are enhanced when at least a base level collection of resources is available at the time they are required by students' (Australian School Library Association, 2001, 30). This is defined as a foundation collection. Recommendations to develop a foundation collection include the need to map the 'collection in specific areas to determine the match between available resource and curriculum need'. Furthermore, a collection development policy should be formulated in relation to an overall school development plan to guide 'the ongoing process of analysis, selection and evaluation, and budget planning'. But breadth should be incorporated into the process, as guidelines recommend that schools take account of 'students' personal interests and needs', not least those relating to 'social justice' (ibid., 26).

This fits in with the prevailing view of the role of school libraries, not least that identified in the UNESCO School Library Manifesto (*The school library in teaching and learning for all*, [2001]), reproduced in Chapter 5. However, the concept of collection mapping can be taken further, as Kachel (1997, 14) suggests that collection development based almost solely on the curriculum is the way forward for school libraries, particularly in a world where fiscal resources are limited. Kachel indicates that public libraries should support the recreational and personal needs of students. Following this approach could provide an even clearer focus and image for a school library and may be within the framework envisaged by the *Investing in children* report (Department of National Heritage, 1995). This report recommended that relevant library services for children and young people in the UK, each with a slightly different focus, comprised school and public libraries, together with a local schools library service. In order to provide a relevant and successful service to user groups, the three services would need to co-operate and liaise closely.

However, local conditions may dictate how far one could take this situation as it will depend on the catchment area for a school and what public library services are available in a local area. Also, thought should be given to how much the approach of strict or close curriculum/collection mapping would change a school library. For instance, would it lose something of its pastoral as well as recreational role? This possible tension of role could be described as 'formula versus tingle factor'. The children's author and active supporter of library services for children, Gillian Cross, refers to the need for school libraries to be wider in appeal:

> But we need to think beyond formal education. Children need access to libraries that are not simply tailored to suit the curriculum. Obviously, the curriculum must be supported, but libraries must be wider and richer than that. And students need to know how to use that richness.   Cross, 1996, 15

So, it should be possible to try to work out a role for sensible and sensitive stock development that is not all formulaic, but also provides for stimulus, excitement and personal discovery for students' reading. In a school library, it is possible not only to understand a curriculum but also to know the users. That knowledge can provide information to aid judicious stock selection to enrich students' experiences. Therefore selection policies can be tailored to a curriculum but also to fit in with students' personal needs.

Policy and development planning

In order to sensibly develop the collections of a school library, it is important to codify and prepare a written stock policy. Such detailed or subsidiary policy (as presented in Chapter 5) can help users understand aspects of library procedure. It also helps to show that a library manager is exercising intellectual rigour in what could be regarded as the under-appreciated role of the school librarian. In particular, with regard to collection management it is important to set out the:

- stock selection, maintenance and editing criteria
- procedure for dealing with complaints/challenged materials (see Appendix I)
- internet access/acceptable use policy
- donations policy.

Policy documentation should be capable of considerable usage, in order to justify the amount of time and energy expended on the process. Using such detailed policy in staff manuals (both electronically and in hard copy) can provide helpful information, even if it is consulted by only a small number of members of the school community.

Conclusion

The wide and varied range of resources that are available, as identified in this chapter, make resource management a challenging job activity for a school librarian. It needs to be approached systematically and must be related to a school's curriculum. Relying, therefore, on good knowledge of the curriculum, learning styles and other individual needs of students, a librarian must manage a considerable asset base for a school and give it a sense of direction. The direction they take is informed and supported by a library's policy so that a collection development plan focuses on identifiable benefits to users and has a clear financial cost base.

10
SERVICE DELIVERY OPTIONS

[School] libraries ought to have a quirky, random quality that makes them worth exploring.   Cross, 1996, 15

Earlier, in Chapter 2, we established that a library facility in a secondary or high school becomes an active library and information *service* in large part through the efforts and expertise of its manager. The services should progress and develop and a good manager will look critically at what is offered to see if they are still relevant. If not, services should be discontinued. If they are still relevant and helpful, it is still possible that they can be improved or streamlined in some way. It is also useful to identify new services or ways of providing the library and information service in a school. Finally, such services need to be promoted to users and potential users.

This chapter will highlight some newer and more innovative ways of providing aspects of a library and information service in a secondary or high school, together with the need to promote the overall service to user groups. It focuses on resources, services and the user, through a consideration of:

- new library collections
- offering a library and information service free from physical restrictions
- reader development
- marketing, promotion and public relations.

New library collections

Library collection development is usually more of an evolutionary development than radical change. It is generally possible to make sweeping or dramatic changes to the library collections only on an irregular basis. But small – perhaps incremental – changes do occur more often and may come about because of new curricular needs, such as new courses or syllabuses. In addition, there may be new specific student needs, for instance those associated with literacy and special needs.

Resources themselves may prompt a new collection or service, such as a newly developed media, e.g. DVD. It may happen that a commercially available media is not represented in a library collection and a decision is made to provide a collection in a new medium, for instance music recordings.

Case study: establishing a music recording collection in the school library

It is thought that musical recordings are not provided as a matter of course in secondary school libraries, though a survey (Sheffield Hallam University, 2000, 45) found that 25% of schools surveyed did provide such resources. If a librarian is considering establishing a collection of music recordings, it is first essential to consider the aims and function of such a section, as it may be used to:

- open and expand listening experiences
- be purely recreational, so supporting the wider curriculum of the school
- support the formal music curriculum (as listening is a major component of a number of courses).

These options could be assessed with regard to the school library policy and informed by liaison with colleagues and students. Then the development is included in the library development plan and the annual budget outline.

Some particular aspects to be considered include:

- Liaison with interested colleagues and students in the school to inculcate a sense of ownership in the project.
- Collection development, involving arriving at solutions to issues such as accommodation and administration and selection of resources.
- Start-up project costs, identifying cost of recordings, appropriate furniture for storage, 'servicing' of recordings and an awareness of VAT or any other purchase tax implications.
- Choice of an appropriate format, reflecting on the variety of types of recorded music and taking into account relevant technology, with especial regard to the machines needed by users to play the selected format. It is helpful to also consider the aim of a collection in this regard. If, for instance, the aim is to provide resources so that *listening* skills are enhanced, then recordings on compact disc may be preferable to DVD, as the video element of the latter means that students will be watching and perhaps not fully concentrating on listening.
- Identifying appropriate specialist suppliers and noting appropriate producers of recordings.
- Strategies for ensuring that legal requirements are complied with, e.g. on lending materials in a certain format, also to deter illegal copying from the particular format.
- Evaluation of the project at given periods of time, involving feedback from users and non-users, criteria having been identified in the planning stages.

Through the case study above, it is possible to identify some common strategies when aiming to introduce new collections in a school library and information service:

- Identify clear aims and objectives for a project that dovetail into or enhance school library policy.

- Liaise and collaborate with colleagues to drive a project forward.
- Clearly identify the project in a school library's development and action plans.
- Think through management implications, for instance, finance and accommodation.
- Identify evaluation criteria and strategies at the outset of a project.

A new media collection can be very visible in a library, so it is especially important that the factors identified above are adhered to and good promotion and marketing will be required in order to establish the collection.

Offering a library and information service free from physical restrictions

Technological developments offer a new way of working for a school's library and information service. As a result, it is possible to imagine ways of using services provided by the library from without the library facility itself. Possibilities include:

- *Subscription services on the internet.* The library department may subscribe to internet databases that are only available through subscription payment. Access to the databases could be made through a password, made available on the school's computer network, or by hosting the access point on the library's webpage. Provided network and other agreements with suppliers are in place, a library could make available general encyclopedias, specific reference works and magazine databases, so that students and staff could use them in classrooms or possibly at home, in addition to accessing them on a library computer network.
- *Library web page.* In addition to the above, a library webpage could contain essential information about the facility, such as policy, rules and regulations. Information on citing references, for example, and compiling a bibliography, and other aids to library services could be included on the web page.

- *Web-based library catalogue.* The traditional skills of cataloguing and key-wording can be given new life and greater importance if it is possible to make a library's automated catalogue available on the web. Provided users are familiar with accessing a catalogue by a number of options (author, title, keyword or subject) – so good user education is important – this could be a valuable way of enhancing use of library resources (especially if websites are also catalogued). Although library web pages are only offered by about 12% of school libraries (Sheffield Hallam University, 2001, 33), the use of a well-constructed web page is a useful tool in extending library and information services in a secondary school.

- *Intranet and e-mail.* A librarian can use a school intranet system to make available electronically curriculum-specific data and other specifically created materials. E-mail facilities can be used to good effect to communicate information about library services and resources to all staff, selected groups and individuals. A selective dissemination of information service, for instance, can be readily used to make staff aware of contents of journals:

Selective dissemination of information (SDI): analysis of contents of a professional journal, e-mailed to a school's staff

Background: As the school is international and new students are accepted from all the continents of the world, staff's interests and needs include knowledge of what is happening in other countries. Also, it will be of interest for colleagues to be aware of developments in their own countries. The curriculum of the school includes following courses to attain International GCSE in various subjects and the International Baccalaureate so any references to these courses are of interest. Finally, the school runs aid projects in Nepal and Cambodia, so information on these countries (plus comparative information on aid projects elsewhere) are of interest. Basically, the librarian reviews the contents of a general educational magazine and extracts relevant information for the benefit of colleagues, based on a knowledge of the curriculum and important issues for the school. Below is a weekly e-mail to provide an example:

From: Librarian

To: School Staff

Sent: Friday, March 08, 2002 2:55 PM

Subject: Times Educational Supplement for 1 March 2002: SDI

TES for 1 March 2002. Articles of interest may include:

Main magazine

page 5 Lifestyle managers for teachers as an extra perk/recruitment incentive

page 13 School for talented children – Johns Hopkins University summer school

page 19 UN report on education in Central and South America

page 19 Violence in Nepal disrupts examinations in schools

page 20 Teachers in Germany told to learn English as part of a drive to increase foreign language education

page 20 Developments in primary education in France

page 20 Banned books in United Arab Emirates include A Town Like Alice, Harry Potter 1 and Animal Farm

page 22 Parental view of language and languages for young children in international schools, etc.

Friday magazine

page 13 Coping with disruptive pupils

page 15 Schools in Zimbabwe

page 16 The big picture: sleeping polar bears

page 22 Student review of GCSE revision guides

page 29 What does it feel like? – giving in-service sessions to colleagues

Children helping Children supplement: UNICEF Afghanistan Appeal

This issue of the TES is available in the reference section of the library.

Technological developments may not be the only way of taking the library service outside of the physical library space. Other options include:

- Deposit collections of library materials for use in classrooms, either on semi-permanent loan or to support specific topics. While librarians would normally prefer students to use a wider range of resources in the library, there may be occasions and situations when a small collection of resources, located in a classroom, can be used to good effect. In such a situation, a teacher could collect relevant materials prior to starting work on a topic or the librarian could offer compilation of such a collection as a service.

- Displays about library resources are perhaps more valuable if they are mounted outside the library facility itself. Displays can obviously promote what a library has to offer, but also can be resources in themselves. For instance, working with staff responsible for health education, information displays (produced as a result of research from library resources) about specific aspects of health can not only inform but associate acquisition of useful information with a school library and information service. So, again, collaboration with other staff (and students) is key. Special (glass-fronted) display units could be used, together with wall-mounted or free-standing notice boards, to provide flexibility in location of such displays.

- Knowledge management (KM). KM is traditionally associated with the 'special' sector (workplace or commercial and industrial libraries) and also with technology. 'While knowledge management may not be seen in its classic form in schools, terminology and concepts can bear translocation – reference to knowledge bases, organisation, "mover and shakers", technology (not least intranet) will not draw blank looks from librarians in schools' (Tilke, 2000, 698). Knowledge gleaned about how learning and the curriculum work in schools, who makes things happen, information needs of staff and communication and management processes in schools will enable a librarian to play a useful role in ensuring that staff can effectively use knowledge that is located within the school community.

Reader development

The concept or at least the phrase 'reader development' is one that has developed over the last few years in a number of countries. It is seen as a contribution to social inclusion programmes and projects and therefore has been of growing interest in public sector organizations, such as public libraries.

'Reader development' initiatives have therefore blossomed in many areas, and include family reading groups, factory reading groups, themed events and promoting reading through technology. So too have partnerships developed, including those between public sector organizations and voluntary and private sector groups.

What constitutes reading?

In this context, it is not reading as a process or a skill per se that is meant, but rather using the skill or technique of reading in order to add a dimension to one's life. Reading is functional but it is more than that. It should be enjoyable and fulfilling in itself. Reading matter takes many forms, but the medium that may be most identified with pleasure is the book. And the form many people think of tends to be fiction.

This said, the children's author Gillian Cross considers that children also 'need non-fiction which is full of fervour and enthusiasm' (Cross, 1996, 19). Reading can therefore be motivated by a variety of reading matter, fiction and non-fiction, book and magazine, in hard copy and electronic format. At any rate a study of reading development in public libraries in the UK found that 'there is overwhelming evidence that through reading the reader's life has been transformed for the better. Reading forms and informs the developing self' (*Checking the books,* 2001).

Of course, schools teach reading. They support and encourage reading. Encouraging *readers* is perhaps the next logical step. As this can only be really developed on an individual basis, there is potential for a firm and individual role for a school library.

Identifying reader development

Is reader development new? One could argue that it is promotion and marketing dressed up in a new guise. However, it is important to identify what is being promoted or marketed. The idea is not to promote goods or services (such as a school or a library service) but a concept: reading. The supplier or service provider is not the principal concern. The concept of developing a reader is the most important thing and this can be accomplished in part through co-operation with other services, organizations and groups.

For a school or school library to prioritize reader development, it is worthwhile identifying the stake-holders in supporting reading and auditing relevant policies and development plans. Otherwise, conditions for a successful project will not be in place.

Within a school, a number of parts of an organization may be involved in reading: the English department, other language departments, specialists in literacy and special needs, parents and volunteers, book club organizers and the school library. It is important that a library's role in supporting reading is understood in a school. Overall a school library is and should be a firm partner in supporting and encouraging reading and readers – as Aidan Chambers, winner of The Library Association (now CILIP)'s Carnegie Medal in 2000 considered: 'librarians are as important as teachers in the reading life of young people' (Chambers, 2001, 21).

Reader development programmes can be extremely flexible, but partnerships seem to be a common factor. It is possible for a school librarian to link into initiatives and umbrella events, such as World Book Day and the shadowing project for the UK Carnegie and Kate Greenaway Awards. World Book Day may be characterized as being very flexible as a vehicle to support reader development. In contrast, the shadowing scheme of the Carnegie and Kate Greenaway Awards may be regarded as being very focused. Local partners may be public libraries, literacy groups and bookshops, among others.

World Book Day

World Book Day has been designated by UNESCO as a day for worldwide celebration of books and reading. The exact nature of the day may vary. World Book Day, as a concept, is adaptable to the needs of an individual school, as it is possible to 'latch' on to the concept and harness media interest to create a link in the minds of the community that a school library serves. In different parts of the world, the day itself is held at different times, in order to fit in with local calendars. Anything can be included and a school can contribute as much or as little as one wishes.

Perhaps the most important thing is to celebrate it *each* year. This builds up a momentum and identity of its own. It was found that this initiative is a popular one for schools and that 65% of school libraries surveyed by Sheffield Hallam University (2000, 33) took part.

Shadowing the Carnegie and Kate Greenaway Awards

The Carnegie Award is given annually for an outstanding work of children's literature, while the Kate Greenaway Award is given for outstanding illustration in children's books. Both awards are in the gift of the Chartered Institute of Library and Information Professionals (CILIP) of the UK. The judges are all children's, youth or school librarians. The awards have earned considerable prestige over a number of years, but considerable development of the concept has taken place in the last decade or so, through involvement of sponsors and an awareness of the importance of promoting these awards to and through the media.

One development has been the shadowing scheme, where children and young people form groups to discuss the titles on the short lists for the awards at the same time as the real judges – hence the term 'shadowing'. These shortlists are announced during April or May and the announcement of the award is made in July each year. This time period gives sufficient time for schools and libraries to organize groups of pupils to read the books, discuss and debate the merits of each and arrive at decisions. The results are forwarded to the organizers in London but the real merit of the shadowing scheme is the involvement of children as readers and judges in a national, indeed international, scheme. It allows children to develop reading tastes, form opinions, understand the writing process, recognize genres and understand many other concepts, including debating and democracy, through using a voting system. (See also Appendix G.)

It is possible to access a website for the shadowing scheme (**www.ckg.org.uk**) and interact with groups in other schools (and in other countries). Insofar as it is very focused, it also allows great scope for involvement. Many hundreds of shadowing groups participate each year. Most groups are in the UK, but a growing number take part from other countries, allowing pupils to communicate electronically:

A Hertfordshire school librarian describes a lunch time Book Circle meeting to shadow the Carnegie Award:

Twenty-seven students turned up to the first meeting together with a member of the English staff and the local children's librarian . . . the enthusiasm was definitely catching. The added bonus was reading and discussing the views of other students we only knew through e-mail . . . .There was added excitement when some of our comments were included on the LA's pages on the internet specifically aimed at Shadowing the Carnegie Medal.

From Glasgow, a librarian commented:

Was the shadowing successful? A resounding yes! It raised the profile of both the school library and reading in general. Books and the scheme were talked about and publicised so much around the school that other pupils were clamouring to join in and couldn't wait for these titles to be added to the junior fiction for borrowing. Will we do it again? Definitely.

Shadowing Carnegie, 1998, 19–21

These national initiatives and others (such as World Poetry Day, organized by the Poetry Society) often generate interest in the national and regional media, thus providing a high profile, and this can enthuse pupils to participate on a local basis. In addition, media coverage may also help to raise the profile of a school library with other colleagues, provided the activity is promoted to them. Practical benefits may also include the use of publicity materials (provided or facilitated centrally) and the fact that the events can provide a springboard for ideas that a school librarian can develop or customize.

Collaborative reading initiatives

A key feature of reader development is collaboration. As we found earlier, there are a number of individuals within the organization and areas of school life who are interested in reading. Within a local community, there will also be a range of services and groups that focus on and celebrate reading.

An example of an initiative where collaboration is internal to the organization is literature circles. The features of this vehicle for enhancing reading are choice, collaborative reading and management of the reading speed. Such initiatives have been found to work well with boys in particular. Students can choose from a selection of multiple-copy texts and then form small groups (made up of other students who are reading the same text). They then decide how much to read in preparation for the sessions and then discuss the material. Focused activities are also used in the groups. Literature circles work well in a library setting (especially if, as was discussed in Chapter 8, the atmosphere of the library is conducive and welcoming and where separate seminar rooms are provided). Collaboration between librarians and teachers is also a key aspect of literature circles (Dawson and Fitzgerald, 1999).

Linking in with agencies in a local community, a school librarian can use Well Worth Reading, formerly an English regional co-operative scheme, but now a national agency that is concerned with producing resources and training for teenage reading development (Hall, 2000, 29). It also seeks to develop partnerships to support this work and links have been made both with youth and prisons services, as well as public libraries and voluntary groups. A particular initiative is BOOX, an occasional magazine written for teenagers by their peers. The standard of production is high, with eye-catching graphics. Multiple copies of issues of the magazine may be purchased by a school and in particular by a school librarian, who can co-operate with other local school librarians in order to purchase and promote at the same time – perhaps with the support of a local schools library service. Once the high-quality materials have been purchased, they can be used for internal promotion at any convenient time. In addition, it may be possible for a school to be part of any local promotion involving BOOX that may be organized by a local public library service. This is true also for the annual British Summer Reading Challenge, organized by the Reading Agency, which is a library development agency whose aim is to promote the value of libraries for children and young people. Many public library services buy into this scheme each year, and good links with a local public library will be useful in order to promote a holiday activity for students in a particular school.

Marketing, promotion and public relations

Marketing

These related areas are traditionally linked together though they are subtly different. Marketing may be considered an over-arching term and is the 'management process responsible for identifying, anticipating and satisfying the requirements of customers' (Jewell, 2000, 195). 'Customers', for a school library and information service, are the school's community. This includes two major user groups – students and staff – as well as others, so marketing is a complex operation for a school librarian.

When marketing a school library and information service, it is important to be clear about what exactly is being marketed. A library manager will also need to be aware of the amount of time and energy that may be required to successfully market a library and information service. The first step should be market research.

Market research should be supported by use of a marketing audit and plan. This is best achieved by use of a SWOT analysis (Gray, 1991, 30) in which the strengths of a specific school library are identified, together with weaknesses, opportunities and threats:

Strengths	Weaknesses
Specific benefits to users	Aspects that are not well carried out or done better by others
Opportunities	Threats
Changes to increase demand or satisfaction	Trends or events to reduce demand and/or satisfaction

For a school library, therefore, the SWOT analysis could look like this:

Strengths	Weaknesses
Curriculum-related stock	Inadequate fiction section
Current awareness service	Lack of technology
Opportunities	Threats
New curriculum initiatives	Library used as a classroom
New members of staff	Demands of curricula on the timetable

It is helpful to be specific when identifying features in each column but important nevertheless to concentrate upon significant issues rather than small details, i.e. those issues that will make a difference should the librarian succeed in achieving any improvement to the given situation.

A few examples have been given to illustrate the use of the SWOT analysis. Issues will be different for each school and indeed should change over time. If they do not, the librarian should use this indicator to further investigate the effectiveness of the library, perhaps looking at a number of other management techniques and aids that are discussed in this book, particular in Chapter 11.

Once an analysis has been completed, it will be clear what should be marketed to users and, crucially, non-users.

The marketing mix is a well-known identifier of the elements in marketing. These are generally known as the 'four Ps': product, place, price and promotion (Gray, 1991, 31). For school libraries, the four Ps could be interpreted as:

- *product*: library and information services and resources; expertise of librarian
- *place*: a school library
- *price*: funding required to obtain the product
- *promotion*: ways of communicating to potential users identifiable benefits from using library services and resources.

Being aware, as a manager, of these basic tenets of marketing will be a helpful discipline for the librarian when applying the results from a SWOT analysis. As Hall recommends, 'consider what you are trying to achieve and the expected outcomes. It will be impossible to evaluate whether or not you have been successful if you do not' (2000, 5). The marketing plan may be over-arching and identify significant job activities and resource implications. In this case, distinct items from it should feed into the library development plan.

Promotion

Large-scale events organized by a school library and information service tend to be an exception rather than the rule as book weeks, author visits and the like require a great deal of planning, time, effort and funding. When organizing such activities, it will be important to liaise prior to events in order to ascertain:

- if an activity or event is wanted and valuable
- how it may be used to support aspects of the curriculum
- where it will take place most comfortably and effectively
- the best time for the event to take place
- who will attend – the target group.

However, momentum is important and to retain a profile for a school library among a school community it is likely that smaller-scale promotions will be more the norm. Examples of such activity include regular updates about additions to the library and current awareness services for members of staff. Because these activities will be regular, there will – over time – be considerable implications in terms of librarian or staff time, so it is helpful to consider whether regular activities have an impact. Specifically it will be useful to:

- Consider the format of information issued by a library. For instance, if a regular update of new stock is issued, identify whether it is best to provide it in printed format, send it as a document file attached to an e-mail or make it available on a library's web page. (An example of an information sheet for students is provided at Appendix E.)
- Think about varying the way of disseminating information and beware of slavishly using one, though it is helpful to identify the best method for users. If sending general, brief information to staff perhaps e-mail is best. For booklists that will involve skim reading and to which subsequent reference is likely to be made, perhaps a printed method is best. (An example is provided at Appendix B.)
- Develop a house style, e.g. with a bold-coloured paper and specific fonts, so that library documentation is clearly identified.
- Remember effective timing. If library staff have spent time on a document, the benefit needs to be maximized. Timing will help – for instance, if issuing a list of additions to the library, try to avoid it arriving in teachers' in-trays at the beginning of a term or when backlogs of communication and mail may fill trays, as any impact of the publicity material will inevitably be minimized.

But it is not enough to develop a relevant collection, the librarian must then promote what the library has to offer. Be as involved in school activities, in educational initiatives, on committees as possible. Bombard the staff and pupils with 'book bites' and 'web bytes' highlighting library resources. Offer to undertake staff in-service training, new pupil orientation sessions, library lessons in developing research skills. As much as possible, work with staff in creating opportunities for the development of pupils' information-handling skills. Remember teachers are busy, stressed-out people – show them how you can make the job of delivering the curriculum easier and they will be eternally grateful.

Anne-Marie Tarter, Librarian, Ripon Grammar School, Yorkshire, UK

Public relations

The term 'public relations' suggests a need to promote a school library to external organizations. A librarian should be aware of the appropriate policy of a school in terms of public relations as senior management may prefer that, rather than (potentially) all members of a staff dealing with outside organizations and individuals, there should be someone specifically directed to deal with external relations. For instance, if the aim is to obtain sponsorship, it will be more effective for a development officer to be involved; if it is in relation to a complaint, the head teacher may insist on dealing with these.

However, it is possible that a librarian will be involved in public relations in more passive but formal ways. For instance, a library web page could be viewed by a wide range of people in a local area or even further afield, so it is important that its content and arrangement are clear and unambiguous. Even though an external audience will not be the group for whom the web page has been prepared, the page is capable of being read by anyone who accesses the internet.

A more formal way of dealing with external organizations is through a press release. A press release is used to communicate specific information about particular developments and events. For a school library, information that a local community might be interested in tends to be related to book events and visits by authors. The aim of a press release is to provide sufficient information for newspapers to make a 'story', so a press release should contain:

- basic information about the event – time, date, place, audience
- background information about the guest and about the school

- readable or memorable quotes from the guest and the head teacher
- contact details for further information.

Press releases may be dealt with by a marketing officer for a school, but it will be helpful to draft the information for this person to put into a school's preferred or 'house' style. Press releases can be issued prior to or immediately after an event, so the document needs to be written in the appropriate tense and clearly written and presented. It is always helpful to liaise with someone on the management or administration of a school in order to check that the contents of a press release are accurate and helpful, especially where names and details of individuals are included. Indeed, with the need to be aware of personal security, care should be taken to protect young people and other individuals from undue and inappropriate attention from persons in the community. (A sample press release is included at Appendix G.)

Nomenclature: the school library as a name or descriptor

When marketing or promoting, it is important to be clear about the name of the service. It is akin to a brand name – people remember it and give it an identity.

What a school library is called can make an important difference to the perception of those to whom marketing is directed. There has been a trend to call a school library by other names. Examples include a learning resource centre, information service, media centre, cybercentre, independent learning centre, and so on. It would be helpful to consider just why it was felt necessary to change the original name or descriptor. Was the name changed because the term 'library' was seen as outmoded, with a bad or negative image?

But at least most people understand what a library is and it has a clear image, though this is not always the image a librarian would wish. Calling a library something else may cause confusion as individuals may not really understand what the new term means. This may have occurred, for instance, in a book about technology in schools where the authors said 'in the school library (or Independent Learning Centre, as it is known)' (Imison and Taylor, 2001, 57). As the book is concerned with technology per se, it may be that it was felt more helpful to present the information in such a way. However, one could argue that, given that the term 'school library' was still used, it would be better to stay with the original term and work on changing the reality and image of a facility.

It is important, however, to recognize that there may be occasions when the term 'school library' in a particular institution has such a negative connotation that there really is no option but to change its name.

The important point for a school library manager to remember is that much time and effort may be spent on considering a new name. To change a name on signs and notices is relatively easy but to change a name in the 'hearts and minds' of members of a school community will take a lot longer. Time and resources, and they are always scarce, spent on this could be used more productively.

Implications for the role of a school librarian

From this chapter we can identify several specific roles for a school librarian:

- project manager
- technological facilitator
- literature expert
- marketeer and promoter.

This possibly sounds a 'tall order' on paper but if a library manager deconstructs what s/he does each and every day, it is probable that the elements identified above can be clearly identified. It may not be appreciated within a school that a librarian is in fact a project manager and a marketeer, and these may well be 'hidden' roles to a certain extent. It is likely, however, that a school community will associate its librarian with a good level of technological aptitude and knowledge of literature. A librarian may become as much a resource as an access point and facilitator to information, knowledge and resources. How much a school librarian would like to develop such a role is a moot point. Students and other users of a school library need to be encouraged to use their information-handling skills, but equally direction and recommendation from a librarian is a valuable part of the role.

It may not be feasible to expect a librarian to 'perform' at will by remembering every website, book and other resource in a library, though a good working stock knowledge should be both expected and appreciated. Fortunately, a number of tools are available to help. Traditional aids such as review journals and other means of keeping up to date with resources may be used, and there are people, not least those in schools library services, available to help. Another useful resource is a computerized library management system. By utilizing keyword and subject aspects of a computerized catalogue in particular, access to available resources may be maximized. Knowledge of the curriculum is an important aid to effectively analysing materials for appropriate keywords and subject terms so that they reflect the needs of the school in question. Most likely this can be done when resources are catalogued but it is possible to add subject terms to resources retrospectively.

A school librarian may not feel that s/he is a natural marketeer and promoter. However, image may do much. For instance, a helpful, welcoming attitude and calm efficiency on the part of a librarian may 'speak volumes'. Appropriate use of written information, web page details and other means of communication can help present a librarian and a library and information service in a positive light. Again, while a school librarian may not wish to lead or speak to large groups of staff at in-service or professional development opportunities, s/he will be an effective networker with individuals in a school, on a more informal but regular manner. In short, 'remember the stereotype of library staff and counteract this by behaving in a businesslike way' (Pantry and Griffiths, 1998, 71).

Conclusion

Reader development in a school may indeed contribute to added value and be part of the mesh of the hidden or wider curriculum (as we identified in Chapter 4). A reader development initiative can provide a relatively small but very significant contribution to the overall rich variety of experiences that students are offered in a school. What is important to remember is that reading, once embedded, provides a reader with a lifetime's pleasure and interest, and that many people, groups and organizations will and should contribute to this process, an important aspect and example of lifelong learning. In order to be successful, a school librarian needs to work not only with but also through others, not least, of course, teachers. This might mean that a library's role may be partially hidden or not readily perceived.

Although reader development initiatives may not raise a library's profile because of the multi-agency approach, the other, newer ways of delivering the library and information service can certainly raise a school library's profile and image. But the real reason for innovation and change is to provide a more relevant and focused service to students, staff and other users. Marketing and promotion should always bear in the mind the requirements of and benefit to users.

Managerial skills of assessment, reflection, negotiation and advocacy may be needed in identifying library roles and benefits to members of a school community and to raise the profile of the library. A librarian will naturally focus these skills more on senior management or administration. Overall, the librarian's use of these skills and aptitudes enables users to perceive a positive image of a school library and associate it with using resources and services that are helpful and relevant to them.

11

MONITORING AND EVALUATION

'Only a novel.' . . . in short, only some work in which the greatest powers of the mind are displayed, in which the most thorough knowledge of human nature, the happiest delineation of its varieties, the liveliest effusions of wit and humour are conveyed to the world in the best chosen language.

Jane Austen, Northanger Abbey, ch. 5 [1818]

Jane Austen, through one of the characters in her novel, gives the reader an assessment of the value of reading novels and identifies the benefit to the reader from so doing. If only educational assessment and evaluation were so easily identified! Nevertheless, Austen's thorough writing style involved the use of a number of revisions to develop the text into elegant, economical language, so the attention given to achieve such high quality in the writing is perhaps a good metaphor for assessment and evaluation.

As the reader will appreciate, this chapter could have been placed at the beginning of the book as the book's contents are circular in nature. We started off by questioning the role(s) of a school library, just as we tried to identify what a school is and does. Throughout the book, references to evaluation and assessment have been made, so it can be seen that evaluation is a management tool. It can tell us useful and helpful things. It can validate the role of a school library and information service, identify its performance, guard against deleterious actions, promote the value of marketing and highlight curricula relevance in terms of library provision and services. What monitoring and evaluation should not be is threatening, whether one undertakes evaluation oneself or has evaluation and assessment thrust upon one by an external body. Unashamedly, this chapter will refer back to aspects discussed earlier in the book, as there are a number of connections to be made (though a discussion about the need for job evaluation for the post of the school librarian has been sufficiently well made).

But already there are grounds for unease and uncertainty. The words 'evaluation' and 'assessment' have been used possibly indiscriminately but there are other words that also could have been used, so it will be helpful to firstly identify relevant terms.

What is meant by monitoring and evaluation?

A number of words and phrases are invariably used, not always accurately, when people in the educational world talk about evaluation. Inaccurate use of terms obscures understanding of the process, aims and benefits of monitoring and evaluation. It may be therefore helpful to define and clarify a number of terms:

- *Assessment* is a 'fact-finding activity, describing conditions that exist at a particular time. No hypotheses are proposed or tested . . . and no recommendations for action are suggested' (Best, 1981, 23). In schools, assessment is usually concerned with pupils' performance and educational development.
- *Monitoring* 'is the process of checking what is happening and the extent to which things have gone according to plan' (ibid.). It is very much an on-going activity.
- *Evaluation*, however, 'involves the collection, analysis, discussion and reporting of evidence which allows judgements to be made about whether we are being successful or not' (Jenkin, Jones and Lord, 2000, 5).

These appear to be the main terms, but there are a number of other related terms, such as:

- measurement
- inspection
- accountability
- accreditation
- goals and purpose
- aims and objectives.

These terms are readily understood enough in themselves, but nevertheless remain aspects of the main terms: assessment, monitoring and evaluation.

Starting monitoring and evaluation

Monitoring and evaluation is really a continuous process. Evaluation of a school library should be identified in a development plan for a library and also in other relevant documentation, including a policy. Evaluation is not an 'add-on' to a project or activity. It needs to be thought about at the outset by asking some basic questions:

- Why does evaluation need to occur?
- What requires evaluation?
- How should library functions, resources and services be evaluated?
- Who will evaluate?
- When will evaluation take place?
- Where will evaluation take place?
- What will be done with evaluation findings?

Why does evaluation need to occur?

As a manager, the librarian will wish to demonstrate the effectiveness of a school library and information service. Indeed, whether for curricular relevance, for budgetary or other reasons, senior management and a governing body may well require a school librarian to produce evidence of the library's effectiveness.

Evaluation can provide evidence to arrive at an understanding of the value of a library and information service to a school. Most helpfully, evaluation can identify a library service's strengths and weaknesses and provide guidance on policy development, set priorities and enable appropriate action to be formulated.

What requires evaluation?

School documentation, such as the overall school development plan, should be able to suggest areas, as 'schools take the quality of teaching and learning as their key monitoring and evaluation focus' (Jenkin, Jones and Lord, 2000, 32). Resource management may also be identified on a global school scale. As far as library management is concerned, it is possible to be very precise and identify a practice or aspect of the library and information service. Examples may include the effectiveness of information skills, relevance of stock and services, or use of methods for promoting the library.

How should library functions, resources and services be evaluated?

This depends on what is to be achieved, what is to be evaluated and what you want to find out. To measure performance it is possible to use a mixture of methods, which divide into quantitative evaluation and qualitative evaluation.

Quantitative evaluation

This is a numerical method of identifying provision, activity or performance. In other words, statistics are collected. Today, through use of a computer library management system, it is easily possible to use a range of data to gauge activity levels or performance of a library's functions. Areas that lend themselves to this method of evaluation include:

- loans of materials from a library
- number of reservations of library items by users
- interlibrary loans received by a school library
- identification of user groups who have borrowed most or fewest materials over a given period of time
- areas of a library collection that are most or least borrowed from.

It is also possible to use other technology in a school library to provide numerical information, such as a photocopier and a library security system in order to, for instance, identify the number of photocopies made by students within a given time period or individuals who have been through a security gate or entrance into a library.

It is also possible to collect figures manually, such as the number of classes who have booked into the library in a given period. This could be identified from consulting a library timetable or booking diary.

In addition, statistical information on aspects of library provision may be purchased from commercial suppliers. For instance, some large library supply (books and other resources) firms, particularly in the USA, can provide a statistical breakdown of the collection of a library. By providing data from a library's computerized catalogue, a firm can analyse data and identify the overall age of a stock and numerical strengths by, for example, parts of the classification. Data can provide valuable evidence for library development and, in particular, collection development.

However, even with readily available figures, it is necessary to think in advance about what areas and issues need the help of data in order to identify performance trends. Then a library manager can identify what method of data collection is most appropriate, which may include statistical information.

Statistics can yield meaningful information. For instance, if a librarian wished to identify how much photocopying has been done by students within a given time period, it is possible to log the rolling total that is typically provided in a photocopier. By dividing the total by the number of students in the school, it is possible to arrive at an average for photocopying from library materials per student.

Again, with a security system gate, it is possible to log the running total of people who have passed through a turnstile or barrier into the library. Divide the total by the number of days in a given time period, and a librarian arrives at an average number of people who visited the library each day.

It will nevertheless be logical to question the validity of these figures and consider their relevance or importance. For instance, take the example identified above of photocopying. A crude figure could be arrived at. Its value could be increased if related to other figures from other time periods, to give a trend. A librarian can then work out if this is an acceptable figure (perhaps by comparing with figures from other schools, etc.) but only if the figures actually provide information to a given question, such as 'Is photocopying by students in this school excessive'? Such information could be used as part of an audit to identify the effectiveness of information skills, e.g. note taking, or to consider financial costs. But the question does need a reason behind it.

Or take the example of visitors to a library. Again, it is possible to use figures from different time periods to identify a trend. Here, though, the figures can only tell a library manager that a number of people came through a turnstile gate, but not identify a purpose for their visits. In other words, they could equally well have come through the gate to go to a toilet or throw something in a wastebin as to use library resources or study. This sort of statistic can only be used with care. Without reasons for visits, the statistics can tell a librarian or others little, unless used with a form of qualitative evaluation.

Qualitative evaluation

This form of evaluation relies mainly on the use of observation and interview, which may then be recorded to use as a basis for evaluation.

It is possible to use this form of evaluation on its own. However it is recommended that a librarian should 'use both quantitative and qualitative methods and both input and output measures to collect and analyze assessment data' (American Association of School Librarians, 1998a, 109). Also, Best (1981, 157) makes the point that neither is better than the other, but

in the past educational researchers have tended to use quantitative evaluation methods. To correct this over-reliance on numerical analysis, a blend
of the two could be used.

To take the example of identifying whether the amount of photocopying undertaken by students in the school library is appropriate, extenuating
circumstances, such as lack of appropriate resources, lack of note-taking skills,
etc., may be identified by interview techniques. Nevertheless, the person
undertaking the evaluation would benefit from looking at the results of quantitative evaluation to pinpoint areas for further investigation.

It is possible to use this method of evaluation on its own successfully, for
instance, observing use of particular newspapers in the library. Interviews
could establish a value for a particular resource that would not be brought
out in a statistical survey.

However, a disadvantage of this method is the amount of time needed
to undertake it effectively. As with other things, a library manager needs to
make a decision about the priority ranking to be accorded to such a management activity, compared with other tasks that could be undertaken in the
given time-frame.

Who will evaluate?

The library manager or colleagues can carry out evaluation; indeed it is
expected that 'subject leaders and heads of department will be monitoring
standards in their subject area' (Jenkin, Jones and Lord, 2000, 13). There
may be a particular value in inviting colleagues to participate in monitoring and evaluating. Observing students effectively use resources and services
in a school library can be more persuasive than any amount of advocacy on
the part of a librarian. There may also be occasions (for instance before an
external evaluation of a library) when it may be appropriate to invite an external contact, such as an SLS librarian to act in a similar manner to colleagues
in the school. It will be important, though, either to set objective criteria
in-house or to recommend the use of standards that are available in published guidelines.

When and where will evaluation take place?

Monitoring and assessment should be regular and continuous. It is a part of a cycle of decision making. If an evaluation of a library facility itself is required, it will clearly need to be accomplished in the facility itself. If, though, an evaluation is concentrating on benefit of using a library in a learning situation, monitoring could equally well be accomplished in a classroom.

What will be done with evaluation findings?

Evaluation informs management decisions that aid the direction for the future of a school library and information service. The American Association for School Librarians recommends that library managers and others should 'make decisions based on the results of data analysis to develop plans and policies for the continuous improvement of the library media program' (1998a, 109).

Evaluation aids both macro (change) and micro (evolution) development of a school library and information service. It is up to a library manager to briefly contextualize the findings, with relevant background information about the particular library, and to present evaluation findings as evidence. This will helpfully support a report (with recommendations) to senior management, as this is the most likely way to advocate large-scale change. For smaller or micro change, it is likely that the result will aid a librarian in directing and quickly fine-tuning aspects of existing school library provision.

Methodology

There are several methods that may be used to monitor and evaluate. These methods could be divided into two areas – those specifically identified by an individual school and those available, more generally, as a standard.

Individually set methods

This method is really concerned with systematic observation and analysis of activity in a library, together with interviews and conversations with users (Jenkin, Jones and Lord, 2000, 49). Once a librarian has identified indicators for evaluation, it is possible to glean data from users of the facility or pre-identified user groups. It is also possible to take data at random, but at certain or identified times, thus gaining a constant 'snap-shot' approach. Qualitative or individual responses and findings may be collated or grouped and information presented in statistical or tabular form, if that is helpful and easier to understand.

A survey or questionnaire may be used, though; Kachel (1997, 36) recommends that surveys 'dealing with a particular type of service or a particular section or format or resources yield the most specific results'. As a survey or questionnaire needs careful analysis, it is more helpful that specific results may be identified. (An example of a survey form produced by an individual school is reproduced in Appendix A). Care should be taken with designing a survey. The questions need to be relevant and focused, eliciting true information, either through optional ('tick-box') answers or free choice. Unless respondees understand the purpose of the questionnaire, there is a tendency to provide an answer that it is thought that the questioner might like. Nevertheless, a survey form can yield sophisticated responses that are capable of being analysed.

Standards

Externally identified standards can act as a target for a school library. A school librarian can measure a performance total or other finding for an individual school against standards and thus identify shortfall or otherwise. It is possible to use a range of guidelines and other standards relating to secondary school libraries. These may be national or regional in nature, general or specialist. Some guidelines are specifically concerned only with aspects of the overall service while others identify very specific aspects or activities. Guidelines may therefore be complementary in nature, rather than mutually exclusive.

In addition, a school library manager could use survey material, again either national, regional or local. It is also possible to generate specifically developed data from local schools or schools that are similar to a librarian's own, for greater accuracy and relevance. Having identified salient features and data, a librarian could either identify an average or other meaningful and relevant figure (which may not be the biggest or best) that provides a realistic goal. Benchmarking a standard that is realistically available can be useful to aid performance management and goal setting for a school library.

Helpful standards and guidelines

Performance measures and input criteria may be identified from guidelines relating to school libraries. These include the American Association of School Librarians (1998a), Australian School Library Association (2001), Tilke (1998a), *Taking a closer look at the SLRC* (2000), developed in Scotland, and specific guidelines published by the (UK) School Library Association. Schools library services may provide local documentation for their individual areas. In addition, surveys can provide full statistical information, especially Sheffield Hallam University (2000) as this also identifies trends (through comparing figures from a similar survey in 1997). The documents identified above agree on the broad areas for indicators:

- *use* – especially students, as regards information literacy competencies, access and opportunity
- *resources (including technology) and funding*
- *management* – policy and development planning; administration
- *services and programmes* – information skills; collaboration between teachers and librarians; inclusive programmes, e.g. varying learning styles and different levels of achievement
- *library staffing*.

For instance, evaluating use of a school library should highlight:

- Whether opening hours are relevant and helpful, so that the library is accessible to students when they can physically do so, i.e. through the

209

school day, and also before and after school, together with breaks and lunch-times. If the school is a residential one, then different access patterns may be relevant.

- Whether library staff show expertise linked to a helpful and knowledgeable manner when dealing with users' enquiries
- Whether use – effective use – is made by students of a library, and the attitude of students towards the facility and its services. This use could be identified in general or in particular, for instance, through use of particular areas, e.g reference and technology areas, and specific resources, e.g. periodicals and newspapers.
- The pattern or trend of use of a library facility by teaching colleagues.

It will be clear from the above that most if not all of these criteria require observation, reflection and analysis rather than use of quantifiable measures, and from several groups of people: library staff, teachers and students.

Examples of evaluation

Guidelines and other documentation can assist a school library manager to achieve a high level of self-analysis in evaluating library functions, resources and services. Self-analysis is therefore very helpful but it can be less objective and rigorous unless indicators and procedure are clearly thought out and identified at the beginning of an exercise. For instance, one web-based document (*Taking a closer look at the SLRC*, 2000), produced as a co-operative exercise by education and school library services in Scotland, provides areas and useful examples for self-analysis.

Example 1: Identifying adequacy of a school library accommodation and its facilities

Specific factors include 'How do you know? Does the library's accommodation and facilities provide a safe, pleasant and stimulating working environment?'

Indicators or features to look for may include the following:

- Is the library featured in a school's health and safety audit and regular inspections?
- Are particular aspects of the physical environment well maintained? For instance, flooring should be suitable for the purpose and safe. In addition, heating, light (both natural and artificial) and ventilation should be sufficient so that users may safely and effectively use the library facilities.
- Is physical access to the library easy for those who are mobile through use of a wheelchair?
- How flexible is the accommodation in terms of concurrently facilitating a range of uses and activities by different groups?
- Whether 'the environment is conducive to different cultural needs' (ibid., 19).

The indicators identified above will provide a librarian with areas for measurement and it will be helpful for a library manager to further identify specific measures, e.g. a local or relevant measurement that is the recommendation for width of door to allow wheelchair access. Some of the measures can be identified through debate with colleagues in a school, such as identifying what local and specific cultural needs may apply to a particular school.

However, this area of functional provision is relatively easy to identify or is one which is more familiar to a librarian. More curricular-based assessment and evaluation, however, may make librarians less confident.

Example 2: Monitoring curriculum use of library resources

This view from a head teacher and senior management team members (Jenkin, Jones and Lord, 2000, 97) is concerned with identifying effective study support for students. As a function of the school library is to support learning 'by servicing curriculum subject areas with materials or use of the facility in delivering their schemes of work', a key role of the library was to support pupils' independent learning and research skills for all curriculum areas. They recommended that the librarian needs to 'support the teaching in the school by having knowledge of when the library can provide relevant materials and equipment for use by teachers and pupils'. In order to monitor how well resources were used, they recommended that the librarian collected data by issuing a record form to each head of department.

Jenkin, Jones and Lord considered that, providing the library has been notified of the requirements of subject departments and could meet these requests for the use of resources, 'monitoring of schemes of work containing reference to the library will become self-evident. Monitoring the actual use of resources is also easily managed by referring to the returns of the pro-formas' (which are completed by students when using the library and can be used to monitor library use).

This example focuses on the use and relevance of library resources to the curriculum, so again is an area that librarians are relatively comfortable and familiar with. Going beyond resource provision in itself to identifying issues concerned with the quality of pupils' learning may well be more contentious. In other words, should school librarians undertake such activities? In Scotland, as elsewhere, the answer is yes, and an example of how to assess the quality of learning in a school library can be seen in:

Example 3: Performance indicator – quality of pupils' learning

This focuses on:

- the extent to which pupils are motivated by their learning experience in the library
- progress in learning, including skills development
- personal responsibility for learning, independent thinking and active involvement in learning
- interaction with others.

Taking a closer look at the SLRC, 2000, 12

Although this performance indicator is well explained through these bullet points, it is still hard to think what the evaluation might look like in reality, so the following provide a more detailed picture:

- A learning environment that encourages pupils to produce work of high quality . . . praise is used effectively to encourage pupils. Pupils are motivated to work well and enthusiastically without close supervision.
- Almost all pupils are making progress in their learning and in particular in the development and use of information/enquiry skills.
- Pupils take responsibility for, and are active in, their own learning. Pupils are frequently required to think for themselves and reflect on their needs, and how to achieve them, in the library.
- Pupils work collaboratively in the library in a variety of circumstances, involving groups of different composition and size.   (ibid.)

Indeed, it is possible to think of many illustrations to aid assessment and to grade them in levels (for more effective analysis), which is what the support pack produced in Scotland has in fact done.

A school librarian can perform the function of evaluation in his role as a service provider, through having responsibility for resource provision and facilities, and as an educator, through identifying the relevance of resources to educational need and in focusing on educational development in individual students themselves. As a theme throughout this book has been effective liaison and collaboration between librarian and subject staff, it can be accepted that assessment by both parties, especially as far as student assessment is concerned, can only be a valuable development and helpfully binds the two roles together even more.

One school librarian's assessment criteria to identify how well the library is working:

- use of the library written into departmental schemes of work
- regular use of the library for research by all year groups, and in all subjects

- regular use of the library for study and relaxation (in a considerate manner to other users) by a full cross section of the school community
- multipurpose use of the library environment by the school community, i.e. sixth form information evenings, parents evenings, etc.
- regular use of the library before and after school hours by the school community
- feedback from teaching staff as to the effectiveness of the library on academic performance
- change of perception (concerning the library) of the school community from 'non-relevance' to 'importance' in their school life
- use of the library environment by teaching staff to deliver occasional lessons
- delivery of information and research skills (generic) to all year groups by the librarian
- tailored information and research skills lessons, delivered by the librarian, to meet the needs of specific research topics
- use of library resources by teaching staff, enabling them to recommend resources to students.

Lynn Winkworth, Librarian, Headington School, Oxford

External assessment and evaluation

Whether assessment and evaluation is external to an organization or internal should – in theory – make very little difference. However, external evaluation in terms of a school inspection has, in the past, caused confusion and concern. This is not to do with the value and methods of an inspection in general. It tends to occur because it has been felt that school libraries either tend to be left out of inspections to a large degree or inspected from a standpoint of little accurate knowledge or unclear criteria.

As with relating library provision to specific curricula in different places, the situation concerning inspections in general changes regularly and therefore this book will not go into any great detail about this. As librarians in home countries in the UK will be aware, inspection arrangements will be handled by different government agencies. For instance, in England, the organization is Ofsted (Office for Standards in Education). An agency with a similar function is separately established for Wales, and Northern Ireland has its own provision, as part of the system of government in the province. In Scotland, responsibility for inspection of schools lies with an education inspectorate. For independent or privately funded schools, there are also separate arrangements for inspection through a non-statutory body (e.g. HMC (Headmasters' and Headmistresses' Conference, for a number of schools). For international schools in the UK and elsewhere, there are accreditation arrangements with another private organization. It was certainly true in the past that inspection of libraries in schools was, at the very least, not consistent. However, there seems to be more harmony in inspection arrangements and procedures now. Overall, it is interesting to observe that, generally, the situation seems to be improving, resulting in more comprehensive or objective coverage of library provision, relating to the development of a school in general. Nevertheless, a survey (Sheffield Hallam University, 2000, 11) found that the proportion of school libraries that were inspected by an external body as part of a school-wide inspection remained (over a three-year period) at about 75%.

In fact, librarians' management skills will stand them in good stead in *preparing* for an external inspection, as library involvement can be identified through:

- communication
- liaison and collaboration
- management data
- time management
- the library being part of and working well within the organization.

School communication channels will be used to provide information about arrangements and preparation for an inspection. In addition, a librarian can usefully liaise and collaborate with colleagues in a school to help prepare. Data collected by a library and information service can and should be part of the information required by inspection agencies. A librarian's management of time will help to allow sufficient time to prepare for an inspection and also assess whether too much time has in fact been spent on the preparation (of a library) for inspection. Overall, being part of and functioning well in an organization will help a librarian to be involved in preparation for an inspection. Of course, preparation may make it apparent that a library and information service is working effectively in a school – hopefully an inspection will be able to bring this out in any findings or report.

In short, the end result is making sure that a school library is involved in and is covered appropriately in an inspection of a school. This result is little different to any other main goal or aim for a school library and information service. It should be treated as such, with the rider that the aim of external inspection is to help a school by providing an unbiased and objective view of the school (as a whole and its constituent parts). This can be of great help to a school librarian.

Conclusion

It may have been felt in the past that it is difficult to measure a facility in a school that has been considered to be invisible (to a certain extent). After all, a school library is there to support all aspects of school life. It has been thought that it is difficult to identify just what the real benefits are as they are hidden and may be only be teased out over the long term, rather than being easily identifiable. However, as has been shown above, it is possible to identify elements for measurement and evaluation, both in terms of provision and educational outcome.

Benefits of evaluation to school management and a school library manager include the provision of accurate and helpful information to aid performance and direction for a library and information service in a secondary school. It also allows expectations to be identified, either those of a librarian, users or of the school's senior management. It is always useful to realize that agendas may be different in different parts of an organization and evaluation should further aid the development of priorities. Documentation about a school library is further developed through the use of evaluation techniques and procedures, thus supporting policy and development planning.

For a manager, and in a management-focused environment, evidence is always helpful, but it must be used or presented by a librarian to a school's senior management team. As Gray (1991, 161) noted with regard to school marketing officers, 'those holding such responsibilities and required to take such actions also need to be given sufficient authority to ensure that the actions will be taken and the improvements made'. The same applies to a secondary school librarian for evaluation is on-going and is part of the evolution of a school library.

It is at the very least helpful if a librarian is a head of department or of sufficient status in a school (for instance, with regard to responsibility for a library budget) in order to quickly and effectively introduce refinements and change based on findings of monitoring and evaluation exercises. For smaller examples of change, evaluation provides evidence and suggests action from a manager, which, as this book has argued, is a firm role of a secondary school librarian. For macro change, however, it is right and proper that a school library manager should be required to recommend necessary action to senior school managers and governors to ensure that a library and information service is and remains relevant to and effective in a secondary school.

12
THE FUTURE FOR THE SCHOOL LIBRARY

Information and communication technology (ICT) has four applications relevant to learning . . . [including that] it has transformed libraries from dog-eared collections of books to CD-ROMs and resource materials on the Internet . . . . By 2050 research will be an integral and essential part of school practice.

Brighouse, 2001, 64

It is tempting, when looking at the future of libraries (and school libraries in particular), to assume that the future is purely technological. However, as Prof. Tim Brighouse implies above, it is more a case of the 'messenger, not the message', as technology may be harnessed to the development of education, or rather, learning. The contrast painted by the words in the comment above may hopefully not be so great in reality. The concept of 'dog-eared collections of books', the words perhaps chosen as hyperbole, to make a point, might be lamented as a commonly perceived *image* of libraries, as was discussed in Chapter 10. Nevertheless, the contrast is well made and the really important words for the future of school libraries are learning and research.

Here is one more vision of the school of the future:

Big libraries, expanded into Resources areas; fed by large wide corridors, each with plenty of alcoves in which there will be many carrels – in fact one for every couple of pupils. And classrooms replaced by tutorial rooms . . . . But remember too that an increasing percentage of work will be done off site . . . and an increasing number of 'students' will not be below the age of 18.

Abbott, 1994, 98

These comments come from eminent people in the educational world. Brig-house, formerly a chief education officer for the largest urban local authority in England, has held a variety of different posts in the educational sphere. Abbott had the distinction of being the youngest person to be appointed a head teacher in England and now heads a policy think-tank called Educa-tion 2000, which is concerned with effective education and learning in the 21st century.

Their visions are thought-provoking, but in writing this concluding chapter, the author will not indulge in crystal ball gazing but rather try to tease out some implications and trends for the development of a second-ary or high school library for the present century. Major areas include:

- political and social policy
- technology
- education and learning.

Political and social policy and secondary school libraries

Even a cursory review of the literature of education, a reading of newspa-pers and reference to the media in general, will indicate that government policies, pressure groups and others all have opinions about educational pol-icy and direction. As one set of writers conclude, 'the possession of political power, and economic and social circumstances all help to shape policy and lead to change in the education system' (Bartlett, Burton and Peim, 2001, 240). Change, as Fullan (1991) has noted, has been a constant but unpre-dictable companion of education systems through recent decades in Britain, as well as other countries.

But what has this to do with a school library, surely a haven of peace and quiet in the middle of a school? As has become apparent in this book, a school library does not exist in isolation, but firmly relates to the rest of an organization. Implications for a school library from political and social policy include:

- *Change*. It is important to accept that change occurs as a result of new policy initiatives from central government. While policy change is designed to improve education provision, it is clear that the process of change brings with it stresses and strains in an organization. This may result in changes to existing development planning and a need to over-ride current priorities. As a manager, a school librarian will need to both accept and deal with any implications that may occur from changes to agreed development for the school's library.

- *Monitoring and evaluation of services*. There are expectations that high standards will be achieved in public services. Systems and procedures have been established to define and identify concepts of best value and good service. This trend for monitoring and evaluation can carry with it unease concerning just what is and can be evaluated. Library managers will wish to be aware of the criteria by which services are examined and clear about any allowance that may be made for differing local and resource baseline factors. However, external monitoring and evaluation are facts of life and any implications need to be managed by a school librarian.

- *Pressure on existing infrastructure*. In recent years in Britain (and elsewhere) there has been pressure on the fabric and structure of educational and library systems. A shift in responsibilities, power and budgets has been seen in local education authorities in England and Wales in particular, a shift that is away from the centre, towards individual schools. For school libraries, a particular aspect of this change can be seen through the provision of schools library services (SLS). SLS have been mentioned throughout this book, whenever relevant to the topic being discussed. It can be seen from the frequency of mention that the roles of SLS are many and varied. Concerns over recent years about their future have been great and indicate the esteem in which these services are held, for the valuable work that SLS have done to raise the standard of school libraries. SLS have generally changed, re-shaping services and work direction, to suit a different political climate. Support for secondary school libraries and their managers, in particular, is necessary, and SLS can still provide such back-up, though inevitably in a different way than in the past. A school librarian may now be a purchaser of services, not necessarily entitled to service provision. This change of emphasis if nothing else is one that needs to be managed by a school librarian.

- *Direct contribution to social and educational policy initiatives.* While it is relatively easy to show a firm role for a school library in supporting specific curriculum developments (and to a certain extent, to provide evidence or this), it is less easy to do so with more general policy changes in the educational area. However, in the areas of social inclusion, literacy development, homework initiatives and lifelong learning approaches, it is possible to advocate a role for school libraries. Some school libraries have been able to do more than that and actually show an involvement in such large-scale developments, not least through being a firm and central part of a school infrastructure. For instance, as regards policy to achieve greater social inclusion, school provision may be monitored so that schools in general do not educate an elite, but rather all who need education in a community. An index for inclusion has been developed. Among other aspects, it asks, as an indicator of whether lessons are responsive to student diversity, 'Is there a variety of activities, including . . . use of library, audio/visual materials, practical tasks and information technology?' (Centre for Studies on Inclusive Education, 2000).

Although seemingly of less direct relevance than specific curricular and technological initiatives, the broader picture of educational and social change can and does affect schools, and, by implication at least, school libraries.

Technology

Where can one start in a discussion of the future of school libraries and technology? The options are many and varied. But are they the same as for other kinds of libraries or are there distinct issues for a secondary school library?

Digitization of library collections

One school librarian in Hertfordshire has identified this as a trend.

> At De Montfort University, the concept of the digital library has taken shape . . . as the university is divided over several campuses, it was decided to digitise the most used parts of their collections to make the resources more accessible to the students. [The] project was carried out in collaboration with Cambridge University Press . . . digitised resources are going to become more widespread.
>
> (Dent, 1998, 17)

The implication for school libraries is that access to other library collections should become more comprehensive, opening up a range of 'new' resources. This may be done on an individual institution basis or an area or regional basis, such as the information technology service development in Croydon, England. Digitization may also appear at national level, with an over-arching project, such as the National Grid for Learning, whereby central government funding has followed a policy decision to develop the technology infrastructure in support of educational needs.

Especially where codified (national) curricula exist, perhaps school librarians, as a group, may recommend that specific heavily used resources be digitized and become available on a nationally provided service. It is unlikely that a school librarian could comprehensively digitize the collection of an individual school library (unless e-books significantly develop in the short term), not least because of copyright implications.

The internet

Issues for school libraries include access to a vastly increasing internet. Most schools are aware of issues concerning appropriate use of the internet by pupils, and have developed policy and procedure to deal with these issues (see Chapter 5). Another aspect is the cost of a hitherto mainly free service. The concept of information on the web being free seems to be less true now. Allied to this is the issue of the quality of resources available in the free web. This highlights the skill and expertise of a librarian in identifying and evaluating potentially useful resources. Of course, this is only possible with a good knowledge of the curriculum, in order to match needs to resources. Recommended sites' details could be incorporated into catalogues of library resources that are computerized (presuming that access to the web from the individual school network is immediate and uninterrupted).

Intranet

Another alternative is that information could be wholly or mainly available in schools on an intranet. Herring (2000) defines an intranet as a facility whereby 'school information resources of different kinds are available via one source i.e. the school intranet's home page and include the school library catalogue, networked CD-ROMs, email and the World Wide Web, curriculum related downloaded websites, instructional websites and school administrative information'. Again, there are management issues, including those of content – updating, maintaining, editing, and so on.

Computerized library management system

Given the time and effort a school librarian will need to put into developing a computerized management system, not least a catalogue of library resources, it makes sense to maximize the benefit from all this work. This can be done through development of a web-based catalogue. A school library's resources could be accessed, not only from a local network in a school library, or even through a school's network, but from a school library's web page. This makes possible access to a library's computerized catalogue from any outlying parts of a school (which may not be included in a local network) as well as by members of a school community from their home.

Access to electronic products

A library web page could also enable users to access databases that are subscribed to by a school library and information service. The entry point to a fee-based product could be through an icon or short description of the product with a hyperlink to enable a library user to directly access the database.

E-books may be another application of this possibility. Currently in its infancy as far as a range of useful titles and ways of using the technology in schools is concerned, it may be the way forward for specific needs. A text of a book may be available electronically as an additional option to (or instead of) a physical or traditionally printed object. For non-fiction needs, e-books will provide another way to access information, but a school library, together with other specialists in a school, may want to consider whether e-novels or e-fiction will make a valuable contribution to sustained literacy levels in themselves. E-journals, where issues of journals are available solely by electronic means (or as an option to a printed version) are more developed and are available as individual title subscriptions and through use of a newspaper and magazine database service. Further information on developing such products is available in Lee (2002).

Management issues

Some management issues have been identified in discussing the individual features above. Issues common to the above include:

- *Time*. Unsurprisingly, time will be needed by a school librarian to develop, explore and become familiar with a range of technology-based resources in order to effectively support the curriculum, to aid literacy and avoid over-reliance on a single form of technology that could become obsolete in the present century. It will probably be on-going use of time too, i.e. for development and maintenance, for already we have seen schools librarians working with second- (and even third-) generation library management systems.
- *Finance*. As well as direct one-off purchasing, there will be a need to be

aware of potentially significant costs incurred by use of subscription or pay-as-you-use services. Control of expenditure and mechanisms for achieving it will need to be worked out in advance by a school librarian and others.

Technology is not surprisingly seen as having huge potential for secondary or high school libraries. Many school librarians and others welcome this but also have reservations, whether they relate to training, hardware, technical back-up, funding, appropriate use and future of specific technologies. The fear is that a school library will be ignored in terms of technological development and be unused as users prefer to gather all their information from electronic or online means. However, there is another scenario, a more positive one for school librarians – as identified by both Brighouse and Abbott, above, as well as by Herring (2000), whereby a school library enables students to use technology in a very practical manner, for real research. It is Herring who identifies a role for a librarian in the school library of the future as a researcher, user and teacher of electronic resources for all users of a school library, perhaps by managing a virtual library. Indeed, with telelearning in its widest sense, a school library becomes a virtual library: 'library systems have to adopt new electronic storage systems. As they do, location ceases to be a serious issue' (Tiffin and Rajasingham, 1995, 77). Such a development will enable librarians to transcend limits to school library development that are caused purely by inadequate and poorly sited physical facilities.

Education and learning

An American school library writer considers that 'curriculum reform has been characterized by the same boom-and-bust pattern that has typified educational restructuring' (Craver, 1994, 87). While she is referring to the situation in the USA, the same viewpoint could be applied to curriculum development in many other countries. Anecdotally, this author, having worked in the UK, has seen similar instances of educational change while working in places as far from the UK and USA as Thailand and Japan.

225

The truth is that a school librarian's skills and aptitudes will enable her or him to work flexibly with whatever a curriculum happens to be. Library collections to be sure are littered with the detritus from previous individual curriculum initiatives that either did not work out or were discontinued for one reason or another. Nevertheless, a librarian's skill lies in getting use out of a range of resources – looking at resources in a cross-curricular manner is almost automatic in the mindset of a school librarian. Use of co-operative systems or services, such as schools library services and electronic means of information, help too in minimizing waste and maximizing access to and obtaining value from resources.

Curriculum initiatives and developments will continue to proliferate, especially those designed for the end of a student's school career. For instance, with the development of baccalaureate-type systems, students may benefit from a range of educational opportunities at an advanced level, and not have to specialize typically in no more than three subjects for the last two years of their life in a secondary school. A school librarian will no doubt become increasingly familiar with a range of these initiatives as schools try to find ways of connecting to a wide variety of student needs, not necessarily purely academic. But two aspects of learning will surely be foundations to education and learning in this century:

Literacy concerns

Although literacy may be generally thought of as basic education, in reality it can be seen that it is a multi-layered concept, not least, for instance, with regard to information literacy. In a major international report in 2001, the Organization for Economic Cooperation and Development (OECD), identified a significant trend in the number of students who drop out from higher education. Having gained a place in a university or college, a number of students find that the pressures and expectations of life in higher education are considerable. Although research in this area is extremely limited, it is interesting to speculate on the extent to which curricular and regular use of a school library can help provide students with the skills, aptitudes and confidence to manage their time, workload and priorities in higher educational institutions (OECD, 2001).

Lifelong learning

Whether for economic reasons or technological needs or indeed personal interests, people are going to need to update skills and acquire new knowledge in order to be successful individuals and citizens in society. Far from students learning what they need to learn for life in secondary and/or higher education, formal education for young people needs to address the need for students to develop their skills and aptitudes for learning, accessing information and understanding knowledge as an on-going activity. Also, students will need to accept and welcome the fact that learning is for life. The role for a school library and its manager lies in teaching aspects of information literacy and enabling students to use a school library to practise and develop these skills and aptitudes. Adults in a school can also play a valuable role in acting as role models, so that students can see that learning is on-going and that techniques and skills to aid learning can be used in a practical manner. A school librarian should have an aim that a student should leave a school empowered to learn through life, at least as far as library and information services are concerned. Indeed, a school may promote its library as a community resource. One school reorganized its site and allocated funds for technology in order to 'develop the library into an exciting independent learning centre which also has the potential to support parents and our local communities. Everyone needs to become an independent learner' (Imison and Taylor, 2001, 7).

But what will learning look like in the future? Intellectually, of course, one can identify principles and aims, but, as managers of building-based services, it is helpful for school librarians to also be able to visualize what learning and library use may look like in the future. Abbott considers succinctly that pupils will move 'by need, not by the bell, [with] pupils working from carrels and going to a teacher when they need specialist advice' (Abbott, 1994, 98).

Implications for the roles of the school librarian and the secondary school library

Inevitably, in any look forward to the future, questions, rather than answers, will predominate. For instance, is it possible to identify any implications for a school library manager from ideas and material presented and discussed in this book? The following points are offered:

Skills, knowledge, aptitudes and roles of a school librarian

In the present century, will we see a common means of (higher) education in order to become a school librarian? Is it possible that all universities that offer courses for library and information studies may provide – inclusively or separately – relevant education for those wishing to become school librarians? However, if all secondary schools in the UK were to offer posts to qualified librarians only, there would, at present, be a shortage of persons with the desired or preferred educational qualifications to apply. Perhaps in-service training and support is a much stronger method of ensuring that librarians in secondary schools have the right mix of skills and education in order to be effective. It is possible that the optimum method of educating and supporting school librarians has not been found.

Issues of employment, salary and status have occupied the minds of individual school librarians, schools library services, professional organizations and others. Local strategies have been identified to improve matters and individuals have forged their own way in particular organizations. The 'educationalization' of school librarians is a significant issue. Clearly, it will be helpful to be familiar with and knowledgeable about educational matters in some detail, but need a school librarian be a teacher, as such? 'Teacher' as in the sense that a librarian is employed as a qualified teacher, for it is accepted that a librarian teaches (as do other certain groups of staff in a school, for instance, laboratory and IT technicians and classroom assistants). Possibly, professional 'jockeying' for position is counter-productive, be it by professional, qualified librarian, teacher or other category of staff. If nothing else, a main thrust of this book is to highlight certain qualities, aptitudes and skills for a school librarian that will be different in each individual, and capable of being developed by a school librarian from the backgrounds mentioned above. In the worst scenarios, when each group – qualified librarian, teacher, 'clerical' assistant – is negative about the other groups (and it appears that this is, anecdotally at least, the case), then school librarianship comes off worst. Pragmatically, it may be that the mix will be much as it was at the end of the last century and as the latest surveys (not least the seminal Sheffield Hallam University in 2000) have identified. In other words the qualification and employment bases for school librarians in the UK are extremely variable.

Perhaps a way forward has been identified in Australia, where guidelines indicate that 'learning in the future in schools will be considerably different, and responsive information services will be dependent on effective co-operation between the information specialists within the school' (Australian School Library Association, 2001, 59). Co-operation, or collaboration, is not only recommended but required and the specialists are meshed into a formal working team. Supported by technical and clerical assistance, the team typically comprises a teacher-librarian and an ICT co-ordinator, plus, as director, a 'person responsible for managing the overall school information service [who] requires skills in management, information science, and information and communication technology as well as an in-depth knowledge of the curriculum' (ibid.). The important point here is to forget about the title 'teacher-librarian' and concentrate on the management skills, aptitudes and knowledge bases identified by the guidelines. This author suggests that they can be carried out by a qualified librarian, a graduate of another discipline and a teacher, as each will inevitably have strong points and, by implication at least, weak ones. It is the blend or match of the skills, aptitudes and knowledge in an individual that are important.

Knowledge management (KM) is a term that has developed in sectors of librarianship, especially in workplace libraries. The concept has not been readily taken up by school librarianship in the UK, but the links are there – knowledge and technology. Stated plainly, 'knowledge management is the field that examines how knowledge . . . might be captured, represented, stored and applied for a range of knowledge intensive tasks – whether that be decision support, computer assisted learning, research or research support' (Knowledge Management Group, 1999). Offering or operating as a KM service may involve learning new skills for school librarians, but it is more likely to indicate the need for positioning in order to be successful. By this is meant that it is important to identify the role of school librarians and their service in an organization, to be pro-active, with a knowledge of the needs of individuals within the organization – basically, to follow through on the management issues identified in this book.

Familiarity with technology and the ability to manage and exploit technologies appears to be a strong common strand or trend for the future for school librarians. And it is management and teaching, not supervision, though this is how it may be perceived – for instance, through monitoring use of the internet, computer games, printing and so on. In among all this activity, it is possible to see a school librarian encouraging students to be confident in their learning, to have pride in their work, to evaluate the information sources available to them, consider alternatives and develop relevant content for their own work (Imison and Taylor, 2001, 58).

Prioritization of user groups for a school library and information service

Do 'we', that is, all members of a school community, as well as the professional community of school and other librarians, perhaps need to accept that a school's library will be relevant or used by *only some* students and staff in a particular school? If so, this implies that our existing thinking, goal and indeed dream about whole-school use of a school library needs to be put to one side. On a practical level, a school librarian may see that the school's library service is only or mainly used by a certain proportion or part of a school community and indeed only by specific individuals. Perhaps the time has come to formally accept such a fact and aim for use of a school library by a certain proportion, perhaps a majority (or not) of a school community, or cater only for specific year groups. Such an approach, accepted by all in a school, could avoid wasted resources and effort, promote more focused use and provide greater value for money for a school from its library and information service.

Different model of library service for children and young people

Do school librarians need to accept that the time has come for a different model of library provision for children and young people in a school, in a community, in an area? The times are characterized by the concept of life-long learning and by technological innovations such as large networks (e.g. the National Grid for Learning). This possibility is of course in direct contrast to the one above. But perhaps it is better, for a variety of societal and educational reasons, for a school to be less specific in its organization and customer base. This would mean that the school, and its library, would be more varied in offering learning experiences to all in the community, as suggested by Abbott at the beginning of this chapter. Possibly dual-use libraries, focused on learning experiences for a local community, offer a better way forward for more people.

Yet another possibility is that a secondary school library should firmly concentrate resource provision on the stated needs of a curriculum, and eschew resources that cater for the wider reading needs of young people, i.e. recreational reading, including fiction. Going further than that, a firm library collection policy for a given geographical area may need to be developed that inherently includes collection policies of secondary school libraries. At the moment, it seems that many of the varied cross-sector networks and co-operative groups do not include individual secondary school libraries (no doubt for very good operational reasons). However, does it help other libraries in an area, for instance, youth (public) libraries to develop effective resource collections and identify relevant services, if school libraries are not part of such a plan? Clearly, duplication of effort could result, though it may be that successful informal liaison in a local area may occur to prevent this. Indeed, complementary roles for library services to children and young people in a given area were recommended in the *Investing in children* report (Department of National Heritage, 1995) and, in this regard, a schools library service may provide a degree of co-ordination.

Nevertheless, can school libraries offer anything in a co-operative sense to any local network? Inevitably, school libraries may be seen as 'poor relations', but the better school libraries may, for instance, have:

- more per capita spending than that for a public library service point
- longer opening hours than some public library service points
- more hours of professional staff per user (if, typically, lacking support staff hours).

They may possibly also be:

- more technology-rich than library service points for the general community
- more effective in a targeted area of specific user groups.

This argument may be irrelevant, certainly on an individual local basis, as provision, functions, access and use of secondary school libraries varies widely, depending on location. But it does highlight a possibility that a secondary school library can have the potential to be involved in various networks of a cross-sector nature, which is a trend among a variety of services in different library sectors. It would be sad if school libraries were left out or even forgotten because of difficulties in co-ordination (which may suggest a role for schools library services).

In 1994, anticipating the new century in good time, American school librarians were set a number of challenges. Among other things, a school library should provide (Craver, 1994, 141–50):

- a range of information and communication technologies to enable pupils to be familiar with and develop skills in using them, thus helping them deal successfully with their school careers
- focused collections to support the concept of lifelong learning among pupils

- services and resources that could bear comparison with state-funded and independent or private schools in a given local area.

In addition, it was recommended (ibid.) that a school librarian:

- assume a leadership function in promoting the use of technologies by teachers and students
- develop products, resources and services that could be successfully monitored and evaluated, so as to justify and obtain funding for school library investment
- gear collections, facilities and services (including information literacy skills) to the societal, cultural and behavioural requirements of students
- analyse school library facilities so that a flexible, responsive service may ensue to users.

These challenges are not geographically specific and they will mostly be familiar, perhaps in part, to school librarians elsewhere. They reflect the issues of the times: social and political policy, technology, education and learning. These issues will be key in determining an effective model for delivering a library and information service to young people, at least in secondary schools. Such a model may not be radically different from the library service currently offered – on the other hand, it may be.

Up to now we have thought of the school library – ideally – as a foundation or centre for the school, and in particular, the curriculum. Rather than thinking purely of a physically centralized location or a centralized resource depot, perhaps it would be more helpful to look further outwards. Loertscher (1999, 4) thinks of the school library as a 'network central', rather like a station where people are both arriving and leaving (see Figure 12.1). His concept grasps hold of the opportunities that technology brings, so that the physical place is not the over-riding feature of a school library. Loertscher sees library and technology developing together, not alongside one another, but firmly entwined. In this concept a school library is:

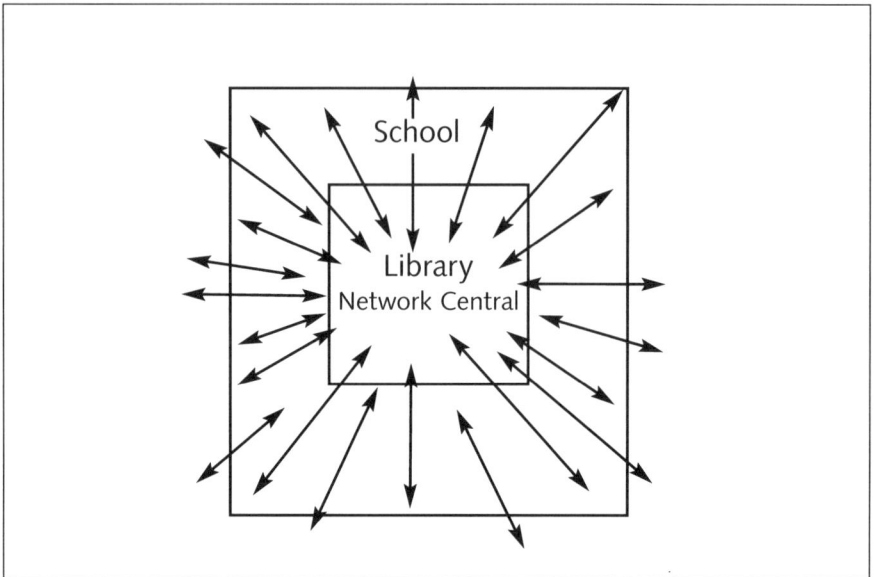

Fig. 12.1 *Uses and functions of a contemporary library in a secondary school*

Reproduced with permission from Loertscher, David V. (1999) *Reinvent your school's library in the age of technology: a guide for principals and superintendents*, San José, Ca., Hi Willow Research and Publishing, 4.

- information rich, irrespective of format; utilizing a wide range of technologies
- both 'centralized and decentralized simultaneously'
- flexible in the way it works, how users use it – where and how
- able to work because it is staffed professionally, with technical support
- a 'busy, bustling learning laboratory' (ibid.).

Conclusion

In the short term, according to Herring (2000), there will be little dramatic change for secondary or high school libraries but in the long term, a school librarian's 'role is likely to change radically as [will] the technology and the mode of learning for most pupils' (ibid.).

Achieving effective learning in a secondary school library is clearly a firm goal for a library manager and others in a school. A study on effective learning and school libraries, discussed in some depth in Chapter 3, concludes that because the research 'has been embedded within the context of *learning*, the findings may provide . . . reflection on the impact of information services, in the broadest sense, on education and lifelong learning' (Williams and Wavell, 2001, 135).

Like an iceberg, so much about a school library is hidden and unperceived, but a library in a school relates to the essential parts of an organization: user groups, management and the wider community. It is concerned with (using current societal, not necessarily educational, terms):

- electronic and technological ways of working
- relating to cultural backgrounds and mores
- understanding lifestyles
- ensuring physical and intellectual access to information
- facilitating useful and helpful knowledge and learning experiences for users.

A good school library adds up to more than the sum of its parts. Its manager can spread the benefits of good service to the whole school community, using a blend of professional, interpersonal and management skills.

If one wanted to sum up the future for secondary or high school libraries in the smallest possible number of words, the following could be used: flexibility and principles. In the future, a school library and its manager will need to cater for different uses and user patterns, a wider range of clientele, new technology and so on. However, too much flexibility weakens provision, so a flexible approach needs to back-bone on firm principles. Principles naturally are expressed in a school's library policy. Principles in themselves should largely be able to stand the test of time. New functions, activities and services for a secondary school library should relate to the principles that an individual school has developed, agreed to and works with, to the benefit of the entire school community.

Appendix A

SPECIMEN QUESTIONNAIRE FOR STAFF LIAISON/CURRICULUM DEVELOPMENT

Schedule for innovation interviews

Innovation: Information Handling Skills Project
Contact: Lynn Barrett &/or Mal Danks

Description of innovation

The Core Lessons that have been developed for Year 7 students cover the following:

- resource selection
- note taking
- skimming and scanning
- validity of internet resources.

The teaching of these skills is spiralled upwards, at increasing levels of sophistication, as students progress through Key Stages 3 and 4. In Year 10, students are reassessed to determine how far they have come on the skills continuum and to identify areas where further teaching is required.

Post-16 students receive an induction to review information handling and to practise their skills in a curricular context. This includes a brainstorming session followed by structuring questions to focus a research task and evaluating a variety of resources to create an annotated bibliography.

Depending on their choice of subjects, some go on to an extended project in which the research process, original thought and presentation skills are emphasized.

In order to disseminate good practice within the Information Handling Skills Project as a whole, regular reports are given to the Individual Needs Representatives with feedback requested as to how the skills are being developed within their departments. The librarians attend departmental meetings annually to discuss the project and avenues for advancing it into new areas of the curriculum. Departmental INSET sessions are held during which teachers are informed about project developments and given practical exercises to help them understand the research problems that students experience. They are taught techniques for differentiating research assignments and are then expected to develop projects in liaison with the librarians that will support the less able students and stretch the more able ones.

The project continues to develop with new concepts being included each year. Trials are currently being planned around questioning techniques and the use of graphic organizers.

Pupil achievement

Has this innovation had any impact on pupil achievement?
Yes.
In what way?

- Students use the library and books more effectively.
- They use the internet with greater confidence and are aware of its inherent problems.
- They use a wide range of skills and progress these year on year.
- They work better independently.
- They are more selective about the resources that they use.

Has there been a different impact for boys compared with girls?

238

No.

Pupil attendance

Has the innovation had any impact on student attendance?
No.

Quality of teaching

Has this innovation had any impact on the quality of teaching?
Yes.
In what way?

- It underpins the National Literacy Strategy. As the work is now in its fifth year, teachers are well prepared for many of the demands of implementing the Strategy.
- Teachers are better able to differentiate their assignments and more aware of what they are asking students to do.
- Teachers are forced to think about the explicit teaching of skills and to recognize the importance of checking that resources match the requirements of an assignment as well as the individual needs of their students.

Management practices

Has the innovation impacted on management practices at the CTC?
Yes.
In what way?

- The information gathered from Year 7 assessments is passed on to subject teachers and also written into documentation for teachers of students with individual needs. This information assists teachers in planning for differentiation
- Library staffing (two qualified librarians and two library assistants)

reflects the additional demands generated by the project's work across the College.

Does it have any effect on levels of teacher non-contact time?
No.

How does this innovation relate to the overall management philosophy of the CTC?

It teaches and encourages students to work responsibly and independently, developing the skills required to become lifelong learners.

Does the innovation affect the way that the CTC covers staff absence.
No.

Does this innovation increase the use of support staff alongside teaching staff in the CTC?

Yes, in that the librarians take a very active role in the development and delivery of skills lessons, the assessment process and the research work that students carry out in the library. The level of expertise and the numbers of library staff reflect this. The Individual Needs Co-ordinator is key to the development of the project and the IN staff offer considerable assistance with the assessment process.

Teacher terms and conditions

Does this innovation require any change in teacher terms and conditions?
No.

Does it affect the way that the CTC covers staff absence?
No.

Teacher workload

Is there any impact from this innovation on teacher workload?
Yes.

In what way does it impact?

- There is mainly a different focus to the workload in that skills are constantly being built into any research work planned for students.
- The work of research and independent learning is positively shared with the librarians.
- Teachers find planning easier because of baseline assessments.

Teacher morale and attendance

Is there any impact from this innovation on overall teacher morale?
   Yes.
In what way?

- Teachers are more confident in setting research assignments.
- Teachers have the support and the resources to experiment with different styles of teaching and learning and are therefore willing to do things differently.
- They feel rewarded when they see that students are more able to cope with the demands and expectations put upon them, therefore achieving a higher degree of success.

Appendix B

EXAMPLE OF REGULAR CURRENT AWARENESS PUBLICITY MATERIAL

Hitting the bookshelves

A monthly library newsletter – no.15   February 2002

WELCOME TO GILLIAN CROSS

Award-winning author Gillian Cross visits Japan for one week at the end of February. We are very lucky that Gillian is spending two days at our school. For more information about Gillian and her books, look at the website **www.gilliancross.co.uk**

New copies of the following novels by Gillian Cross have arrived in the Library: for older readers, *Born of the sun, Chartbreak, A map of nowhere, On the edge, Pictures in the dark* and *Tightrope*, and for younger readers, *The prime minister's brain* and *The mintyglo kid*. In Japanese, we now have: *Ayatsurareta gakko, Sori daijin no zuno, Zoh to futari no dai dassoh* and *Ki no ue no i-shiro*.

Also, see our website: **www.yis.ac.jp/Library/visiting_authors.htm**

NEW additions to the library collection include:

New books to help you study

Cottrell, Stella	The study skills handbook	371.3 COT
Fry, Ron	The great big book of how to study	371.3 FRY
Gilbert, Sara Dulaney	How to do your best on tests	371.3 GIL
Letts revision skills: a survival guide		371.3 BRE
Peck, John	Student's guide to writing: grammar, punctuation and spelling	808 PEC
Varley, Ann	Good essays: every student's indispensable guide to effective writing	808.042 VAR

•**plus** *revision guides* – please see individual subject areas, below.

Art and Design

Gaff, Jackie	1940–60: art in emotion	709.044 GAF

Biology/Health educators

Llewellyn, Claire	The facts about arthritis	616.72 LLE
Parker, John	Biology AS revision notes	574 PAR
Taylor, Dave	Endangered desert animals	591.90954TAY
Trueman, Terry	Stuck in neutral (novel about cerebral palsy)	FIC TRU

Chemistry

Gannon, Paddy	Revise AS Chemistry	540 GAN
Ritchie, Rob	Chemistry AS revision guide	540 RIT

Drama

Berry, Cicely	Your voice and how to use it	808.5 BER

English language, English literature/world literature translated into English

Collins, Billy	Picnic, lightening	811 COL

| Handley, Graham | Songs of innocence & experience (Brodie's Notes) | 821 BLA |
| Foster, Malcolm | Margaret Atwood's 'The handmaid's tale' (Max Notes) | 813 ATW |

To help readers to select fiction, the listing below gives a letter to indicate what sort or genre of fiction the book is. The code is as follows:

A = Adventure	Al = Allegory	An = Animal stories	C = Crime/Murder
F = Fantasy/ghost	H = Historical	Ho = Horror/Gothic	Hu = Humorous
J = Japan	M = Mystery	R = Romance/Love	Re = Relationships
SF = Science Fiction	Sst = short stories	S = Situation	So = Social issue
Sp = Sports stories	Su = Horror/Suspense		

Fiction for high school and adults *includes*

Card, Orson Scott	Ender's shadow	SF
Faulks, Sebastian	Birdsong	H
Glazebrook, Philip	The electric rock garden	H
McEwan, Ian	Atonement	H
Matsumoto, Seicho	Points and lines	M
Mitchell, David	Ghostwritten	J

Fiction for junior high *includes*

Beere, Peter	Kiss of death (Point Crime s.)	C
Breslin, Theresa	Dream master nightmare!	Hu
	also Names games	
Burgess, Melvin	Billy Elliot	S
Cross, Gillian	see above	
Crossley-Holland, Kevin	Arthur at the crossing places	H
Gibbons, Alan	Julie and me . . . and Michael Owen makes three	Re
Gleitzman, Morris	Adults only	Hu

Glover, Sandra	The nowhere boy	M/S
Leeson, Robert	Liar	S
Lingard, Joan	A secret place	So
McCaughrean, Geraldine	Stop the train	H
Martin, Les	E.B.E. (X-files)	SF
Matsumoto, Seicho	Points and lines	M
Paulsen, Gary	The Transall saga	SF
Trueman, Terry	Stuck in neutral	So

Geography/Environmental science

Doherty, Gillian	Usborne book of peoples of the world *Internet-linked*	910 DOH
	Earth sciences	REF 550 EAR
Goddard, Peter	Geography AS revision notes	910 GOD
Gore, Al	Earth in the balance: ecology and the human spirit	363.7 GOR
Powell, Julian	World Wildlife Fund	361.1 POW
Schultz, Warren	Organic suburbanite	635 SCH
	Ukraine: in Russia's shadow (Understanding Global Issues s.)	Topic Files 947.7 UKR
Witherick, Michael	Environment and people: an integrated course for A and AS Geography	333.7 WIT

History/Social studies

Beeching, Cyril Leslie	Oxford Dictionary of Dates, 2nd ed.	REF 902 BEE
Burleigh, Michael	The Third Reich: a new history	943.086 BUR
Faulks, Sebastian	Birdsong	FIC FAU
Scaife, Michael	History, modern British and European AS revision notes	940.2 SCA
Service, Robert	The Russian Revolution 1900–1927, 3rd ed.	947.083 SER

Information Technology

| Doherty, Gillian | Usborne book of peoples of the world *Internet-linked* | 910 DOH |

Japanese studies

	Hiroshima mon amour. Video Tape	Fic Hir
Matsumoto, Seicho	Points and lines	FIC MAT
Mitchell, David	Ghostwritten	Fic MIT
Rowling, J.K.	Harry Potter to Kenja no ishi	JAPANESE FIC ROW

Mathematics

| Cope, Lee | Revise A level in a week: Maths | 510 COP |

Media Studies

| Connolly, Sean | Steven Spielberg (Heinemann Profiles s.) | 791.43 CON |
| Sibley, Brian | The Lord of the Rings official movie guide | 791.43 SIB |

Music

	GCSE Music. Your personal tutor	CD-ROM 781.1 GCSE
Isserlis, Steven	Why Beethoven threw the stew and lots more stories about the lives of great composers	780.9 ISS
Jensen, Eric Frederick	Schumann	780.92 SCH
	Les miserables (in concert) Video Tape	782.14 LES
Rosenthal, Ethel	The story of Indian music and its instruments	781.6 ROS

Compact discs

[Dylan, Bob]	Bob Dylan's greatest hits, Volume 3
Haydn, Joseph	Symphonies 94, 99, 101 (Clock, Surprise, etc.)
[Piaf, Edith]	Edith Piaf …
[Simon & Garfunkel]	Simon & Garfunkel's greatest hits

Sports

Lovitt, Chip	Michael Jordan	796.323 LOV
McManners, Hugh	Complete wilderness training book	613.69 McM
	Match annual 2002	796.334 MAT
	The official Liverpool FC annual 2002	796.334 OFF
	The official Manchester United annual 2002	796.334 OFF
Olsen, Larry Dean	Outdoor survival skills, 6th ed.	613.69 OLS
Wallechinsky, David	The complete book of Winter Olympics 2002	796.98 WAL

Theory of knowledge

Laing, R.D.	The politics of experience and the bird of paradise	128.4 LAI
Zizek, Slavoj	On belief	291.2 ZIZ

Videos *(All fiction unless otherwise stated and shelved in the fiction area)*

	Animal crackers (Marx Brothers)	[PAL]
Dahl, Roald	The BFG (animation)	[PAL]
	Crouching tiger, hidden dragon (Ang Lee; Yeoh)	[NTSC]
	Hiroshima mon amour (Resnais; Okada; Riva)	[PAL]
	Les miserables (in concert)	Video Tape 782.14 LES

	Seven years in Tibet (Pitt; Annaud; music – J.Williams)	[PAL]

Plus general non-fiction

Beeching, Cyril Leslie	Oxford dictionary of dates, 2nd ed.	REF 902 BEE
Dowswell, Paul	Tales of real survival	613.69 DOW
Hollinger, Carol	Mai Pen Rai means never mind	959.3 HOL
Middleton, Haydn	Diana, Princess of Wales (Heinemann Profiles s.)	941.085 MID
Olsen, Larry Dean	Outdoor survival skills, 6th ed.	613.69 OLS
Rees, Rosemary	People and communities	307 REE
Schultz, Warren	Organic suburbanite	635 SCH
Varley, Ann	Good essays: every student's indispensable guide to effective writing	808.042 VAR

Recommended websites, etc. (the following have received positive reviews/citations)

Festivals	**www.holidayinsights.com/**
Interactive frog dissection	**http://curry.edschool.virginia.edu/go/frog/**
Mycal Cinema	**www.warnermycal.com/schedule/honmoku.html**

Sanagitachi homepage (nonprofit organization working with the Kotobukicho people)

www.fuumaru.hoops.livedoor.com/sanagiframe.htm

Sleep: adolescent sleep needs

www.sleepfoundation.org

YIS LIBRARY & INFORMATION SERVICE

Webpage: **www.yis.ac.jp/Library/index.htm**

Info Web Database available through **www.yis.ac.jp/Library/index.htm**

Kristin Scott Thomas, stage and film actress (*The English Patient, Four Weddings and a Funeral, Richard III, Gosford Park, Life as a House*) 'talking passionately about . . . her choice of authors: Julian Barnes, Saki, Ian McEwan, Jane Austen, Ruth Rendell'.

(Ref: Daily Yomiuri 20.i.02)

Appendix C

Specimen job description for a school library assistant

Based on a job description developed by Hertfordshire Schools Library Service, England. This is a companion job description to the librarian's job description discussed in Chapter 2.

Job Description: Library Assistant
Responsible to: Head Librarian
Responsible for: the routine task necessary for the smooth, day-to-day running of the school library so that the Head Librarian can fulfil professional tasks and a managerial role, together with teaching/instructional commitments.
Role:
Directing
   The rota and work of volunteers
Operating
   The circulation system – issuing and returning books; operating the reservation system, generating and sending out notices for overdue books and other resources. The monthly booking system for class visits to the Library.
Ensuring
   That the library stock is in good order – shelving and filing new and returned books and materials and maintaining resources in their correct order

Progressing

New library materials going through the cataloguing cycle, prior to being available in the library collection

Processing

And maintaining the system for recording and storing newspapers and magazines

Maintaining

The catalogue – entering details onto computer catalogue for stock; deleting catalogue records for withdrawn stock

Records of users on the computer system

Developing

Skills to use IT facilities in the library

Looking after

The library environment

Helping

With enquiries from readers and colleagues.

Appendix D

Example of a policy statement dealing with donations to a school library

DONATION OF BOOKS TO THE SCHOOL LIBRARY: policy and information

The school is grateful to parents who have donated books to the school library. In addition, many parents have asked for advice about donating books to the library. It is hoped that the following information will be helpful in this regard.

The school library is guided by a policy that has been agreed by the school community and also has a thriving collection policy and development plan (copies of which are available in the library). Books, audiocassettes, videos, compact discs, CD-ROMs, magazines and newspapers are continually being added to stock. Library resources are selected and purchased with the needs of the curriculum in mind.

Although it is tempting to think that all books must be useful for a school library, this is not always so. Overall, books for donations should be:

- in good physical condition – adequate binding, strong cover, unmarked pages, etc.
- at a text level suitable for the 11–18 year age range.

In addition, for most non-fiction items, books suitable for donation to the school library should not have been published more than ten years ago, as pupils need to have access to accurate information and generally speaking older books are not so useful in this regard.

As we encourage pupils to read for pleasure, fiction books (especially) should be attractive and appealing. The school library may well already possess copies of classic English literature texts and will not need to shelve any donated items of this kind on the open shelves.

However, the librarian would be grateful for donated items in the following areas of knowledge:

- botany
- artists
- sport (only if published in the last two years)
- US history.

The donation of suitable magazines (on a regular basis) is welcomed.

Unfortunately, it is not possible to accept books on long- or short-term loan to the school library.

Parents who are interested in donating books to the library should please see the librarian in the first instance.

For books not suitable for the school library, we hope that it would be possible to donate books (through the school library) to a book charity, or possibly to be exchanged/sold for books required in the school library. Please note that donated items that are added to stock are treated in the same way as other books in the library, i.e. once books become out of date or physically deteriorate (owing to use), they are withdrawn from stock. (Please see our library collection policy for further information.)

Thank you for your interest in the school library. The school is grateful for the support of parents.

Appendix E

EXAMPLE OF AN INFORMATION SHEET DESIGNED TO HELP STUDENTS USE THE SCHOOL LIBRARY MORE EFFECTIVELY

SCHOOL LIBRARY AND INFORMATION SERVICE
LIBRARY RESOURCES FOR A LEVEL AND GCSE

BUSINESS STUDIES AND ECONOMICS

The school library contains a number of resources to assist you in your work in Business Studies and Economics.

The Dewey Decimal Classification, by which *non-fiction resources* in the library are arranged, groups books and other resources on a subject together. Books are arranged on the shelves in number order, starting at 000 and finishing at 999. Guiding on the shelves will also assist you to find the section you need.

To find relevant items, you can use the computer catalogue or printed subject indexes. Below are several subjects within the Business Studies and Economics syllabuses, with their 'Dewey' number that may be of interest to you.

Administration (Business)	650
Advertising	659.1
Business	650
Commerce	380
Communications	302

Computers	005
Economic development	338.9
Economic growth	338.9
Economic history	330.9
Enterprise	338
Entrepreneurs	338
European Community	382.9142
Industries	338
Inflation	332
Law	340
Management	658
Marketing	658.8
Mathematics	510
Media	302.23
Money	332.4
Office practice	651
Population	304.6
Single currency	382.9142
Social trends	303.44
Statistics★	310
Statistics – Mathematics	519.5
Trade unions	331.88
Transport	338

(★See especially the Reference Section.)

The other section that may contain useful information is the *Reference section* where dictionaries, encyclopaedias, statistics and other material on specific subjects are available. Examples include directories of company information and government statistics. (Resources in this section have a notice attached to the spine saying 'for reference only' meaning for use in the library only.)

In addition to books and other items, it will be helpful to consult *news-*

papers and periodicals (or magazines). Current copies are displayed, whilst previous issues or 'back copies' are located in the reference section. Periodicals to help with your studies in Economics and Business Studies include:

- *Business Review*
- *Economic Review*
- *Economics Today* ★★
- *Economist*

(★★ Available in the Economics and Business Studies Department.)

The financial sections of daily and weekly national newspapers may assist to update your information about current trends and issues.

Useful websites

The internet can provide access to a wide range of information, which *may* be up to date and authoritative. The better sites will ensure that you receive high-quality information. This is not always the case, so please evaluate sites as you use them. Some recommended sites include:

- The Educational Business and Economics website – 'Bized': **www.bized.ac.uk/**
- OECD: **www.oecd.org/**
- UN: **www.un.org/**
- The World Bank (IBRD): **www.worldbank.org/**
- DTI: **www.dti.gov.uk/**
- Bank of England: **www.bankofengland.co.uk/**
- Banks: **www.lloydsbank.co.uk/** and **http://www.natwest.co.uk/**
- Penn World Data tables: **http://bized.ac.uk/dataserv/pennhome.htm**
- Statistics from countries (UK, Japan and Australia): **www.ons.gov.uk/** and **http://www.stat.go.jp/1.htm** and **www.statistics.gov.au/**

- Companies: FTSE 100 company websites:
  www.bized.ac.uk/companies/comlist.htm/
- Thomson directories: **www.inbusiness.co.uk/**
- Individual firms, e.g.: **www.tesco.co.uk** and **www.marks-and-spencer.co.uk** and **www.glaxowellcome.co.uk/**
- Newspapers: **www.the-times.co.uk/** and **www.independent.co.uk/**

This information sheet is also available at the school library web page, where you will also be able to access the Info Web Database. The library subscribes to this web-based product, allowing you to access many sources of information, including newspapers, periodicals, broadcast transcripts, digests of science journals and other sources.

Please ask the librarian for any help you may require.

Appendix F

CILIP Solo Workers' Questionnaire 2002

Pay and Status

Information gathering exercise (questionnaire)
Spring 2002

These questions are aimed at discovering something about your **current** employment. If you are between jobs, we would be interested to learn about your previous post. Please complete the following questions as fully as possible, and send to the address at the end of the form.

Place of work

1 Which sector do you work in?
e.g. health, government, industry, law, voluntary, media, finance, school, HE or FE, public

2 How many staff are employed in your organisation?

3 How many locations are covered by your service?

4 Are there other libraries or information services serving the organisation?

a. How are you linked?

5 Mobility – how far do you travel to work?

Nature of the job

6 What is your job title?

7 What is the scope of your job?
e.g. do you have full responsibility for providing an information service, or do you have responsibility for a specific area, e.g. desk research, acquisitions, etc.?

8 Do you have staff management responsibilities?

a. If yes – how many staff?

9 Please indicate which band your salary fits within (please circle or highlight):

>£10000	£10000–£15000	£15000–£20000
£20000–25000	£25000–£30000	£30000–£35000
£35000–£40000	£40000–£45000	£45000>

10   Do you receive any additional benefits as part of your employment package?
e.g. Pension, car, bonus, private health insurance, gym membership

11   Working arrangements – do you work on a full-time or part-time basis?

12   Do you experience any variation from the traditional full-time (or part-time) working arrangements?
e.g. flexible working, job-share, working from home, etc.

13   Perceptions of the job, i.e. how valued do you feel (please circle or highlight the most relevant)?

Very valued
Valued
Accepted
Unrecognised
Under valued

14   What is the most satisfying aspect of your job?

Personal characteristics

15 Please indicate which age band you fit within (please circle, or highlight):

>20yrs   20–29yrs   30–35yrs   36–40yrs

41–45yrs   46–50yrs   51–55yrs   56yrs>

16 Please indicate what qualifications you have:

17 What additional skills (i.e. non-traditional librarianship) do you draw upon to meet the demands of your position?
e.g. management, personnel, marketing, budgeting, negotiation, etc.

18 Please list the organisations (professional or other) that you are a member of.

a. How do they help you in your career?

19 What one thing could CILIP do to dramatically improve your professional standing within your organisation?

And finally...

Please consider whether you would be prepared to help us further in our mission to improve the pay and status of library and information professionals. If you would like to help, please provide contact details:

Name:

Organisation:

Address:

Tel:

Fax:

E-mail:

Please return to:

Lyndsay Rees-Jones
CILIP
7 Ridgmount Street
London WC1E 7AE

Appendix G

PRESS OR MEDIA RELEASE

An example of a press or media release is shown below. This is a press release prepared by the Marketing Department of CILIP which is included in the pack of materials made available to schools who participate in the Carnegie and Greenaway shadowing scheme, as discussed in Chapter 10. The press release should contain the basic elements of the project in clear language. The text of the document should be short, but further information may be provided in background notes for editors.

The press release may be customized by an individual school, and background information about the school could be provided in the notes. An example of how to customize the text of the press release itself is given at the end of this Appendix.

Press release provided by CILIP

MEDIA RELEASE ... MEDIA RELEASE ...

CARNEGIE/GREENAWAY SHADOWING SCHEME
RAISING LITERACY STANDARDS THROUGH READING FOR PLEASURE

800 library-based reading groups across the UK, with over 10,000 children will shadow the national judging of the most prestigious of the children's

book prizes, CILIP's Carnegie and Kate Greenaway Medals. Groups will read shortlisted titles and choose their favourite books, in time for the announcement of the Medal winners on 13 July, in the largest programme of its kind in the UK.

Shadowing offers schools and public library reading groups a key strategy to support young people's reading and literacy. Many schools have adopted it as a support mechanism for the National Literacy Strategy at Key Stages 1 and 2. Secondary schools are linking it to literacy work at Key Stage 3, currently a core government concern.

The structured reading and discussion of the very best in writing for young people engages and inspires those taking part, providing a vital catalyst in encouraging and motivating students' reading. Shadowing enables schools to take reading beyond literacy. It supports youth and school libraries' holistic approach to reading, creating a fun, informal way of learning.

The scheme is used to support literacy and learning with pupils who have a wide range of ability. Shadowing the Greenaway Medal for picture books is used as a strategy to support the development of visual literacy – frequently with special needs students. Shadowing the Carnegie Medal is increasingly recognized as a stimulating project for gifted and talented pupils – addressing another key area of current educational concern – by offering more challenging and critical reading experiences.

The project features the opportunity for innovative ICT use, enhancing the impact of initiatives such as the National Grid for Learning and enabling young people from different parts of the UK to form a web-based reading group and exchange reactions and reviews across the net.

- ends -

27 April 2001

Editor's notes and background

1. The process

Once the shortlist is announced on 27 April, all kinds of organizations including schools, reading groups, young offender institutions, parent and child groups, home educators and special needs colleges start the process. The books are read and discussed, with reviews e-mailed to the shadowing website (**www.cilip.org.uk/shadowing**).

The books are used as a springboard for a creative approach to the whole reading experience. Activities include:

- creating their own websites
- exchanging reviews online
- chatting online with fellow shadowers – and even shortlisted authors
- linking up with other schools for live book debates
- dramatizing and videoing scenes from the books
- organizing paired reading with younger readers
- reading aloud to younger children from local primary schools
- creating displays both for their organization and local bookshops
- working with the Greenaway shortlist in art and design classes
- video conferencing with other schools.

2. Example Groups

Cramlington 'Litcritters,' Cramlington High School, Northumberland

15 volunteer students reading the Carnegie shortlist, other groups working with the Greenaway.

- E-mail/video conference with other schools and RNIB New College in Worcester.
- Whole school vote for winners.
- Special needs – redesigning picture books as a CDT project, televised 'book bites'.

- Health and Social Care – testing picture books in a first school (opportunity for real reader-to-reader interaction)

The Hollyfield School, Surbiton, Surrey

The school has a new after school reading group of Year 7s (having won an Education Extra Award) who will be working with the Carnegie titles.

- Presentations to the rest of the year in English lessons.
- Reviews posted and scanned on to the intranet.
- Discussions made public on the web via webcam and digital images.
- Short drama pieces.
- Mass vote for Year 7 – videoed.

Sutton Central Library Reading Group

An existing 12–15 Reading Group of seven girls who meet in the library once a month will be shadowing the Carnegie Medal.

- Writing reviews for their bi-monthly magazine.
- Events with local schools.

Customizing the text, such as:

BOOK SECONDARY SCHOOL LIBRARY CLUB GOES NATIONAL
Students of Book Secondary School's library club become book award judges by taking part with 800 other library-based reading groups across the UK – over 10,000 children – 'shadowing' the national judging of the most prestigious of the children's book prizes, CILIP's Carnegie and Kate Greenaway Medals. Groups will read shortlisted titles and choose their favourite books, in time for the announcement of the Medal winners on 13 July, in the largest programme of its kind in the UK.

School librarian, Sam Catalogue said 'taking part in the shadowing scheme is a key strategy to support young people's reading and literacy'. Secondary schools nationwide are linking it to literacy work at Key Stage 3, currently a core government concern.

Head of English Tara Bronte considered that 'the structured reading and discussion of the very best in writing for young people engages and inspires those taking part, providing a vital catalyst in encouraging and motivating students' reading. Shadowing enables schools to take reading beyond literacy.' Sam Catalogue added 'It supports youth and school libraries' holistic approach to reading, creating a fun, informal way of learning.'

The scheme is used to support literacy and learning with pupils who have a wide range of ability. Shadowing the Greenaway Medal for picture books is used as a strategy to support the development of visual literacy – frequently with special needs students. Shadowing the Carnegie Medal is increasingly recognized as a stimulating project for gifted and talented pupils – addressing another key area of current educational concern – by offering more challenging and critical reading experiences.

The project features the opportunity for innovative ICT use, enhancing the impact of initiatives such as the National Grid for Learning and enabling young people from different parts of the UK to form a web-based reading group and exchange reactions and reviews across the net.

Head teacher Gwendoline School said 'taking part in this national scheme is a fine opportunity for our students. I'm sure they will have an enjoyable time reading the shortlisted books and discussing which one they consider to be the winner'.

- End -

Date: ....

Notes for editors:

Appendix H

LISTSERVS FOR SCHOOL LIBRARIANS

Communication and networking among school librarians is valuable, especially where librarians work as solo librarians. One relatively new way of communicating is electronically, via e-mail. More accurately, it is through a listserv, whereby a librarian may join a group of librarians who communicate via a certain mailbase. Typically, a message is sent to all librarians who are registered on the list. The message may ask for views about library developments, best methods of doing things, new initiatives, and for recommended resources and products. Replies may be sent solely to the enquirer or again to the members of the mailbase. A regular discussion may be started for the benefit and interest of all members of the mailbase. There are several listservs for school librarians, including:

Lis-educ

This is a web list set up for librarians working in institutions concerned with educational research and teacher training, as well as librarians in colleges and schools. It is moderated for ELG, the Education Librarians Group of CILIP. It is a free and open list. A message to join may be sent to **lis-educ@mailbase.ac.uk**. Although naturally it is focused on the UK, librarians from other parts of the world may become members.

LM_NET

LM_NET is a worldwide discussion group for school library media specialists, and is not open to general librarians. All discussion is therefore focused on school library media matters. Over 14,000 subscribers, from over 60 countries, are registered with the list. Details may be found at **http://askeric.org/lm_net/**

Listservs set up for specific organizations

Local or other special interest listservs may be set up formally or informally as the size and nature of the group dictates. Listservs may also be hosted by organizations for their members, such as the listserv maintained by ECIS (the European Council of International Schools) for librarians in international schools. To join, visit **http://listserv.ecis.org/archives/library.html**

For schools who offer the International Baccalaureate at diploma level, support includes a listserv maintained at the IBO (International Baccalaureate Organization) site. This works through a password, which may be obtained from the individual school's IB co-ordinator.

Appendix I

EXAMPLE OF COMPLAINTS POLICY AND PROCEDURE

Policy and procedure concerning challenged materials or complaints concerning resources in the school library collection

In establishing and following policy and procedure relating to concern from members of the school community about resources held in the school library, the following factors will be relevant:

a. Stock management principles need to be identified in the general school policy (even if the detail is covered elsewhere), together with a statement about the rights of the individual and/or freedom of information
b. Members of the school community should be aware that a policy and procedure concerning complaints is in place. This needs to be stated in appropriate documentation and display signs.

The procedure for dealing with a complaint should include:

a. Formal notification of receipt of notification. Such a letter should outline the procedure followed.
b. Evaluation of the item in the light of comments or complaint detail.
c. A decision, which should be reached by the librarian and headteacher and/or senior management team. A member of any school library steering committee or other specialist in the school (e.g. if the item concerns

sex education, various individuals in the school dealing with this aspect of the curriculum should be consulted) may be involved.

d. A mechanism for obtaining the views of others, such as the local schools library service or LEA advisory service, which may also be helpful.

e. Communication of the decision as soon as possible to the person complaining. The decision should be recorded and filed. (It may be appropriate to also record details of the decision on the catalogue entry for the item in any computerized catalogue.)

A complaint or expression of concern over library resources (but also for other aspects of library service or provision) may cause a review of library policy and practice. There may also be a tension between a statement about the rights of the individual and/or freedom of information and libraries' role in enabling individuals to access information and ideas. There may too be an issue concerning media, such as access through the internet. However, the school may indeed have particular values and an ethos so that a balance will normally be possible. Identifying these issues in policy, developments plans and other documentation will be very helpful in the long term.

BIBLIOGRAPHY

Abbott, John (1994) *Learning makes sense. Recreating education for a changing future*, Letchworth, Hertfordshire, Education 2000.

Abbott, John and Ryan, Terry (2000*) The unfinished revolution: learning, human behaviour, community and political paradox*, Stafford, Network Educational Press, 2000.

American Association of School Librarians/Association for Educational Communications and Technology (1998a) *Information literacy standards for student learning*, Chicago, American Library Association.

American Association of School Librarians/Association for Educational Communications and Technology (1998b) *Information power: building partnerships for learning*, Chicago, American Library Association.

American Association of School Librarians (2001*) Position statement on the role of the school library media specialist in site-based management*, Chicago, American Library Association, available at
www.ala.org/aasl/positions/ps_sitemgmt.html

Ashcroft, Maggie (2000) Loose cannon or guided missile? St Ivo School aims for community partnerships in teaching and learning, *School Libraries in View*, **13** (Spring), 10–12.

Australian School Library Association; Australian Library and Information Association (2001) *Learning for the future: developing information services in schools,* 2nd edn, Carlton, Victoria, Australia, Curriculum Corporation.

Barber, Michael (2001) Beware snake oil, the brain story is not yet told, *Times Educational Supplement*, (27 April), 21.

Barrett, Lynn (1999) Connecting minds and machines, *School Libraries in View*, **11** (Spring), 5–8.

Bartlett, Steve, Burton, Diana and Peim, Nick (2001) *Introduction to education studies*, London, Paul Chapman Publishing.

Best, John W. (1981) *Research in education*, 4th edn, Englewood Cliffs, NJ, Prentice Hall Inc.

Branch, Jennifer (2000) A day in my life, *School Libraries Worldwide*, **6** (1) (January), available at
www.iasl-slo.org/day_branch.html

Brighouse, Tim (2001) Delivering the Caldecote Memorial Lecture to the Royal Society of Arts, *RSA Journal*, **CXLVIII** (5496), 63–5.

British Library (1990) *Crossing the great divide: with support the school librarian can enhance pupils' learning*, British Library Research and Development Report 6014, London, British Library.

Brookes, Christopher (2002) Life sentence? The concept behind lifelong learning needs to be rebranded, *RSA Journal*, **1/6**, 30–1.

Bush, Gail and Kwielford, Merrilee Andersen (2001) Advocacy in action, *Teacher Librarian*, (June), 8–12.

Bush, Tony et al. (1999) *Educational management: redefining theory, policy and practice*, London, Paul Chapman Ltd.

Centre for Studies on Inclusive Education (2000) *Index for inclusion: developing learning and participation in schools*, Bristol, CSIE.

Chambers, Aidan (2001) A link in the chain, *Youth Library Review*, **29** (Summer), 12.

Charlton, Leonore (2002) *Planning and designing a secondary school library resource centre*, 2nd edn, Swindon, School Library Association.

Checking the books: the value and impact of public library book reading (2001) Sheffield, Centre for the Public Library and Information in Society, Sheffield University.

Craver, Kathleen W. (1994) *School library media centers in the 21st century: changes and challenges*, Westport, CT, Greenwood Press.

Cross, Gillian (1996) Libraries: rain forests of the mind, *International Schools Journal*, **xvi** (1), 10–23.

Czerner, Thomas B. (2001) *What makes you tick? The brain in plain English*, New York, Wiley.

Dawson, Darrell and Fitzgerald, Lee (1999) *Literature circles: reading in action*, Wagga Wagga, Centre for Information Studies.

Dent, Angela (1998) School libraries go digital for the next millennium, *School Libraries in View*, **10** (Autumn), 17–18.

Department of Education and Science (1989) *Better libraries: good practice in schools – a survey by HM Inspectorate*, London, Department of Education and Science.

Department of National Heritage (1995*) Investing in children: the future of library services for children and young people*, Library and Information Services Council (England) Working Party on Library Services for Children and Young People, London, The Stationery Office.

Dewe, M. (1996) *Planning and designing libraries for children and young people*, London, Library Association Publishing.

Dirda, Michael (2001) Manchester, *The Guardian* (10 May).

Drake, Barry (1998) Pastoral care: the challenge for international schools. In Hayden, Mary and Thompson, Jeff (eds) *International education: principles and practice*, London, Kogan Page.

Driessen, Karen C. and Smyth, Sheila A. (1995*) A library manager's guide to the physical processing of nonprint materials*, Westport, CT, Greenwood Press.

Ecclestone, Kay (2001) Seeking new horizons: creating a used and usable LRC, *School Librarian*, **49** (2) (Summer), 62–4.

Fang, Josephine Riss (ed.) (1995*) World guide to library archives and information science education*, 2nd edn, K. G. Saur.

Fullan, Michael G. (1991) *The new meaning of educational change*, 2nd edn, London, Cassell Educational Ltd.

Gordon, Carol (2000) *Information literacy in action*, Saxmundham, Suffolk, John Catt Educational Ltd.

Gray, Lynton (1991) *Marketing education*, Milton Keynes, Open University Press.

Hall, Christine (ed.) (2000) *Read smarter, not harder: reading promotions for children's libraries*, London, Youth Libraries Group.

Heeks, Peggy and Kinnell, Margaret (1992) *Managing change for school library services*, Library and Information Research Report 89, London, British Library.

Herring, James (1996) *Teaching information skills in schools*, London, Library Association Publishing.

Herring, James (2000) The 21st century school librarian: educator, information manager and expert adviser, *Impact, Journal of the Career Development Group of the Library Association*, **3** (6), available at **www.careerdevelopmentgrou.org.uk/impact/0600/herringJ.htm**

Hertfordshire Schools Library Service (1995*) Inspection and the secondary school library – preparing the paperwork: a workbook*, Hatfield, Hertfordshire Schools Library Service.

Hones, Kay Ellen (1997) "Not extinct!" School libraries for learning and leadership. In Lightall, Lynne and Haycock, Ken (eds.) *Information rich but knowledge poor? Emerging issues for schools and libraries worldwide*, Seattle, International Association of School Librarianship.

Howard, J. and Hopkins, D. (1988) *Information skills in TVEI and the role of the librarian*, Research Paper 51, London, British Library.

Hyams, Elspeth (2001) Seizing the opportunity in Cambridgeshire, *Library Association Record*, **103** (7) (July), 420–1.

Imison, Tamsyn and Taylor, Phil (2001) *Managing ICT in the secondary school*, Oxford, Heinemann Educational Publishers.

Jenkin, Mazda, Jones, Jeff and Lord, Sue (2000*) Monitoring and evaluation for school improvement*, Oxford, Heinemann Educational Publishers.

Jewell, Bruce R. (2000) *An integrated approach to business studies*, 4th edn, Harlow, Essex, Pearson Educational Ltd.

Jones, Jeff, Jenkin, Mazda and Kirkham, Sue (1996) *The head of department's handbook*, Oxford, Heinemann Educational Publishers.

Jones, Patrick and Shoemaker, Joel (2001) *Do it right! Best practices for serving young adults in school and public libraries*, New York, Neal-Schuman Publishers, Inc.

Kachel, Debra E. (1997) *Collection assessment and management for school libraries: preparing for cooperative collection development*, Westport, CT: Greenwood Press.

Kitani, Maki (2000) *Secondary school librarians: their role in making the library central and visible*, MRes dissertation, University of London [unpublished].

Klein, Naomi (2000) *No logo*, London, Harper Collins.

Knowledge Management Group, available at

www.csu.edu.au/research/kmg/

Kuhlthau, Carol C. (1993) Implementing a process approach to information skills: a study identifying indicators of success in library media programs, *SMLQ* (School Media Library Quarterly), **22** (1) (Fall), available at

www.ala.org/aasl/SLMR/slmr_resources/select_kuhlthau1.html

Lacey Bryant, Sue (1995) *Personal professional development and the solo librarian*, London, Library Association Publishing.

Lance, Keith Curry; Rodney, Marcia J. and Hamilton-Pennell, Christine (2000) *How school librarians help kids achieve standards: the second Colorado study*, San José, CA: Hi Willow Research and Publishing.

Lee, Stuart (2002) *Building an electronic resource collection*, London, Facet Publishing.

Levacic, Rosalind et al. (1999) Modern headship for the rationally managed school: combining cerebral and insightful approaches. In Bush, Tony et al. (eds) *Educational management: redefining theory, policy and practice*, London, Paul Chapman Publishing Ltd.

Lighthall, Lynne and Haycock, Ken (eds) (1997*) Information rich but knowledge poor? Emerging issues for schools and libraries worldwide*, Seattle, International Association of School Librarianship.

Loertscher, David V. (1999) *Reinvent your school's library in the age of technology: a guide for principals and superintendents*, San José, CA, Hi Willow Research and Publishing.

Lowe, P. (1992) *The LEA adviser and inspector: changing demands, changing roles*, London, Longman.

MacDonell, Colleen (2001) Implementing a library programme, *International*

School: European Council of International Schools, **3** (2) (Spring), 15.

McKenna, Barbara J. and McKenna, John J. (2000) Selecting topics for research writing projects, *English Journal* (The Journal of the Secondary Section of the National Council of Teachers of English), **89** (6) (July), 53–8.

Markuson, Carolyn (1999) *Effective libraries in international schools*, Saxmundham, Suffolk: John Catt Educational.

Morgan, Gareth (1998) *Images of organization: the executive edition*, San Francisco, Berrett-Koehler Publishers Inc.

Morris, Betty J. (1995) *Administering the school library media center*, 3rd edn, R. R. Bowker.

Mortimore, Peter (1992) Issues in school effectiveness. In Reynolds, David and Cuttance, Peter (eds) *School effectiveness: research, policy and practice*, London, Cassell.

Murphy, Joseph (1992) Effective schools: legacy and future directions. In Reynolds, David and Cuttance, Peter (eds) *School effectiveness: research, policy and practice*, London, Cassell.

National Sleep Foundation (2000) *Adolescent sleep needs and patterns: research report and resource guide*, Washington, DC: National Sleep Foundation. Also available at
www.sleepfoundation.org

Norman, Sandy (1999) *Copyright in school libraries*, 4th edn, London, Library Association Publishing.

Office of Arts and Libraries (1986) *School libraries: the foundations of the curriculum. Report of the Library and Information Services Council's Working Party on School Library Services*, London, HMSO.

Organization for Economic Cooperation and Development [OECD] (2001*) Programme for international student assessment*, available at
www.pisa.oecd.org/

Pallett, Helen (2000) School improvement for school librarians, *School Libraries in View*, **13** (Spring), 6–7.

Pantry, Sheila and Griffiths, Peter (1998) *Becoming a successful intrapreneur: a practical guide to creating an innovative information service*, London, Library Association Publishing.

Pass, Christopher (1995) *Collins dictionary of business*, 2nd edn, London, Harper Collins.

Phinn, Gervase (1999) *The other side of the dale*, London, Penguin Books.

Powell, Marion (1999) The implications of the National Literacy Strategy for Key Stage 3 and beyond, *School Libraries in View,* **12** (Autumn), 8–10.

Preedy, Margaret, Glatter, Ron and Levacic, Rosalind (1997) *Educational management: strategy, quality, and resources*, Buckingham, Open University Press.

The primary school library guidelines (2000) London, Library Association.

Primrose, C. (1993) English as a foreign library. In Blue, G. M. (ed.) *Language learning and success: studying through English. Developments in ELT*, Hemel Hempstead, Hertfordshire: Phoenix ELT.

Reynolds, David and Cuttance, Peter (eds) (1992) *School effectiveness: research, policy and practice*, London, Cassell.

Reynolds, David and Packer, Anthony (1992) School effectiveness and school improvement in the 1990s. In Reynolds, David and Cuttance, Peter (eds), *School effectiveness: research, policy and practice*, London, Cassell.

Schmoker, Mike (1996) *Results: the key to continuous school improvement*, Alexandria, VA: Association for Supervision and Curriculum Development.

The school library in teaching and learning for all: IFLA/UNESCO School Library Manifesto [2001]
http://infl.org/VII/s11/ssl.htm#3d

Shadowing Carnegie (various contributors) (1998) *School Libraries in View*, **10** (Autumn), 19–21.

Shakeshaft, Gillian (1998) *Survey of independent school libraries: library provision in secondary schools of the Headmasters' and Headmistresses' Conference*, LISU Occasional Paper 17, Loughborough, Loughborough University, Library and Information Statistics Unit.

Sheffield Hallam University, Survey and Statistical Research Centre (2000) *Survey of secondary school libraries: main findings. A report prepared for the Library Association*, available at

www.cilip.org.uk/

Shoemaker, Joel (2001) Library heaven. In Jones, Patrick and Shoemaker, Joel, *Do it right! Best practices for serving young adults in school and public libraries*, New York, Neal-Schuman Publishers, Inc.

Slevin, James (2000) *The internet and society*, Cambridge, Polity Press.

Small, Ruth V. (2002) *The teaching role: are librarians teachers?* (Comments and review of literature), Chicago, American Library Association: American Association of School Librarians, available at
www.ala.org/aasl/SLMR/eric.html

Smallwood, Carol (1997) *Insider's guide to school libraries: tips and resources*, Worthington, OH: Linworth Publishing, Inc.

Southcombe, Dianne (1999) *Setting the scene: local studies resources in the school library*, Swindon, School Library Association.

Spink, Sian (2000) Good behaviour: how school librarians can reap if they sow, *School Librarian*, **48** (4) (Winter), 175–82.

Streatfield, David (1999) Do you seriously want to be ICT trained?, *School Libraries in View*, 11 (Spring), 17–18.

Streatfield, David and Markless, Sharon (1994) *Invisible learning? The contribution of school libraries to teaching and learning*, Library and Information Research Report 98, London, British Library.

Streatfield, David and Markless, Sharon (2001) Do your services make an impact?, *School Libraries in View*, **15** (Autumn), 3–5.

Sykes, Simon (2000) The benefits of primary partnerships for secondary LRCS, *School Libraries in View*, **14** (Autumn), 16–18.

Sykes, Simon (2001) Measuring performance to survive and thrive: evaluating stock and the physical environment to increase effectiveness, *School Librarian*, **49** (3) (Autumn), 118–21.

Taking a closer look at the SLRC (2000), available at
www/slainte.org.uk/slicpubs/schoolpis.x.pdf

Thompson, Paul (2001) quoted in *Newsday*, (26 May), 17, syndicated in other newspapers.

Tiffin, John and Rajasingham, Lalita (1995*) In search of the virtual class: education in an information society*, London, Routledge.

Tilke, Anthony (1997) Advisory roles of Schools Library Services in the United Kingdom, *New Review of Children's Literature and Librarianship*, **3**, 11–38.

Tilke, Anthony (ed.) (1998a) *Library Association guidelines for secondary school libraries*, London, Library Association Publishing.

Tilke, Anthony. (1998b) *On-the-job sourcebook for school librarians*, London, Library Association Publishing.

Tilke, Anthony (1999) *The school librarian, core competencies, curriculum development and staff liaison. The role of the school librarian in providing conditions for discovery and personal growth in the school library.* Paper delivered at the open session of the section of school libraries and resource centres, Conference of the International Federation of Library Associations, Bangkok [unpublished].

Tilke, Anthony (2000) Knowledge manager/Farmer Duck, *Library Association Record*, **102** (12) (December), 698–9.

Todd, Ross (2001) *Keynote paper. Transitions for preferred futures of school libraries: knowledge space, not information space; connections, not collections; actions, not positions; evidence, not advocacy* at International Association of School Librarianship conference 2001, available at **www.iasl-slo.org/virtualpaper2001.html**

Turner, Philip M. (1993) *Helping teachers teach: a school library media specialist's role*, Englewood, CO: Libraries Unlimited, Inc.

Usherwood, Bob (2002) Let's be professional, *Library Association Record*, **104** (2) (February), 98–9.

Valentine, Pearl and Nelson, B. (1988) *Sneaky teaching: the role of the school librarian*, London, British Library.

Waddell, Martin and Oxenbury, Helen (1991) *Farmer Duck*, London, Walker Books.

Williams, Dorothy and Wavell, Caroline(2001) *Impact of the school library resource centre on learning. A report on research conducted for Resource, the Council for Museums, Archives and Libraries*, Aberdeen, Robert Gordon University.

Yates, Barbara (1997) Our patch v. their patch: information technology and literacy in schools. In Lightall, Lynne and Haycock, Ken (eds) *Infor-

mation rich but knowledge poor? Emerging issues for schools and libraries world-wide, Seattle, International Association of School Librarianship.

Yucht, Alice H. (2001) Guiding principles, *Teacher Librarian*, (June), 38–9.

INDEX

Library Association Guidelines for Secondary School Libraries

School libraries are, or should be, an integral part of the educational process. The Library Association (now CILIP) has consistently argued for better training of teachers in information skills, for the appointment of professional librarians in schools and for the school library to be regarded as an aspect of curriculum development.

The Secondary School Guidelines deal specifically with secondary school libraries, placing them in the context of current educational imperatives and thinking. The contribution of schools library services towards educational effectiveness in secondary schools is especially emphasized. Amongst other key topics the Guidelines cover:

- level of provision
- exploitation of resources
- management
- funding
- ICT
- information skills
- evaluation and inspection.

The Guidelines provide comprehensive service level recommendations and promote high standards of professional practice. They are essential reading for school librarians, teacher librarians, head teachers, governors, LEA and HMI inspectors, local education officers, chief librarians, and government and other policy makers.

Edited by **Anthony Tilke** for the Youth Libraries Committee of The Library Association (now CILIP).

2nd edn; 1998; 96pp; paperback; 1-85604-278-2; £15.95

The On-the-Job Sourcebook for School Librarians

Anthony Tilke

Those responsible for library provision in secondary schools often work in isolation without on-the-spot advice or assistance and usually have little immediate access to professional input or feedback.

This book has been written to fill that advice gap by offering a survival guide full of tips and suggestions on every aspect of a school librarian's daily work-life and responsibilities in a secondary school library. Written in a clear, readable style, it is designed to be dipped into as and when needed, and is arranged into handy sections for ease of reference.

Content includes:

- the role of the school librarian: training, status and support
- school and library policy: mission statement and development planning
- managing and making your case for funding, budgeting, ICT
- the curriculum and the library: lesson planning, departmental liaisons and links
- information skills: supporting examinations, vocational courses and homework needs
- resources: accommodation, collection development policy and Internet use
- promoting the library: user training opportunities, negotiating skills
- important information for the school librarian: specimen job descriptions, criteria for evaluation, courses and qualifications.

Essential reading for librarians, teachers and others employed in secondary school libraries in the UK and beyond, this publication will also be of great interest to head teachers, advisers, school inspectors and others involved in school policy-making.

1998; 184pp; paperback; 1-85604-270-7; £19.95

Public Internet Access in Libraries and Information Services

Paul Sturges

Public access to the internet is arguably the most important current development in library and information services. Public concerns about harmful internet content and inappropriate use, particularly by children, continue to be debated. All this is against a background of ongoing debate about how new technology affects legal and human rights areas such as copyright and other intellectual property;confidentiality, privacy, data protection and official secrecy; freedom of information; and harassment, obscenity and defamation.

This book is a much-needed guide for information professionals requiring a fuller understanding of these areas of law and ethics, and provides essential guidance on access policy and management. Whilst working on the basic principle that freedom of expression and freedom of access to information are simultaneously human rights and fundamentals of librarianship, it also takes into account the ethical and legal ambiguity of internet provision and uset. A step-by-step guide to developing an internet access policy is offered, including guidance on controversial aspects such as surveillance and monitoring of use, and software filtering and blocking.

Illustrated with a broad range of international case studies and scenarios, this is an invaluable guide to internet access management for practising information professionals across all sectors. It will also be essential reading for students on library and information studies courses offering modules covering internet access and broader legal and ethical issues.

Paul Sturges MA PhD FCLIP is Reader in Libraries in Social Development at the Department of Information Science, Loughborough University.

2002; 240pp; hardback; 1-85604-425-4; £34.95

Marketing Concepts for Libraries and Information Services
Eileen Elliott de Sáez

The most successful organizations in a fast changing world are those that are genuinely market oriented. If librarians and information professionals are to ensure the survival and prosperity of their services, then marketing is a tool they must master, and market research is an essential element of their work.

This well-known textbook introduces to practitioners a wide range of marketing concepts and techniques suitable for library and information services. Fully revised and updated, this second edition contains an extensive new chapter on marketing in the digital age, which explores the potential of e-marketing for librarians and information managers; data mining and customer relationship management; and the current marketing focus. Other major areas covered in the book include:

- what is marketing?
- the corporate mission
- marketing strategies for librarians and information professionals
- the marketing mix
- promotion and public relations

- market segmentation
- marketing research and market research
- corporate identity and corporate image
- the marketing plan.

This essential LIS-specific text will alert information professionals in all sectors to all the latest marketing strategies, and offers a comprehensive foundation and structure for effective strategic marketing. It is also an invaluable core text for undergraduate and postgraduate courses on LIS marketing and management.

Eileen Elliott de Sáez BPhil MCIM DipMRS DMS is a Chartered Marketer, one of the first in the UK, and was until recently Senior Lecturer at the School of Information Studies, University of Northumbria at Newcastle.

2nd edn; 2002; 240pp; paperback; 1-85604-426-2; £29.95